The Work-Ready Graduate

Neil B. Niman • Jennifer R. Chagnon

The Work-Ready Graduate

Preparing Tomorrow's Workforce

palgrave
macmillan

Neil B. Niman
Peter T. Paul College of Business and Economics
University of New Hampshire
Durham, NH, USA

Jennifer R. Chagnon
Peter T. Paul College of Business and Economics
University of New Hampshire
Durham, NH, USA

ISBN 978-3-031-33909-7 ISBN 978-3-031-33910-3 (eBook)
https://doi.org/10.1007/978-3-031-33910-3

This Palgrave Macmillan imprint is published by the registered company Springer Nature Switzerland AG.
The registered company address is: Gewerbestrasse 11, 6330 Cham, Switzerland

None of this would have been possible without the support of my family.
To Debbie, Joshua, and Isaac.
N.B.N.
To my Matt, Amelia, and Sonja, as well as my brother, Matt,
and my parents, Děda and Gigi.
J.R.C.

Preface

Employers have expressed frustration that students are not graduating with the requisite skills, while graduates have voiced similar concerns that they do not feel well prepared to enter the workforce. Clearly, there is more that higher education can be doing to prepare students to transition to the workplace. This, however, did not seem very important nearly 50 years ago when I first walked on campus at UCLA as an entering first-year student. What would happen at the end of four years was the last thing on my mind. Little did I know at the time that I would graduate into an economy that was experiencing both high inflation and unemployment, with few opportunities for employment (even if I knew what I wanted to do). Fast forward 20 years when Jen arrived on the campus of Juniata College only to discover that four years later, she would have a similar experience. The tech bubble of the 1990s had burst and in a post-9/11 environment, career opportunities were fairly limited.

We both appreciate the quality of our educations. Looking back, however, we wish that more had been done to ensure that we had graduated with a better understanding of what was needed to embark on a professional career. For Neil, that would be having a better understanding of what work-ready capabilities he might have developed while completing his liberal arts degree. For Jen, it was to have more substantial work experiences and a network to tap for opportunities (in a competitive labor market). Fortunately, we both had a chance to change all of that when I became Associate Dean of Academic Programs at the Peter T. Paul College of Business and Economics at the University of New Hampshire (UNH) and Jen came to work as the Assistant Manager for Academic Programs shortly thereafter.

Around that time, my previous book, *The Gamification of Higher Education* (also published by Palgrave Macmillan), appeared in print and served as a set of guiding principles for a slew of programs we would create to redefine the undergraduate experience. We remain grateful to the Dean of the College at the time, Deborah Merrill-Sands, who let me push the envelope in new and creative ways, and Peter Paul, whose commitment to the college provided much of the funding needed to turn these ideas into a reality.

Even before Deborah arrived on campus, I had pitched an idea for a new first-year program called FIRE (first-year innovation and research experience). I could speak to my own personal experience as a first-generation student who didn't have a clue about how to navigate the higher education experience that saw me two years later transferring to the University of California, Santa Cruz, hoping for a much different experience. These memories remain with me today and remind me of the importance of looking at *all* facets of the undergraduate experience.

We believed then, and believe now, that it is important for students to begin thinking about what they need to do to make themselves "work-ready" from the minute they step onto campus. This does not mean they need to have a career in mind, but, rather, that they begin to take steps to help create a broad range of experiences that will position them to determine their professional careers (rather than having to settle for whatever might be available based on the state of the economy). Using game design and storytelling principles, we were able to see how simple mechanics could influence behavior and make students take action, whether in terms of attending events, creating social and professional networks, or building a solid foundation for a professional future.

When I started as Associate Dean, I had no idea that I would be spending every Thursday morning with a group that, for the most part, interpreted and implemented academic policies for the entire university. It was my first experience looking beyond a single college and it led to assignments that found me writing a report on the state of our general education program, chairing a task force looking at student retention for the entire university, and working across colleges to develop courses and degree programs applicable across disciplines. During this same period, Jen and I guided the preparation process for accreditation and wrote the continuous improvement report for AACSB (Association to Advance Collegiate

Schools of Business) that gave us great insight into program design and assessment, as well as how to effect change. It is these experiences (and others) that have informed much of what we have accomplished in creating a tight-knight community that encourages the development of what we will later define as work-ready capabilities in all of our students.

Housed in a business school, we observed that of our 2500 students, only about 300 were actually taking advantage of the multiple opportunities provided so that they could make the most out of their undergraduate experience and very likely receive a job offer before the start of their senior year. What was less obvious was what was happening to the remaining 2200 students, many of whom were struggling to obtain their first job offer. What were their stories? How could we build a program that would benefit *all* students in the college and set them on a path toward a life well lived? Our solution was Business in Practice (BiP).

Business in Practice, a curriculum enhancement that started as a way to make the existing business administration major more relevant, current, and adaptable, quickly morphed into a vehicle for helping to accelerate the professional development of our students. What sets the program apart is that we create learning experiences that are crafted to take advantage of the unique knowledge and work experiences from a group of talented industry professionals recruited to take part in what we think is a very special program. They teach two-credit courses that are designed to help our students develop those soft/smart skills that are desired by employers in a way that complements our core curriculum. The program is structured to bring an internship-like experience to campus, giving the vast majority of students a quality work-related experience under the guidance of industry professionals interested in the students' professional development—an experience that was previously only available to a small percentage of students.

What really sets the program apart is its scale and scope. We offer over 70 courses led by industry professionals each academic year. The sheer number of learning experiences we have developed, when combined with our other experiences working in the Dean's Office, has helped us to understand how to design a course, generate an engaging learning environment, and provide students with an opportunity to further their professional development. At this point we know what works and what is likely to fail (even as we continue to innovate under the auspices of continuous improvement).

While we call it Business in Practice, a similar type of program can be developed for many majors, colleges, or universities. Everyone can benefit from being exposed to the latest tools, techniques, and approaches that reflect what is currently happening in a variety of organizations across the professional world.

Durham, NH
March 2023

N. Niman
J. Chagnon

Acknowledgments

We extend much gratitude to Susan Mattioni and Jacqueline Sampson for their keen abilities to support the continued growth of the Business in Practice program in a variety of ways, and especially for their care and kindness for the students and instructors, and for keeping our team together. Thank you, Susan, for jumping into this journey from the start.

Thank you to Martine Grenier-Burtis for your efforts on this book project and being a sounding board for our work.

We'd especially like to thank several UNH students (some now Paul College alumni) who traveled on this journey with us. Their contributions, insights, and personal experience as students in BiP helped evolve the program and keep us going. Special thanks to our foundational student team: Alice Butcher, Hannah Donahue, Isabella Ronson, Kemal Warouw, Sarah Wilkinson, and Hannah Wirth. Additional appreciation to Aubrey Benoit, Jack Bouchard, Genevieve Cannon, Leah Glidden, Caroline LeBlanc, and Annabelle Stott.

Additionally, we're grateful for the Paul College students who served as BiP Student Guides. Their work has been essential in supporting our working professionals.

Much appreciation goes to the BiP instructor community—the working professionals. As an even greater community, we are indebted to your involvement and dedication, especially in how much you do to help each student on their journeys. Additional thanks to Kim Clark, Krystal Hicks, and Ed Miles who've been with the program since its launch and continually serve the BiP community. Also, Duncan Craig and Brian DeKoning of

Raka Creative who helped launch Voice Z Digital and taught some of our first pilot courses.

Deborah Merrill-Sands (Dean of Paul College during much of the development of the BiP program) deserves special recognition and gratitude for believing in this initiative, as well as providing the resources and the latitude needed to transform our collective vision into a reality. Thank you, Deborah.

Thank you also to the members of the Paul College faculty and staff who have supported and contributed to the development of the program. Special thanks to the Paul Undergraduate Curriculum Review Task Forces that we were a part of and brought forth the concept and proposal for the program: May Bao, Rachael Campagna, Khole Gwebu, Paul Harvey, Yixin Liu, Lee Mizusawa, Robert Mohr, Bruce Pfeiffer, and Tamara Rury. Additionally, we'd like to thank Tara Belanger, Diane Devine, Tom Gruen, Riane Metcalfe, Russ Miles, and Suzanne Roberge.

Thank you to the Business in Practice Advisory Board and the Paul College Dean's Advisory Board for their advocacy of this initiative. Special thanks to Mike Hickey and Liz Gray for your insights and always being in our corner.

We have sustained and developed the program, including the Forge experiential learning space, through the generous financial support of donors. An extended thank you to the following individuals and families for their contributions and belief in this program: T. and A. Boucher; T. and E. Collins; E. and R. Dodier; J. and S. Faro; J. and E. Franson; the Freedman Family; M. and M. Hickey; K. Hicks; P. T. Paul; T. and R. Youngman; and W. and V. Zagrobski.

Lastly, an extended thanks to our families and friends for their encouragement and patience.

Contents

List of Figures

Introduction

"Jobs do not require four-year degrees. Employers do." So begins a report published by the Burning Glass Institute describing what they believe is the coming great reset where skills rather than degrees form the foundation for the hiring decision. Currently, employers use the bachelor's degree as a filter to effectively shrink the pool of candidates to a manageable number by eliminating 64% of the working-age population. From this perspective, degree requirements serve as a proxy for hard-to-detect qualifications often associated with soft skills.[1] One consequence of this action is that individuals from underrepresented communities or who do not have access to applicable work experiences are never considered for jobs that could easily be performed by someone who has a high school education.[2]

Employers, however, no longer have the luxury of using a single measure to exclude job candidates in one swath. A careful look at the data suggests that the current exit of workers from the labor market, while impacted by the global pandemic, is actually the continuation of a historic trend.[3] Tight labor markets will continue to pressure hiring managers to consider nondegree candidates. As a result, there is growing interest in looking at alternate credentials to help determine whether an individual possesses the requisite skills to perform at a job.[4]

Changes in the supply side and higher education's position as an important source of new workers are not the only factors affecting the labor market. National studies that look at the role of higher education, such as

N. B. Niman, J. R. Chagnon, *The Work-Ready Graduate*,
https://doi.org/10.1007/978-3-031-33910-3_1

the one produced by Bates College and Gallup on Forging Pathways to Purposeful Work, suggest that, while the focus of entering college students is still on getting a "better" job, what that means is changing. The concept of a better job has become associated with the idea of purposeful work. One outcome from the national study was that four out of five college graduates affirmed the importance of finding purpose in their work; further, graduates with high purpose in work are almost 10 times more likely to have high overall wellbeing.[5] This is echoed by an earlier Gallup report that suggests millennials, the previous college-aged generation, are also placing increased importance on finding purpose in their work.[6] These findings are consistent with the view of many hiring managers that employees who can find purpose in their work will be more engaged, productive, and likely to stick around.[7]

All of this poses two major challenges for higher education. The first is that, despite the recognition of benefits associated with purposeful work, fewer than half of the graduates surveyed by Bates-Gallup succeeded in finding purpose in their work.[8] The second challenge is that the premium associated with a college degree might eventually disappear with the continued use and acceptance of alternatives to the bachelor's degree.[9] This should serve as a wakeup call for higher education.

A growing number of prospective students (and their parents) question whether a bachelor's degree is worth it.[10] When coupled with a trend suggesting that employers are growing increasingly disappointed by what they perceive as a lack of preparedness for entry into the workforce, it should come as no surprise that some employers are offering their own training programs and making them available to potential job candidates or are considering alternate credentials as a substitute for a bachelor's degree.[11]

As viable alternatives emerge that offer a different path to acquire the hard and soft skills valued by employers, higher education will be left with little choice but to turn its attention toward producing a more work-ready graduate. This will be even more important as colleges and universities become more competitive amid a declining pool of potential college students.[12] Thus, while college administrators seem most focused on changing demographics, we believe that the response to changes in the labor market (rather than demographics) will drive, to a large extent, the coming transition to a new model for higher education.

If there is to be a revolution in higher education, what will propel this change is not the availability of new technologies that will reduce the high cost of an education (though this dynamic will come into play), but rather the search for job candidates who have demonstrated their work-readiness and the willingness of employers to cast a wider net to find them.[13] With rising costs and growing debt burdens, we have perhaps finally reached the point where higher education must start delivering on its promise of creating a path to a life well lived.[14]

The Triple-Threat Graduate

Instructure, the company that produces Canvas (a popular learning management system), published its own report in 2022 on the State of Student Success & Engagement.[15] Echoing many of the themes in the Bates College & Gallup study, Instructure defines student success as career-readiness, skill competency, and student educational goals. Put another way, success encompasses more than the graduating senior successfully completing a major; it also includes developing skills desirable to a potential employer and completing the foundational work needed to embark on a career.[16]

All of this sounds great, but the challenge for higher education is to put some substance behind the rhetoric. What does it mean to be career-ready? Can it truly be measured by how many times a student visits career services on their college campus? Or, what about skill competency? Which skills are we talking about within the context of future employment? How will those skills be developed?

One pathway forward is offered by Brandon Busteed, Chief Partnership Officer and Global Head of Learn-Work Innovation at Kaplan. Kaplan is one of the largest providers of online education; it is from this perspective that Busteed contends that for higher education to remain relevant, it must produce what he calls triple-threat graduates.

A triple-threat graduate is one who leaves college with a bachelor's degree that contains three important elements: (1) several long-term projects, (2) extensive work experience, and (3) an industry-recognized credential.[17] He goes on to contend that these elements need to be demonstrable, as in the form of a line on a resume, transcript, or part of a portfolio. It is not enough to have done something; there must be a way of demonstrating in a credible way that a graduate has the skills and experiences needed to succeed in a given job or industry.

Without a standard means for assessing the value of a credential or an experience, it can be difficult to send a credible signal to a potential employer.[18] Hence, for the foreseeable future, the current system that relies on a college degree where the institution is accredited, is potentially ranked, and has an established brand will still have an advantage. Secondly, work experiences and long-term projects are not all created equally; skill development for these students may vary greatly, as well as the feedback and coaching the students greatly need. Thirdly, certifications also vary widely, and the market has expanded quickly from 334,114 unique credentials in the US in 2008 to 967,774 in 2020, and 1.076 million in 2023.[19]

Many credential programs are designed for employees looking to upskill or reskill, giving the most benefit to those that already have established work experience. For many undergraduate students, the experience can sit in a vacuum, where they may watch a series of videos, complete elements of assigned "work," or pass the exam required to gain a certificate. They may not receive any real hands-on experience that would teach them how or when to apply a particular tool, technology, or knowledge in a given set of circumstances—the knowledge remains siloed from the context of the workplace.

Higher education distinguishes itself from training by teaching individuals how to think and broadly apply that knowledge to new and changing circumstances. It is not the mastery of a skill that one necessarily repeats over and over again to an unchanging set of conditions. A work-ready graduate is one who can embrace innovation because the capabilities they have developed are transferable to new and existing ways of doing things. Thus, Busteed's triple threat might be a desired outcome and indicative of what we will later call a work-ready graduate, but it highlights the importance of how we get there. Projects that do not reflect the realities of the business world, skills that are years out of date, and certificates that do not require putting skills and knowledge into practice may represent a triple, but not much of a threat.

Purposeful Work

Bates College, through their Purposeful Work program, attempts to reach a similar set of outcomes with one important addition: preparing graduates who are ready to engage in purposeful work. Returning to the Bates & Gallup Study, "…too many graduates appear unprepared to find pathways to work that is truly meaningful to them. The result is often dissatisfied workers, frustrated employers and graduates still searching for the return on investment (ROI) from their college education."[20] The authors go on to note that there are four key undergraduate experiences (percentages reflect student response rate) that align with graduates finding purpose in work:[21]

- an internship or job that allowed the student to apply what they were learning in the classroom (56%)
- someone who encouraged the student to pursue their goals and dreams (39%)
- provision of realistic expectations for postgraduation employment prospects (23%)
- participation in a class/program that helped the student think about looking for meaning in work (28%)

Bates created a Center for Purposeful Work that offers programming designed to provide these four key experiences and a collection of career services similar to those found at most colleges and universities but defined by the theme of purposeful work. All services are designed to help their students obtain an internship that can satisfy the first key experience.

Recognizing that faculty may not have extensive experience with a job function, company, or industry and thus may not be the best source for advising students who are interested in entering the workforce rather than postgraduate studies, Bates created a mentorship program designed to match interested students with business professionals who can provide advice about careers and life.[22]

To create realistic expectations for what life might be like after graduation, Bates offers several programs, most notably one that provides an opportunity for students to shadow an alumnus or parent to gain a better understanding of a day in the life of an occupation within a particular organization. In addition, they offer roadshows and spotlights that put students in contact with business professionals.

Finally, Bates offers a limited number of practitioner courses, and their Purposeful Work Infusion Project integrates touchpoints in a number of courses. These touchpoints might include a guest speaker, reading, structured writing assignment, or presentation of course material through a lens of how a course topic might intersect with the concept of purposeful work.

In total, these experiences offer multiple touchpoints, but to what extent do they develop those skills coveted by potential employers? One might argue that programs like this promote a purposeful mindset, very much like brief interventions can create a growth mindset.[23] However, we will discover that creating the appropriate mindset is only the first step in developing what we will later call a work-ready set of capabilities, and to make a graduate truly work-ready, they must be provided with a series of experiences that enables them to put their skills and knowledge into practice within a context similar to what they are likely to encounter after graduation.

Mindsets must be coupled with action, and hence we believe that the appropriate path forward should be grounded in experiential learning. Experiential learning is, at its core, learning by doing.[24] It stands in stark contrast to conventional forms of learning in which knowledge and exercises are provided and, at the end of the process, students are examined on how well they have retained that knowledge. While it can take many forms, from our perspective, learning by doing places the student in an authentic context where, by working collaboratively in a supportive community, they are able to develop work-ready skills and capabilities.

Business in Practice

Returning for the last time to the Bates & Gallup Study, the observation is made that both hiring managers and parents stress the importance of gaining real-world experience. In response to questions surrounding what can be done to develop more engaged workers, the study found the most common answers to be:[25]

- Stress and teach analytical/critical thinking and problem solving, allowing students to think for themselves.
- Exposure to real-world situations/teaching real-life scenarios.
- Require or encourage internships, mentorship, or apprentice programs.
- Teach more soft skills along with technical/focus on practical/real skills curriculum.

Many of these recommendations underlie our own Business in Practice program offered at the Peter T. Paul College of Business and Economics.

Our odyssey began in 2017, while Neil was Associate Dean of Academic Programs and Jen was the Assistant Manager of Academic Programs. At that time, we started to question whether higher education was meeting the needs of the external business community and what (if anything) we could do to bridge the disconnect between theory and practice. Business

Administration is the largest major at the University of New Hampshire and serves approximately 2500 students. The goal of the review was to look at whether the curriculum was up to date and meeting the needs of today's economy. A survey of employers and a review of the literature suggested that we were not turning out graduates who were distinctive and essentially work-ready.

After encountering a great deal of resistance to changing the core curriculum or what is taught in those courses, a proposal was drafted to create what is now called the Business in Practice program. Here we created an entire program comprised of guided experiences that are led by working professionals and carefully crafted around well-defined learning and developmental goals. It is experiential learning by design, a design that attempts to accelerate the learning process by giving the student an opportunity to gain insights as they learn by doing with the assistance of a professional who has seen much of it before.[26]

What makes the program distinctive is that all the courses (with one exception) are taught by working professionals and are customized around the interests, passions, and work experience of that professional. The program consists of a collection of two credit courses that sit on top of the core curriculum. Every Business Administration student is required to complete four Business in Practice (BiP) courses. Students are allowed to substitute one equivalent experiential learning opportunity for a BiP course.

Our two credit learning experiences use what we call ISA^2 (Informal, Situated, Active, and Applied) learning to transmit knowledge. It is designed to be *informal* so that our students can take advantage of the tacit knowledge and experience of our working practitioners. Learning is *situated* within the culture, standards, and way of doing things that our practitioners bring with them into the classroom. It is both *active* and *applied*; students learn by doing as they actively engage with the material, each other, and the practitioner/instructor.

By providing learning experiences that are both relevant to business and offer a glimpse into what it would be like to solve a certain type of problem, work in a particular environment, or use a current tool or technique, our students are in a better position to know what they like and what needs to be done to pursue a particular career or work for a particular type of company. Each course focuses on the development of a set of soft, or what are sometimes referred to as smart, skills that better position our students to be successful once they embark on their career.[27] The sum total of the program is designed to turn those skills into capabilities that prepare our students not only to meet current needs but also for a future that is currently unknown.

All of this has led to the creation of a structured path designed to make our students work-ready. All students, not just those who join clubs or are part of an academic group, have multiple opportunities to put their skills into practice under the guidance of working professionals and leave the program with a collection of narratives that can point to tangible projects and experiences that closely approximate what they might find in a real work environment. It is our way of bringing the internship experience on to campus in a substantive way that provides context and relevance for the development of a set of capabilities that allow our students to solve both current and future problems as they emerge in the business world.

Moving the Conversation Forward

When we first envisioned this book project, we thought we would tell the story of Business in Practice. The more we shared our story, however, the more we were surprised by the consistent reaction we received; overwhelmingly, we heard "that is truly impressive, and I wish we could do that." But then the conversation would devolve into all of the reasons why doing something similar is impossible at their own institution. We slowly realized that there is a myriad of ways to develop work-ready capabilities, but for these to occur, someone first needs to get the conversation started. This is our attempt to start a broader conversation. Rather than spending a great deal of space on whether or not higher education should respond to the needs of the marketplace, we start from the position that it should and move on to talk about those realistic steps that can be taken to advance the development of a work-ready graduate.

We have structured the conversation to take place in two parts. The first looks broadly at higher education and why creating a work-ready graduate is important. The second focuses on curricular changes and how working professionals might be integrated into any academic experience.

Part I looks at higher education and why creating a work-ready graduate is important. In the chapter, "Unrealized Opportunities", we introduce six unrealized opportunities preventing higher education from developing work-ready graduates. In the next three chapters, we discuss in more detail these unrealized opportunities. The next chapter, "Human

Capabilities", makes the case that higher education should develop capabilities rather than skills. The chapter, "Self-Discovery and Curriculum", suggests changes in how, from a work-ready perspective, higher education might support a discovery process that focuses on learning what types of work might lead to a prosperous and fulfilling career. It explores how changes in the curriculum could support this process and assist in the selection of a major, along with various choices, that could support the development of work-ready capabilities. The chapter, "Connections and Signals", looks at the power of professional networks and how students might be supported to make these very important connections from the time they arrive on campus. It also discusses the development of alternate credentials and evaluates them as a signaling device for potential employers. Finally, the chapter, "EdTech to the Rescue?", explores EdTech and asks whether this growing complement (and substitute) to higher education can, through its own efforts, assist higher education to realize these six opportunities.

Part II looks more closely at the changes needed to reimagine how courses and curricula could be repositioned to create a more work-ready graduate. It is informed by the work done in our Business in Practice program. The chapter, "Practice-Based Learning", looks at practice-based learning and discusses the value of offering learning experiences guided by ISA^2 (informal, situated, active, and applied) principles. The chapter, "Designing Learning Experiences", details how we design our learning experiences using the $STAR^2$ (situation, task, action, the results, and reflection) design method. The next chapter, "Industry Professionals in the Classroom", explores the rewards associated with bringing in working professionals and the efforts required to prepare them for the classroom. The chapter, "A Practice-Based Journey", discusses how to integrate the principles underlying practice-based learning into a more traditional curriculum. The chapter "Outcomes" focuses on the challenges associated with measuring the development of soft skills and work-ready capabilities. It provides an approach for collecting evidence of program success and how we use that to engage in a process of continuous improvement.

We draw to a close with the final chapter, "Forces of Change", that provides recommendations for integrating practice-based learning into any college or university. It offers helpful suggestions of steps that can be taken to enhance the undergraduate experience and promote the development of a work-ready graduate.

Where We End Up

If higher education is to avoid a race to the bottom, then it must focus on meeting the needs of tomorrow's workforce. This involves looking at complementary forms of education that can enhance traditional curricula by making them relevant, better connected to career pathways, and able to develop relevant professional capabilities. It is not about repackaging existing courses (or partial courses) in the form of micro-credentials, but instead, higher education must take a fresh approach to experiential learning.

Throughout this volume, we will be making the case that higher education should do what it does best—turn out a generation of independent thinkers who are adaptable to changing circumstances and who can meet the global challenges of tomorrow. Higher education distinguishes itself from training by teaching individuals how to think critically and apply that knowledge broadly to new and changing circumstances. That being said, what hiring managers are looking for and businesses are demanding is not just graduates who can think; they also want job candidates who are able to do. This is captured in the ability to take action based on a developed set of work-ready capabilities that will enable today's graduates to grapple with tomorrow's challenges.

Notes

1. Burning Glass Institute (2022).
2. The data reveals that of the number of bachelor's degrees conferred in 2018–2019 by race/ethnicity, 62.3% identified themselves as White, 10.3% as Black, 14.9% as Hispanic, 8.2% as Asian/Pacific Islander, and 0.5% as American Indian/Alaska Native, and 3.9% are those who identify with two or more races. NCES. Degrees conferred by race/ethnicity and sex (National Center for Education Statistics, 2022).
3. Evaluating the state of the labor market, Domash and Summers (2022) look at various measures of unemployment and conclude that the labor market is very tight. They also believe that the labor market will continue to be tight unless there is a considerable slowdown in demand. This is a level of tightness that would historically have been associated with an aggregate unemployment rate below 2% (Domash & Summers, 2022, p. 24) and a total shortfall of 6.9 million workers.

   The issue is not only the shortage in the number of workers, but also the skills needed by employers (Society for Human Resource Management, 2019).

4. Belkin (2020).
5. Gallup and Bates College (2019).
6. Adkins and Rigoni (2016).
7. Dhingra and Schaniger (2021).
8. Four out of five responding college graduates in the Gallup and Bates study said it was very important or extremely important to have a sense of purpose in their work (Gallup & Bates College, 2019, p. 11). However, only a minority of graduates strongly agree that they found purpose in the work (Dhingra & Schaniger, 2021, p. 12), thereby creating a fairly wide "purpose gap."
9. There are a number of studies that lead to roughly the same conclusion that the future lifetime earnings of a graduate exceeds that of a high school graduate by $2.8 million. See, for example, Carnevale et al. (2021).
10. Whether college is worth it depends on whom you ask. That is the conclusion of a survey by the Bipartisan Policy Center and the Association of American Colleges and Universities (Finley et al., 2021). How much a graduate earns and thus whether a degree makes good financial sense depends upon major. A closer look at the earnings and debt associated with 37,000 college majors at 4400 institutions can be found in "Buyer Beware" (Carnevale et al., 2020).
11. Finley et al. (2021, p. 16). Share of employers who report that recent graduates are "very well prepared" on a particular skill:

    - Digital literacy (49%)
    - Work effectively in teams (48%)
    - Creative thinking (46%)
    - Communicate effectively through writing (44%)
    - Work with numbers and statistics (44%).

12. Grawe (2018).
13. See, for example, *The Economist* (2014) and Christensen and Eyring (2011).
14. The problem is nicely defined in a study undertaken by Cengage, one of the leading textbook publishers. Here it is summarized: "Today, there are 7 million jobs but 15 million un-or-underemployed Americans. Part of the reason for the gap is because our society believes all good jobs require a college degree-for which the average graduate takes on $30,000 in debt to attain-only to find out they haven't developed the right skills for entry-level work" (Cengage, 2021, p. 3). Information about college debt can be found in the Board of Governors of The Federal Reserve System's (Board of Governors of The Federal Reserve System, 2022) report on "Economic Well-Being of U.S. Households" in 2021, pp. 71–76.
15. Instructure is the maker of Canvas, a leading Learning Management System used in higher education (Instructure, 2022).

16. This dovetails nicely with the Bates-Gallup Study that proposes: "Students can no longer assume that a college credential alone is enough to guarantee career success. As a result, colleges and universities must be more intentional in the design of curriculum and programs that will provide graduates with the skills, experiences and self-awareness to be strong and competitive job candidates" (Gallup & Bates College, 2019, p. 7).
17. Busteed (2020).
18. The difficulty of evaluating credentials is laid out in a special report by *The Economist* (2017).
19. Credential Engine (2023). More information is also available from Tyler (2022).
20. Gallup and Bates College (2019, p. 8)
21. Gallup and Bates College (2019, p. 14)
22. From the same Gallup and Bates College (2019) study: Participants shared the view that their professors and advisors did not offer a sense of what work would be possible with their degree. They discovered instead that what they believed might qualify was only available to graduates with advanced degrees. Many spoke of the disconnect between their academic experience and the realities of the workplace.
23. Yeager et al. (2019) showed that a brief intervention of less than an hour had a positive impact on the development of a growth mindset in adolescents. For more information on growth mindsets, see also Dweck (2016) and Dweck (2006).
24. One of the leaders in experiential learning is David Kolb. His influential book is *Experiential Learning: Experience as the Source of Learning and Development* (Kolb, 1984).
25. Gallup and Bates College (2019, p. 18).
26. Niman and Chagnon (2021).
27. Padurean (2021).

References

Adkins, A., & Rigoni, B. (2016, June 1). *Paycheck or purpose: What drives millennials?* Gallup, Inc. Retrieved March 21, 2023, from https://www.gallup.com/workplace/236453/paycheck-purpose-drives-millennials.aspx

Belkin, D. (2020, November 12). Is this the end of college as we know it? *The Wall Street Journal.* Retrieved March 21, 2023, from https://www.wsj.com/articles/is-this-the-end-of-college-as-we-know-it-11605196909?mod=article_inline

Burning Glass Institute. (2022, February 9). *The Emerging degree reset: How the shift to skills-based hiring holds the keys to growing the U.S. workforce at a time of talent shortage.* Burning Glass Institute. Retrieved March 21, 2023, from https://www.burningglassinstitute.org/research/the-emerging-degree-reset

Busteed, B. (2020). College Should Produce Triple-Threat Graduates. *Forbes*. https://www.forbes.com/sites/brandonbusteed/2020/04/28/college-should-produce-triple-threat-graduates/?sh=727e325d56bc

Carnevale, A. P., Cheah B., & Wenzinger. E. (2021). *The college payoff: More education doesn't always mean more earnings*. Center on Education and the Workforce, Georgetown University. Retrieved March 21, 2023, from https://cew.georgetown.edu/wp-content/uploads/cew-college_payoff_2021-fr.pdf

Carnevale, A. P., Fasules, M. L., & Campbell, K. P. (2020). *Workplace basics: The competencies employers want*. Georgetown University Center on Education and the Workforce. Retrieved March 21, 2023, from https://cewgeorgetown.wpenginepowered.com/wp-content/uploads/cew-workplace-basics-fr.pdf

Cengage. (2021). Graduate employability report. *Cengage*. Retrieved March 21, 2023, from https://cengage.widen.net/content/e5oqtwwrw1/pdf/Graduate_Employability_Report%2D%2D-May-24-FINAL.pdf?u=fn2gt2

Christensen, C. M., & Eyring, H. J. (2011). *The innovative university: Changing the DNA of higher education from the inside out* (1st ed.). Jossey-Bass.

Credential Engine. (2023). *Credential Engine*. Retrieved March 21, 2023, from https://credentialengine.org/

Dhingra, N., & Schaniger. B. (2021). The search for purpose at work. *The McKinsey Podcast*, McKinsey & Company. Retrieved March 21, 2023, from https://www.mckinsey.com/capabilities/people-and-organizational-performance/our-insights/the-search-for-purpose-at-work

Domash, A., & Summers, L. H. (2022). *How tight are U.S. labor markets?* National Bureau of Economic Research. Retrieved March 21, 2023, from https://www.nber.org/papers/w29739

Dweck, C. (2006). *Mindset: The new psychology of success*. Ballantine Books.

Dweck, C. (2016, January 13). What having a "growth mindset" actually means. *Harvard Business Review*. Retrieved March 21, 2023, from https://hbr.org/2016/01/what-having-a-growth-mindset-actually-means

Finley, A., Aborn, M., Ruddy, S., & Miller, K. (2021). *Is college worth the time and money?* Bipartisan Policy Center and Association of American Colleges and Universities. Retrieved March 21, 2023, from https://bipartisanpolicy.org/download/?file=/wp-content/uploads/2021/09/BPC_Fed-State_Brief_R05.pdf

Gallup, & Bates College. (2019). *Forging pathways to purposeful work: The role of higher education*. Gallup, Inc. Retrieved March 21, 2023, from https://www.gallup.com/education/248222/gallup-bates-purposeful-work2019.aspx#:~:text=of%20Higher%20Education-,Forging%20Pathways%20to%20Purposeful%20Work%3A%20The%20Role%20of%20Higher%20EducatioE,and%20success%20in%20their%20work

Grawe, N. D. (2018). *Demographics and the demand for higher education*. Johns Hopkins University Press.

Instructure. (2022). 2022 state of student success & engagement in higher education. *Instructure*. Retrieved March 21, 2023, from https://www.instructure.com/resources/research-reports/2022-state-student-success-engagement-higher-education

Kolb, D. A. (1984). *Experiential learning: Experience as the source of learning and development*. Prentice-Hall.

National Center for Education Statistics. (2022). *Fast facts: Degrees conferred by race/ethnicity and sex*. The Department of Education's Institute of Educational Sciences. Retrieved March 21, 2023, from https://nces.ed.gov/fastfacts/display.asp?id=72

Niman, N. B., & Chagnon, J. R. (2021). Redesigning the future of experiential learning. *Journal of Higher Education Theory and Practice, 21*(8), 87–98.

Padurean, L. (2021, April 19). *The 10 smart skills of the future*. Association to Advance Collegiate Schools of Business. Retrieved March 21, 2023, from https://www.aacsb.edu/insights/articles/2021/04/the-ten-smart-skills-of-the-future

Society for Human Resource Management. (2019). *The global skills shortage: Bridging the talent gap with education, training and sourcing*. Society for Human Resource Management, The Skills Gap. Retrieved March 21, 2023, from https://www.shrm.org/hr-today/trends-and-forecasting/research-and-surveys/documents/shrm%20skills%20gap%202019.pdf

The Economist. (2014, June 28). *Creative destruction*. The Economist Group, Ltd. Retrieved March 21, 2023, from https://www.economist.com/leaders/2014/06/28/creative-destruction

The Economist. (2017, January 12). *Established education providers v new contenders*. The Economist Group, Ltd. Retrieved March 21, 2023, from https://www.economist.com/special-report/2017/01/12/established-education-providers-v-new-contenders

The Federal Reserve System, Board of Governors. (2022). *Economic wellbeing of U.S. households in 2021*. The Federal Reserve System. Retrieved March 21, 2023, from https://www.federalreserve.gov/publications/files/2021-report-economic-well-being-us-households-202205.pdf

Tyler, K. (2022, June 7). *How alternative credentials can help you find employees*. Society for Human Resource Management. Retrieved March 21, 2023, from https://www.shrm.org/hr-today/news/hr-magazine/summer2022/pages/alternative-credentials-help-increase-talent-pool-.aspx

Yeager, D. S., Hanselman, P., Walton, G. M., et al. (2019). A national experiment reveals where a growth mindset improves achievement. *Nature, 573*, 364–369. https://doi.org/10.1038/s41586-019-1466-y

PART I

The Tide of Change

Unrealized Opportunities

Did February 28, 1967, change higher education forever? According to Dan Berrett, it triggered a debate that is still raging today. It was the day that Ronald Reagan, then Governor of California, declared that austerity would be the new watchword with a state budget in crisis; not only would everyone need to tighten their belts, but there were certain "intellectual luxuries" that he believed the State could do without. So began what has become a long-standing conversation about the purpose of higher education: Is the role of higher education to prepare students for a career or should it foster a broad set of knowledge and capabilities whose immediate value is less clear?[1]

In a Gallup & Lumina report on the State of Higher Education in 2022, 94% of those who made the decision to enroll in higher education agreed that an additional credential beyond high school was important for obtaining their ideal job. The number falls dramatically to 51% for US adults who are not enrolled or did not consider enrolling in the past two years.[2] The number one reason for not enrolling (54%) was cost. In the 1960s, the average cost of tuition, fees, room, and board was $10,973 for a four-year college or university (in 2020–2021 dollars). By 2020, that price had ballooned to $29,033. At public universities, costs increased from an average of $7923 to $21,337.[3] Many believe that these increases can be attributed to a decrease in public funding. Following the recession of 2008, funding at the state level decreased by approximately $6.6 billion.[4]

N. B. Niman, J. R. Chagnon, *The Work-Ready Graduate*,
https://doi.org/10.1007/978-3-031-33910-3_2

It is unclear how much longer academia will be able to continue in this direction. In a survey of high school students performed by the ECMC Group in 2020, they found as the result of four surveys conducted over a year and a half that the likelihood of attending a four-year school decreased from 71% to 48%.[5] The cost and amount of student loan debt was the number one concern, with 46% responding that their ideal post-high school plans would require three years of college or less.[6] This has led many to question the value of an undergraduate degree. In a survey undertaken by the Federal Reserve, four in 10 people who went to college said they incurred some debt.[7] The median amount of outstanding education debt in 2021 was between $20,000 and $24,999.[8] What was previously a debate between politicians and academics now takes place at the kitchen table as parents and their children decide on what can or should be sacrificed to earn a bachelor's degree.

With numbers like these, higher education needs to reconsider the entire four-year undergraduate journey, taking a holistic approach that includes the social, professional, and academic experiences.[9] In combination, these experiences offer the potential to provide both a vibrant world of personal and intellectual discovery *and* the development of capabilities valued by employers. At many institutions, however, whether that potential is ever realized is more a matter of happenstance than a coordinated strategy designed to prepare a student for life after graduation.

A Series of Unrealized Opportunities

The undergraduate student living on campus is in a 24/7 immersive environment populated by a selected group of individuals at an identical stage of life with comparable academic profiles and, at many institutions, similar socioeconomic backgrounds. Universities provide a large number of opportunities to explore and discover who you are and what you want out of life, but they vary greatly in terms of the level of involvement by the administration in creating a holistic environment that promotes social, academic, and professional development. Some students will prosper no matter what, while others will struggle and unfortunately drop out before completing their degree. Many students will wait until their final year before focusing any effort on preparation to enter the workforce or pinpointing a career path. This forms the foundation for what we consider to be the unrealized opportunities that exist in higher education today.

Though the list is long, we have identified here what we consider to be the six most significant unrealized opportunities:

1. *Human Capabilities*—In today's tech-driven environment, it is common to talk about the development of skills. We find it meaningful to distinguish skills (abilities for meeting today's challenges) from capabilities (the ability to respond to future challenges) and emphasize that the development of capabilities provides the best opportunity for higher education. This distinction between skills and capabilities is elaborated in the chapter, "Human Capabilities".
2. *Self-Discovery*—Growing up is complicated. Universities could do more to help students evaluate and set expectations associated with their majors and finding a career, as well as taking steps to become work-ready within the workplace and their field. This discussion is presented in the chapter, "Self-Discovery and Curriculum".
3. *Curriculum*—Given the high cost of a bachelor's degree, career opportunities have moved to the forefront of conversations related to whether higher education is still worth the price. Instead of focusing on a narrow career path, there is an opportunity for curricula and majors to guide students toward things they like to do and how they can use them to make a living. This will also be included as part of the chapter, "Self-Discovery and Curriculum".
4. *Connections*—Who you know is as important as what you know; universities have extensive alumni networks and close ties to the local business community but often leverage these assets in a limited way. If made accessible to all students, these connections can contribute to a student's development of professional networks, capabilities, and experiences. This is discussed in the chapter, "Connections and Signals".
5. *Signals*—Whether a graduate is work-ready depends on both what they have accomplished and their ability to communicate those accomplishments. While certain schools have brand recognition, an academic record alone does not speak to work-ready capabilities. Students learning to effectively translate important accomplishments to employers should be an integral part of the undergraduate experience. This will also be more thoroughly covered in the chapter, "Connections and Signals".

6. *Technology*—The rise of EdTech along with new technologies like ChatGPT are threatening to radically change higher education as we know it. Universities have an opportunity, however, to use this same technology to promote social learning and leverage the assets comprising the residential collegiate experience to better prepare their students to enter the workforce. This topic will be the focus of the chapter, "EdTech to the Rescue?".

Human Capabilities

New technologies such as generative artificial intelligence (AI) is dominating the conversation within higher education as it threatens to disrupt long-held practices that surround both teaching and learning.[10] Perhaps the greatest impact of these technologies surrounds how we will conceptualize and experience work in the future[11] as technology shifts and displaces traditional career paths that current university and college students expect to gain after graduation. As noted by Lee Raine and Janna Anderson of the Pew Research Center, "Machines are eating humans' jobs talents. And it's not just about jobs that are repetitive and low skill. Automation, robotics, algorithms, and artificial intelligence (AI) in recent times have shown they can do equal or sometimes even better work than humans…."[12]

These new technologies such as AI will have an inordinately large impact on what it means to be a work-ready graduate going forward.[13] If higher education is to remain relevant, it must formulate a response to the increasingly loud voices calling for change.[14] The response, however, is not to just add more tech-based AI courses to the curriculum. AI is slowly and steadily infiltrating each and every industry and therefore requires a renewed laser-like focus to identify complementary human skills and intelligence. Looking at the landscape of AI and humans, it is clear that there are distinctly human capabilities that will be needed to complement, guide, and harness the potential of AI in the workforce.[15]

Self-Discovery

Who I am, what is required of me, where I would like to be ten years from now, and what is the best path to achieve success are all important questions that many first-year students cannot answer, let alone identify how to go about answering. Why is it so difficult? Do students select a major because they are good at a particular subject or because that is what their parents would like them to study? A major may be selected not because someone is particularly good at it but because it is the clearest path to a well-paying career. How is someone truly supposed to commit themselves to an area of study and potential career when they are still trying to figure out who they are and what they like?

In a survey undertaken by Ellucian (a company that sells enterprise resource planning systems to higher education), it was found that more than half of college students change their majors at least once, and approximately two-thirds of students feel overwhelmed by the process of selecting a major[16] This is in keeping with data from the US Department of Education that finds that approximately 30% of undergraduates change their major at least once within three years of initial enrollment and approximately 10% change their majors more than once.[17] Further, in a survey conducted by Best Colleges, 61% of college graduates indicated that they would change their majors if they could go back.[18] If this provides an accurate reflection of the attitudes of college graduates, higher education needs to do a much better job of matching students with a major.

One possible explanation for why some students switch majors (multiple times) is that many majors do not provide a clear career path, and the skills they do develop are not immediately transferable to a first job. A finding in the report "Robot Ready" commissioned by Emsi and the Strada Education Network is that for many liberal arts graduates, it often takes the third job before they can make best use of their education."[19]

For many institutions, investing in a strong career services office is thought to be the solution for how to best place students in majors and career opportunities that will serve them well. Beginning to understand what you are good at and how those skills can translate into a fulfilling work life can contribute to better decisions in selecting a major. In addition, resume reviews, networking nights, and mock interviews are all effective tools for preparing a student for their first interview. The reality is most students wait until their senior year to work with career services. In a 2017 Strada-Gallup survey, 40% of the undergraduates who participated revealed that they never utilized career services.[20]

The consequence of not having sufficient time and direction to make what are potentially life-enabling opportunities creates a tremendous amount of uncertainty paired with a fair amount of anxiety.[21] These feelings are often exacerbated by underdeveloped time management skills that are essential for balancing the social, academic, and professional components of the undergraduate experience.[22] That being said, this is a challenge exacerbated by the fact that 70% of university students work, thereby placing additional constraints on time.[23]

Curriculum

The structure of higher education has remained largely unchanged since the formative years between 1890 and 1940.[24] Here, breadth of understanding is generally encapsulated in some type of general education program, while depth is reserved for the major, which represents a more focused area of study. Students are required to attend class, and are assessed through an examination process that, for the most part, judges individual effort and understanding.

Nevertheless, there are some skills required for academic success that transcend disciplinary boundaries. The ability to express oneself through the written word is one of them. Writing, similar to many other skills, requires practice to gain improvement. While many universities require a composition course for all first-year students, they also recognize that it takes multiple opportunities spanning all four years to develop someone's writing ability. As a result, the idea of writing across the curriculum was born. In short order, many universities adopted this approach, where opportunities to write were embedded in discipline-based courses that a student would encounter as they made progress toward earning their degree.[25]

A student, however, can become a good writer and not necessarily possess those written communication skills that are very much in demand by employers. If writing is to transition from a means for expressing discipline-based knowledge into a work-ready capability, there must not only be multiple opportunities to practice the skill of writing, but also opportunities to put that skill into practice in a variety of different applications (thereby transforming writing from a skill into a capability). For majors that have a tightly coupled career path (e.g., nursing, accounting, or engineering), this may be a nonissue. For other majors, such as physics, economics, or history, where multiple career paths exist that may only be tangentially related to the degree, a substantial disconnect might exist.

If higher education is to embrace the concept of creating a work-ready graduate, then comparable programs like one that would feature some form of capabilities across the curriculum need to be created. This would require faculty and administrators to look outward to identify a set of essential skills and then create multiple opportunities to develop those skills through multiple applications. However, to turn those skills into capabilities, those opportunities will need to be tightly coupled to the needs of the workplace rather than defined by a specific academic discipline.

Connections

Alumni play a key role in how universities assess, rate, and market work-readiness, and institutions often emphasize the professional success of their alumni as a proxy for their ability to produce work-ready graduates. Alumni are frequently asked to share their wealth of experience with students as a way to impart professional skills and lessons. These interactions, however, are rarely integrated into the curriculum or classroom, and are unknown or inaccessible to the majority of students.

To take advantage of the professional experience of their graduates, many institutions have created mentorship programs. A mentor is meant to take an interest in the student as a person and is able to offer guidance that leads to career success. A 2018 Strada and Gallup Alumni Survey revealed, however, that only 43% of those surveyed either strongly or somewhat agreed that they had a mentor who encouraged them to pursue their goals and dreams. Further, of the 43% of students who agreed they had a mentor, 64% identified that person as being a faculty member, instead of an external professional or alumni mentor.[26]

This is problematic because many faculty members have spent their entire lives in academia. They are intimately familiar with a particular body of knowledge or the internal politics that dominate life in a university but have limited contact with the so-called "real world." In fields where there are not direct pathways to careers, the quality of advice offered by faculty is not necessarily aligned with providing future success outside of academic institutions. Additionally, the connection or network that might influence gaining an interview or first job is, in many cases, nonexistent.

Universities are trying to bring in more external mentors and cultivate these professional networks for students, but they are careful to limit access to alumni or business affiliates so that these connections are not over-burdened by requests. This means that fewer students benefit from meaningful connections, mentorship relationships, or career opportunities.[27] There exists an unrealized opportunity to extend these alumni and professional relationships to the majority of students, which may ultimately translate to more work-readiness.

Signals

A 2017 benchmarking report published by The Society for Human Resource Management (SHRM) found that the average recruitment cost per hire was $4425, and it took 36 days to fill the position.[28] If you asked an economist why companies invest that much time and effort to recruit a new employee, they would attribute it to the problem of asymmetric information. Asymmetric information is an academic way of saying 'I know something you don't know.' A candidate knows what they have to offer to an organization, and a recruiter knows the demands of the job. By reviewing a resume, the recruiter can make a series of educated guesses, but it often takes more to determine whether a candidate is worth the investment to invite into the organization.

According to economist Bryan Caplan, it all comes down to signaling.[29] Do the choices that a student makes in terms of major, courses taken, extracurriculars, and other activities send strong enough signals to justify the investment of time and money? In other words, to what extent do these signals reflect the degree to which an undergraduate is work-ready?

These signals are important because the capabilities that position a graduate to be work-ready are not always obvious by looking at a student's choice of major, course work, or experiences. Students with majors such as sociology, biology, or communications that do not provide a clear pathway to a first job might find it more difficult to send a clear signal of how they can perform at a specific job.[30]

A more granular approach of looking at individual courses does not necessarily add clarity as courses often fulfill multiple goals that can make it challenging for a potential employer to determine what has been learned and which skills have been developed. These goals include the following:

- Identify or sustain an area of interest (major, minor, concentration, credential, etc.)
- Create a broader understanding and appreciation of a wide diversity of ideas, events, and perspectives
- Acquire a deeper understanding of a body of knowledge
- Develop useful skills
- Career Preparation

It should therefore come as no surprise that a transcript review of courses taken provides a sense of what a graduate presumably learned, but with instructors trying to achieve multiple goals, it can be challenging to connect them to a graduate's work-readiness.

Technology

Technology has increasingly become an important part of the life of every faculty member either as the creator or, now, curator of knowledge and information that encompasses the academic experience. New avenues for self-expression allow a broader range of voices to be heard. With the explosive growth in ideas easily accessible to everyone, there is an increasing need to determine which voices or ideas merit further consideration and which are adding noise rather than substance to important conversations.

This change has also created an opportunity for artificial intelligence and machine learning to subsume part of the role of a faculty member. Artificial intelligence can be used to determine what information is of value within a given area, and machine learning can, over time, refine what is determined to be relevant. Moreover, the same technology can be used not only to put together a course of study for a group of students but also to personalize learning for individual members of a class. The technology can be used to assess individuals and put together a list of readings or exercises that match a learner's needs. With technology and the development of individualized learning plans, each student has a chance to master a body of knowledge and achieve academic success.

The promise of new technology is that it can offer a personalized and more robust academic experience, coordinate social and professional activities that contribute to the undergraduate experience, and open up new opportunities to connect with alumni and members of the broader business community. It can become an important tool for the development of a work-ready graduate.

At the same time, these technologies are opening the door to a slew of new competitors that are challenging what has traditionally been the domain of higher education. EdTech in all of its different forms can both support existing institutions and create a slate of offerings that serve as a substitute for the traditional collegiate experience. Ultimately, this will either strengthen or seriously weaken colleges and universities as they grapple with deciding how much to embrace this changing technological landscape.

A Way Forward

Those in favor of the status quo point to the premium that college graduates earn relative to those with a high school degree and conclude that nothing truly needs to change. Looking at the 2021 report produced by Georgetown University's Center on Education and the Workforce, it is estimated that the lifetime earnings of full-time workers with a high school diploma are $1.6 million while those who have a bachelor's degree have a median earnings of $2.8 million,[31] thereby serving as justification for the current higher education model.[32]

In the minds of many, if a problem exists, it must be a messaging one. The solution is for higher education to do a better job of explaining how students are developing needed job skills even if they are not readily apparent at the time of graduation. Better messaging, over real reform, is needed to compete effectively against the explosion of certificate programs, non-degree programs, online courses, and the growing list of alternative forms of obtaining education.

We disagree, and with good reason: a 2019 survey of entering first-year students undertaken by the Higher Education Research Institute (HERI) at UCLA suggests that the number one reason for enrolling in college (82.4% listing as very important) was the ability to get a better job. However, a Pew Research Study found that while 62% of college graduates felt that their time in college was useful in helping them grow personally and intellectually, only 49% said it was very useful in helping them develop skills and knowledge they could use in the workplace. In addition, a McGraw-Hill-Hanover survey found that only 21% of college students felt very prepared for a professional career.[33]

In our opinion, these outcomes indicate that there is a larger issue than just a messaging problem. Students come looking for better employment opportunities, and many leave feeling disappointed that the experience did not meet their expectations. If higher education is to maintain its position as the premier source for talent by hiring professionals, then more must be done to support both the acquisition of knowledge *and* the development of work-ready capabilities.

Notes

1. Berrett (2015).
2. Gallup and Lumina Foundation (2022).
3. National Center for Education Statistics (2021).
4. The $6.6 billion dollar figure comes from Mitchell et al. (2019).

   Recent changes in state funding for higher education and prospects for the future are discussed in depth in "The Higher Ed Funding Rollercoaster: State Funding of Higher Education During Financial Crises" (National Education Association, 2022).

   See also Urahn et al. (2019).
5. Dickler (2021).
6. This is part of a growing trend that questions the return associated with the investment in a college education.
7. Board of Govenors (2022, p. 71).
8. Board of Governors (2022, p. 72).
9. We will be making the case for strengthening the residential collegiate experience. An alternate view is offered by Ernst & Young. Identifying the forces that are driving change in higher education, traditional values are cast aside in their view of the future of higher education (Friday, 2022).
10. See, for example, Huang (2023).
11. For a description of Industry 4.0 and what it means for the future of work, see McKinsey & Company (2022). A more extensive discussion can be found in Schwab (2017).
12. The Future of Jobs and Jobs Training: As robots, automation and artificial intelligence perform more tasks and there is massive disruption of jobs, experts say a wider array of education and skills-building programs will be created to meet new demands. There are two uncertainties: Will well-prepared workers be able to keep up in the race with AI tools? And will market capitalism survive? Raine and Anderson (2017).
13. On a more positive note, an often-cited World Economic Forum report reaches the conclusion that "...by 2025, 85 million jobs may be displaced by a shift in the division of labour between humans and machines, while 97 million new roles may emerge that are more adapted to the new division of labour between humans, machines and algorithms." This represents a net gain of 12 million jobs. However, there is, of course, no guarantee that such a transition will in fact lead to a net gain in jobs (World Economic Forum, 2020).
14. See, for example, Wilkie (2019), Hansen (2021), and Carnevale et al. (2020).
15. "We needn't be intimated by AI. The human brain is incredible. It is far more complex and more powerful than any AI in existence. So rather than

fearing AI and automation and the changes this will bring to workplaces, we should all be looking to harness our unique human capabilities and cultivate these softer skills—skills that will become all the more important for the future of work" (Marr, 2020).

16. The Higher Education Research Institute (HERI) at UCLA surveys high school seniors to get a sense of who they are, what they have accomplished, and their goals and dreams. In the most recent survey, approximately 9% of entering first-year students are undecided about their major, 10.9% estimate that there is a very good chance that they will change their major, and, related to that, 11.6% estimate that there is a very good chance they will change their career choice. See Stolzenberg et al. (2020) for further data.
17. Leu (2017).
18. Johnson (2020).
19. For more details, see Weise et al. (2018).
20. Strada Educational Network and Gallup (2018).
21. For an in-depth discussion of mental health issues, see chapter 6 in Fischman and Gardner (2022). See also Van Der Meer et al. (2010).
22. Time Management is one of the most important skills listed in the Wiley University Services (2023) report. It is also included as a top skill in the governmental report on Workforce Automation (United States Government Accountability Offices, 2022).
23. Seventy percent of students work and they must balance that time commitment as well. This disproportionately affects low-income students and students of color (Carnevale & Smith, 2018).
24. An interesting discussion of the formative years of higher education can be found in Goldin and Katz (1999).
25. A history of writing across the curriculum can be found in Palmquist et al. (2020).
26. Strada Educational Network and Gallup (2018).
27. A Gallup survey in 2019 found that only 9% of graduates reported that their alumni network has been very helpful or helpful to them in the job market. For more details, see Auter and Marken (2019).
28. See Society for Human Resource Management (2017) for more data.
29. See Caplan (2018).
30. That is why, in many cases, unless a student is committed to earning a graduate degree in the field, many might shy away from the major because there is not a clear career pathway.
31. For more information, see Carnevale et al. (2021).
32. Of course not all majors generate the same return. See, for example, Winters (2022). A real-time interactive tool developed by the Federal

Reserve Bank of New York (2023) can be found at: https://www.newyorkfed.org/research/college-labor-market/index.html#/outcomes-by-major.

33. The view from the employer's perspective is captured in Finley et al. (2021).

References

Auter, Z., & Marken, S. (2019, January 15). *Alumni networks less helpful than advertised*. Gallup, Inc. Retrieved March 21, 2023, from https://news.gallup.com/opinion/gallup/245822/alumni-networks-less-helpful-advertised.aspx

Berrett, D. (2015, January 26). The day the purpose of college changed. *The Chronicle of Higher Education*. Retrieved March 21, 2023, from https://www.chronicle.com/article/the-day-the-purpose-of-college-changed/

Board of Govenors Federal Reserve System. (2022, May). *Economic Well-being of U.S. Households in 2021*, from https://www.federalreserve.gov/publications/files/2021-report-economic-well-being-us-households-202205.pdf

Caplan, B. D. (2018). *The case against education: Why the education system is a waste of time and money*. Princeton University Press.

Carnevale, A. P., Cheah, B., Van Der Werf, M., & Gulish, A. (2020). *Buyer beware: First year earnings and debt for 37,000 college majors at 4,400 institutions*. Center on Education and the Workforce, Georgetown University.

Carnevale, A. P., Cheah, B., & Wenzinger, E. (2021). *The college payoff: More education doesn't always mean more earnings*. Center on Education and the Workforce, Georgetown University.

Carnevale, A. P., & Smith, N. (2018). *Balancing work and learning: Implications for low income students*. Center on Education and the Workforce, Georgetown University. Retrieved March 23, 2023, from https://cewgeorgetown.wpengine.powered.com/wp-content/uploads/Low-Income-Working-Learners-FR.pdf

Dickler, J. (2021, November 5). Less than half of high schoolers want to go to a four-year college, survey finds. *CNBC*. Retrieved March 21, 2023, from https://www.cnbc.com/2021/11/05/interest-in-four-year-college-sinks-post-covid-as-costs-concerns-rise.html

Federal Reserve Bank of New York. (2023). *The labor market for recent college graduates*. Federal Reserve Bank of New York. Retrieved March 21, 2023, from https://www.newyorkfed.org/research/college-labor-market/index.html#/outcomes-by-major

Finley, A., Aborn, M., Ruddy, S., & Miller, K. (2021). *Is college worth the time and money?* Bipartisan Policy Center and Association of American Colleges and Universities. Retrieved March 21, 2023, from https://bipartisanpolicy.org/download/?file=/wp-content/uploads/2021/09/BPC_Fed-State_Brief_R05.pdf

Fischman, W., & Gardner, H. (2022). *The real world of college: What higher education is and what it can be.* The MIT Press.

Friday, C. (2022, January 24). *Are universities of the past still the future?* Ernst & Young Global Ltd. Retrieved March 21, 2023, from https://www.ey.com/en_sy/education/are-universities-of-the-past-still-the-future

Gallup and Lumina Foundation. (2022). *The state of higher education 2022 report.* Gallup, Inc. Retrieved March 21, 2023, from https://www.gallup.com/analytics/391829/state-of-higher-education-2022.aspx

Goldin, C., & Katz, L. (1999). The shaping of higher education: The formative years in the United States, 1890 to 1940. *Journal of Economic Perspectives, 13*(1), 37–62.

Hansen, M. (2021, May 18). The U.S. education system isn't giving students what employers need. *Harvard Business Review.* Retrieved March 21, 2023, from https://hbr.org/2021/05/the-u-s-education-system-isnt-giving-students-what-employers-need

Huang, K. (2023, January 26). Alarmed by A.I. Chatbots, universities start revamping how they teach. *The New York Times.* Retrieved March 21, 2023, from https://www.nytimes.com/2023/01/16/technology/chatgpt-artificial-intelligence-universities.html

Johnson, R. (2020). New survey finds most college grads would change majors. *Best Colleges.* Retrieved from https://www.bestcolleges.com/blog/college-graduate-majors-survey/

Leu, K. (2017). *Data point: Beginning college students who change their major within 3 years of enrollment.* National Center for Education Statistics. Retrieved March 21, 2023, from https://nces.ed.gov/pubsearch/pubsinfo.asp?pubid=2018434

Marr, B. (2020, September 28). 9 soft skills every employee will need in the age of artificial intelligence. *Forbes.* Retrieved March 21, 2023, from https://www.forbes.com/sites/bernardmarr/2020/09/28/9-soft-skills-every-employee-will-need-in-the-age-of-artificial-intelligence-ai/?sh=1f6fddb554b8

McKinsey & Company. (2022, August 17). *What are Industry 4.0, the fourth industrial revolution, and 4IR?* McKinsey & Company. Retrieved March 21, 2023, from https://www.mckinsey.com/featured-insights/mckinsey-explainers/what-are-industry-4-0-the-fourth-industrial-revolution-and-4ir

Mitchell, M., Leachman, M., & Saenz, M. (2019, October 24). *State higher education funding cuts have pushed costs to students, worsened inequities.* Center on Budget and Policy Priorities. Retrieved March 21, 2023, from https://www.cbpp.org/research/state-budget-and-tax/state-higher-education-funding-cuts-have-pushed-costs-to-students

National Center for Education Statistics. (2021). *Digest of Educational Statistics; Table 330.10: Average undergraduate tuition, fees, room, and board rates charged for full-time students in degree-granting postsecondary institutions, by level and control of institution: Selected years, 1963–64 through 2020–21*. The Department of Education's Institute of Educational Sciences. Retrieved March 21, 2023, from https://nces.ed.gov/programs/digest/d21/tables/dt21_330.10.asp

National Education Association. (2022). *The higher ed funding rollercoaster: State funding of higher education during financial crises*. National Education Association. Retrieved March 21, 2023, from https://www.nea.org/hefunding_report

Palmquist, M., Childers, P., Maimon, E., Mullin, J., Rice, R., Russell, A., & Russell, D. R. (2020). Fifty years of wac: Where have we been? Where are we going? *Across the Disciplines, 17*(3), 5–45. https://doi.org/10.37514/ATD-J.2020.17.3.01

Raine, L., & Anderson, J. (2017, May 3). *The future of jobs and jobs training*. Pew Research Center. Retrieved March 21, 2023, from https://www.pewresearch.org/internet/2017/05/03/the-future-of-jobs-and-jobs-training/

Schwab, K. (2017). *The fourth industrial revolution*. Crown Business.

Society for Human Resource Management. (2017). *SHRM customized human capital benchmarking report*. Society for Human Resource Management. Retrieved March 21, 2023, from https://www.shrm.org/hr-today/news/hr-magazine/0918/pages/accentuate-the-positive.aspx

Stolzenberg, E. B., Aragon, M. C., Romo, E., Couch, V., McLennan, D., Eagan, M. K., & Kang, N. (2020). *The American freshman: National norms fall 2019*. Higher Education Research Institute, UCLA. Retrieved March 21, 2023, from https://www.scribd.com/document/510883541/The-American-Freshman-2019#

Strada Educational Network and Gallup. (2018). *2018 Strada-Gallup Alumni Survey: Mentoring college students to success*. Gallup, Inc. Retrieved March 21, 2023, from https://go.stradaeducation.org/strada-gallup-alumni-survey

United States Government Accountability Office. (2022, August). *Workforce Automation*. GAO-22-105159

Urahn, S. K., Irwin, M., Stauffer, A., Oliff, P., Foard, C., Thiess, R., Reese, M., Samms, B., Bryant, M., Pontari, L., Spence, E., & Einsiedler, J. (2019). *Two decades of change in federal and state higher education funding: Recent trends across levels of government*. The PEW Charitable Trusts. Retrieved March 21, 2023, from https://www.pewtrusts.org/-/media/assets/2019/10/fedstatefundinghigheredu_chartbook_v1.pdf

Van Der Meer, J., Jansen, E., & Torenbeek, M. (2010). 'It's almost a mindset that teachers need to change': First-year students' need to be inducted into time management. *Studies in Higher Education, 35*(7), 777–791. https://doi.org/10.1080/03075070903383211

Weise, M., Hanson, A., Sentz, R., Saleh, Y., Ashburn, E., & Botkin, D. (2018). *Robot ready: Human+ skills for the future of work*. Strada Institute for the Future & Emsi. Retrieved March 21, 2023, from https://www.luminafoundation.org/resource/robot-ready-human-skills-for-the-future-of-work/

Wiley University Services. (2023). *Closing the skills gap 2023: Employer perspectives on educating the post-pandemic workforce*. John Wiley & Sons, Inc. Retrieved March 23, 2023, from https://beyond.wiley.com/resources/skills-gap-report/

Wilkie, D. (2019, October 21). *What happened to the promise of a 4-year college degree?* Society for Human Resource Management. Retrieved March 21, 2023, from https://www.shrm.org/resourcesandtools/hr-topics/employee-relations/pages/what-happened-to-the-promise-of-a-4-year-college-degree.aspx

Winters, M. (2022, February 12). The best- and worst-paying college majors, five years after graduation. *CNBC*. Retrieved March 21, 2023, from https://www.cnbc.com/2022/02/12/the-best-and-worst-paying-college-majors-five-years-after-graduation.html

World Economic Forum. (2020). *The future of jobs report*. World Economic Forum. Retrieved March 21, 2023, from https://www3.weforum.org/docs/WEF_Future_of_Jobs_2020.pdf

Human Capabilities

For futurists such as Kevin Roose who see a technology-driven economy gradually becoming dominated by AI, the key to successfully navigating this new reality is to focus on areas where humans excel. In his book *Futureproof*, Roose proposes a mantra that is predicated on capabilities that fall within the categories of: surprising, social, and scarce. In their totality, they put forth a strategy designed to prepare for a future infused with AI.

Surprising refers to dealing with unexpected, sporadic, or non-static situations and environments. People who can more easily adapt, be flexible, pivot, or adjust to change will thrive in this new work environment. This is a trait that AI has a difficult time addressing. Because AI is 'educated' through specific source information or cases, it has difficulty responding to environments that fluctuate, are changing beyond its current learning, or do not conform to set parameters.

Social is a broad set of skills that higher education and employers alike yearn for in undergraduates. Skills in verbal and written communication, collaboration, ethics, emotional intelligence, and various forms of leadership are all in high demand and highly desirable to work in the AI landscape.

Scarce, in this context, is "work that involves unusual combinations of skills, high-stakes situations, or extraordinary talent,"[1] "work that will be either impractical or socially unacceptable to automate," or work that mandates problem-solving or critical thinking and requires a combination of skills or knowledge. Humans have robust capabilities to generate or apply ideas across situations or disciplines and posess the ability to see

N. B. Niman, J. R. Chagnon, *The Work-Ready Graduate*,
https://doi.org/10.1007/978-3-031-33910-3_3

potential applications and connections—human capabilities which are not yet appearing in the design of AI. The goal is to create human capabilities that complement AI, rather than challenge it.

If today's graduates are to be prepared for this coming revolution, higher education needs to focus on critical thinking as it is applied in non-static environments that reflect various shades of gray. Students, especially undergraduates, need to learn how to function in changing situations and how to assess the options before them. Many undergraduates are trained to follow a syllabus, respond in a certain way to a fixed set of parameters, or give a 'safe' answer.[2] They often struggle or become anxious when structure is pulled away or processes are not clearly defined. Rather than tackling flexibility and adaptability head on, higher education frequently turns away or delegates this learning to experts, internships, or life experiences.[3]

Work-Related Intelligences

In a bitter ironic twist, AI has advanced to the point where it may be outperforming some students in writing essays and papers. [4] However, despite these advances, communication still plays a crucial role in those positions that will not be displaced as the technology becomes increasingly prevalent in the workplace. The collaboration and leadership qualities needed for team performance are more nuanced and often built on human capabilities such as situational awareness and emotional intelligence, or they call on motivational or persuasive skills.

The commonalities of employers' most in-demand skills are in their nature, whether looking at AI/futureproof skills, soft skills, smart skills, or twenty-first-century skills. They are woven into our fabric as humans and are structured in our own coding and neural networks. These are human capabilities that we have appreciated for years, and should continue to be cultivated.

From a business perspective, this might begin with a strategic analysis based on an emerging opportunity created by new advances in technology. It might include the creativity of extending existing technology in new and purpose-driven ways that requires the formation of a well-functioning team to bring together a collection of expertise to fashion a solution. Alternatively, it may require the ability to assess a given situation, process the requisite information, and act decisively in response to random factor, the ability to communicate with different sources of information to assess their relevance to the current set of circumstances and respond accordingly, or the ability to plan for a future based on the current available information.

Capabilities provide the means to enhance human intelligence in a direction that supports distinct work-related intelligences. In doing so, they will place higher education in a stronger position by preparing students to apply their knowledge in a manner that will have an impact in the workplace or broader society. In a networked economy where solutions require resources and human capital spread across multiple organizations or disciplines, *social intelligence* in the form of being able to navigate complex social and organizational relationships is crucial for success. The existence of a wealth of data requires the ability to make evidence-based decisions that utilize *analytical intelligence*. In a world where diversity in all of its richness is something to be celebrated, *competitive intelligence* captures the strategies required to respond to a truly global marketplace. Finally, *professional intelligence* is seen as the ability to put knowledge into practice in actual business situations.

Thinking in terms of work-related intelligence may be higher education's best response to the changing landscape created by the rise in AI for purpose-driven work. From the perspective of Deloitte, a global accounting and consulting firm, the largest impact that AI will have on organizations is by making operations more efficient, supporting better decision-making, and freeing up workers from repetitive tasks to be more creative. In characterizing the future, Deloitte researchers "propose reimagining work not as a set of tasks arranged in a predefined process but, rather, as a collaborative effort in which humans define the problems, machines help find the solutions, and humans verify the acceptability of those solutions."[5]

Skills, Competencies, and Capabilities

If we are to reimagine work, what is the best way to prepare for a new future? 'Work-ready' is a collection of words that may mean one thing for some people and something entirely different for others. Is it all about the acquisition of skills? What about experience? Isn't someone more capable if they have put their skills into practice in some meaningful way? Is this just a way of talking about competency—the real currency for determining if someone is work-ready? Or is it truly about capability—the capacity to grow and become better positioned to perform sometime in the future? When we talk about skills, competency, and capabilities, the words are often used interchangeably. For the purposes of identifying what makes a work-ready graduate, it makes sense to be more precise in how we use these terms.

Skills are generally viewed as a type of work or action that is performed in relation to finite parameters (such as amount of time or specific environment), and often tied to a person's current capacity (a limited degree of execution).

Competencies are a demonstrated set of knowledge, skills, and behaviors that have been utilized to achieve a desired performance in the present. Successive performance that achieves that task (either once or multiple times) confers information about one's capacity to perform in a particular role.

Capabilities refer to the potential ability to take knowledge and skills that have been learned and/or practiced and apply them to new and unfamiliar circumstances at some point in the future.

The distinction between competency and capability is important for understanding talent development. Think of professional development as representing a spectrum with skills at one end, competency in the middle, and capability at the other ending point. Or alternatively, meeting the needs of the present in contrast to preparing for the challenges posed by the future. It is not an either/or, but rather a matter of degree (Fig. 1).

These distinctions take on special significance when identifying what it means to be work-ready. Being work-ready means that a graduate has the ability to contribute in a meaningful way to advance a shared set of goals related to their employment. To do that, a graduate needs to enter the workforce with a set of foundational capabilities that are transferable and therefore applicable to a number of different uses and employers. This is not a one-size-fits-all exercise but rather reflects the natural aptitude, skills acquired, knowledge gained, and set of experiences that enable them to put that knowledge into practice. In summation:

> Work-ready capabilities are developed from meaningful experiences that give students an opportunity to put their knowledge, behavior, and skills into practice within a work-related context. It is a *process* that requires multiple iterations that occur across a variety of authentic situations.

Capabilities develop from the interaction between skills, knowledge, and experience. It is a dynamic process that requires the acquisition of skills, the ability to understand when and how to use those skills in a particular

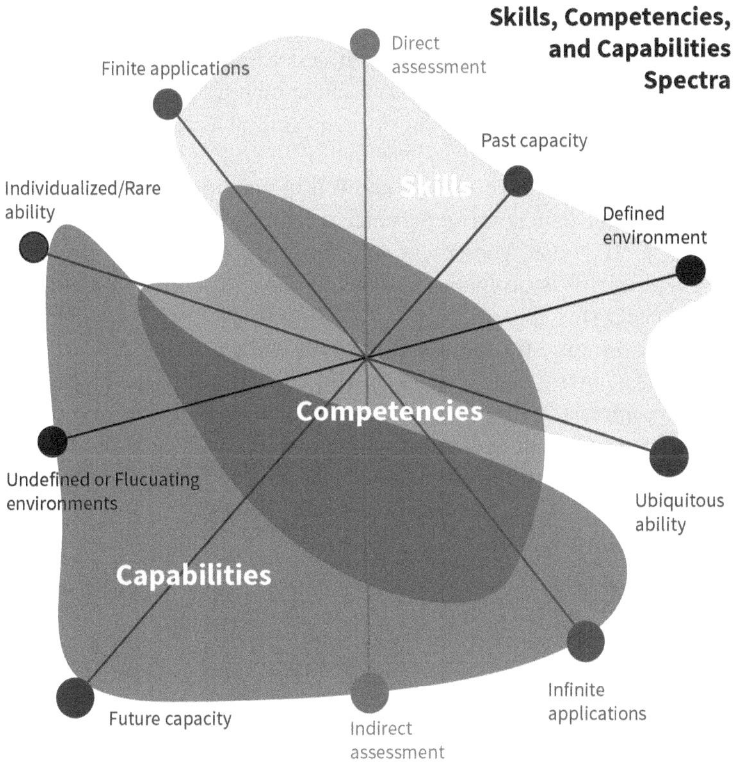

Fig. 1 Skills, competencies, and capabilities are visualized across spectra that define these terms. Spectra include past to future capacity, defined to undefined/fluctuating environments, ubiquitous to individual/rare abilities, finite to infinite applications, and direct to indirect assessments

context, and the appropriate experiences where skills can be put into practice in a meaningful way. Capabilities are developed over time in a variety of contexts with a number of different applications. The goal is not to become proficient in performing a task in a single situation but rather to become forward thinking and able to perform when facing future opportunities or challenges.

Twenty-First-Century Skills

The World Economic Forum has identified what they believe are the top 15 skills for 2025 (see Fig. 2 below).[6] These include a mix of skills that can be acquired in a typical classroom or on an online learning platform where a student for the most part passively listens (learning by listening) as ideas are presented. The entire experience might include exercises or simulations designed to gain some experience working with those ideas and then engaging with some assessment mechanism to measure the amount learned. All of this is designed to develop a baseline level of competency. One often sees this approach as part of a certificate program designed to foster the development of industry-focused skills.

In contrast, many of the skills on the list are better developed with a more active approach that can be characterized as experiential learning or, put another way, learning by doing. These skills are not something easily taught but rather acquired over time through a series of structured learning experiences. It is possible to teach someone why flexibility is

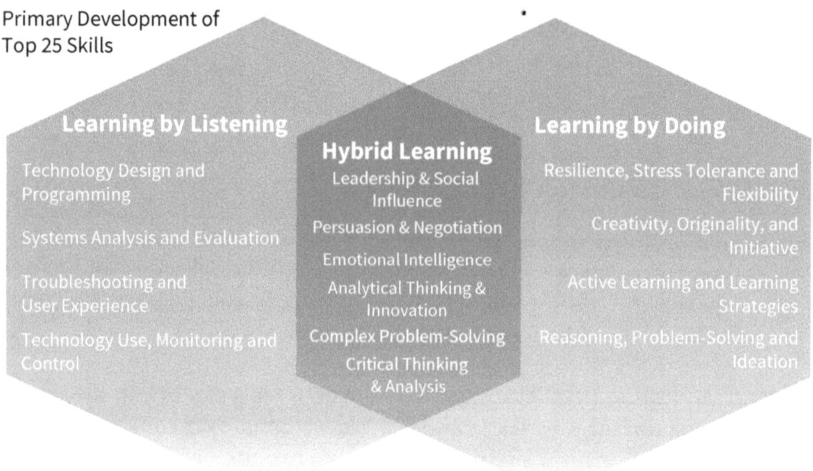

Fig. 2 The top 25 skills as forecast by the World Economic Forum for 2025 represent a combination of technical and smart/soft skills. The diagram categorizes the list of skills by the primary way in which these skills would be developed: learning by listening, learning by doing, and a hybrid approach

important, but it is something entirely different for them to actually become more flexible. Typically, they need to be placed into several structured experiences where they are required to exhibit flexibility and then have an opportunity to reflect on those experiences.

In many instances, it is not an either this or that proposition. It is possible to teach the principles underlying negotiations in a standard course. However, students will only feel secure in their knowledge after they have an opportunity to place that knowledge into practice. Sitting across the table from someone and having to negotiate a lower price or more favorable contract terms provides much needed context and introduces a confluence of factors that have a bearing on the final outcome. These skills might be best developed through a hybrid approach that combines both learning by doing and by listening (Fig. 2).

According to data from the Future of Jobs Survey, formal upskilling appears to be more closely focused on technology use and design skills, while human skills are less frequently targeted in that formal reskilling provision.[7] In addition, data from Coursera (a major player in the EdTech space) confirms this finding.[8] On the other hand, with regard to important human skills such as active learning, resilience, stress tolerance, and flexibility, there is a dearth of skill development opportunities.

Opportunities for learning how to be more adept at what are traditionally thought of as soft or smart skills, are better developed as part of a process. While some of the skills can be taught in a classroom alone, the majority (and arguably all) are personalized skills that require the learner to interact with them intimately. Skills like creativity, originality, innovation and problem solving cannot easily be mapped from one individual onto another.

Embedding learning in meaningful activity is a necessary and effective means to teach such skills and develop them into capabilities.[9] This development is the result of an informal learning process that relies more on figuring things out than applying a set of abstract principles.

Essentially, context is everything. Because we all learn how to learn informally (think of speaking, walking, brushing our teeth),[10] fostering capabilities is not about discovering the best way to do something in the abstract, but rather about how to best navigate an existing set of circumstances to solve a problem or accomplish a specific end goal, which we all do differently.

Becoming more resilient, for example, depends on the ability to bounce back when encountering adversity. Resiliency is a capability that develops over time as a series of obstacles are encountered. It represents the type of learning that emerges from the application of knowledge and behavior in a particular situation.

Storytelling: An Example

One thing that we have learned as part of the assurance of learning (AOL) process that Paul College adopted for Association to Advance Collegiate Schools of Business (AACSB) accreditation is that there is more to creating a work-ready graduate than fulfilling a course requirement. Take, for example, verbal communication.[11] As part of the AOL process, an industry professional serving as an adjunct instructor and a UNH professor from the communications department were asked to evaluate a number of student presentations. While the professional chose to evaluate the presentations primarily from a content perspective, the communication professor looked more closely at presentation skills. What surprised the Paul College committee most was that despite the reviewers' very different perspectives, both were consistent in their evaluations of the students' presentations.

What was concluded from both reviewers was that in all but a small number of cases, the students were just meeting expectations. The presentations reflected more of what happens when a student is simply trying to meet the requirements of an assignment, rather than what it might look like if a young professional were making a similar presentation to colleagues or the senior leadership team. Both the evaluators and committee wondered how that gap might be closed so that students could perform at a level that does more than merely meet expectations.

In the work world, the need for effective communicators requires more than standing in front of an audience or putting together a series of coherent slides or sentences. Employers are looking for storytellers—the ability to construct a story capable of engaging an audience by forming an emotional connection that can inspire, motivate, or persuade.[12] It is about providing a context for conveying important information in a manner that is impactful and (hopefully) leads to action. Of equal value is the ability to extract a subset of numbers from a dataset and use them to construct a compelling story.

At the heart of any good story is the larger narrative.[13] The narrative provides order to the events or pieces of information that are subsequently communicated. It affects how a story is perceived and ultimately the impact that it might potentially have on the reader or listener.

When communication skills are developed into the ability to construct and deliver a compelling narrative, a work-ready capability is born. Communication as a set of skills represents demonstrated abilities such as translating/expressing ideas or concepts into words, transferring knowledge to others, or presenting information orally or visually.

Storytelling as a capability represents the ability to take a set of data or collection of ideas and structure thoughts in a manner that makes an impression, potentially serving as a call to action and, at the very least, a lasting memory.[14] Like many other capabilities, creating a narrative is often a deeply personal skill that cannot be learned through a lecture. It must be practiced and made one's own. How you and I construct narratives will necessarily be a reflection of who we are as individuals.[15]

The power of storytelling was used as a compelling learning tool in an early effort to rethink how to teach the principles of economics, under the direction of Neil when he was the Associate Dean of Academic Programs. The project was called EconJourney and utilized storytelling as a mechanism for both learning and applying economic principles.[16] Each week, students were introduced to a select number of microeconomic principles and then asked to use them in a highly structured writing assignment that extended across the entire semester. The idea was for the student to create a story where the main character needed to overcome a problem rooted in the concept of scarcity, in which foundational ideas were used to overcome a challenge so that the main character could advance to the next stage of their journey.

Fashioned on Joseph Campbell's *Hero's Journey*, the course design used a common story archetype to help the student think creatively, problem solve, and learn basic economic principles.[17] Students could rely on a digital guide called Story Coach that would assist in the construction of a coherent structure that kept the story moving forward based on the new economics concepts added that week. Weekly writing assignments were submitted electronically and evaluated by trained peer graders. The frequent feedback was used to improve more than just the weekly writing. Every fourth week, students were required to take their writing and combine it into a finished chapter that would comprise part of the final story they would turn in at the end of the semester. In this way, communication became a fundamental part of the learning process, and students were given ample opportunities to improve their storytelling abilities. The EconJourney project is an example of how the development of human capabilities can be tied to context and become an integral part of a course.

The Future of Work

Preparing the next generation for purpose-driven lives where tight labor markets are providing a myriad of opportunities that offer a variety of working conditions should prompt us to think differently about how we prepare a work-ready graduate. In addition to developing those capabilities required to transition to the workplace, we need to help prepare graduates for a more flexible work environment where they have an opportunity to make choices that will have a profound impact on job satisfaction, career advancement, and the ability to create a positive work–life balance.

In a post-COVID-19 world, how we work has become as important as what we work on.[18] This is the premise behind what some have called the Great Reflection, where work–life balance has for many become more important than compensation or the path to advancement within an organization.[19]

A Future Forum survey conducted in November 2021 found that 95% of respondents wanted flexible hours and 78% were looking for location flexibility[20] Along with greater flexibility has come a change in how we collaborate and how work is evaluated. Appearance-based indicators (being present and looking busy) are giving way to value creation assessments.[21]

As entire organizations seek to attract and retain the best talent by embedding greater flexibility into their organizations, new challenges are emerging. When employees are scattered across time zones and physical locations where some are in the office and others may never be, how and when they collaborate is also changing. A new type of balance is coming into play between collaboration time and focused time for individual work.[22] What is emerging is the concept of asynchronous work, where employees are able to create a work schedule that best suits their lives *and* the needs of the organization. The concept of teamwork has expanded to include working effectively with others in multiple modalities and according to different conceptions of time and the structure of the workday.

All of this has grown in importance as, for many, work is no longer tied to maintaining a physical presence in a specific location, and flexibility is more the exception than the rule.[23] The residential collegiate experience consisting of *Attendance* (a student is mandated to show up to class at a specific time and place), *Assignments* (a specific set of activities designed to enhance knowledge-based understanding), and *Assessments* (a measurement of how well a student performs relative to a predefined rubric) at one time might have at one time been closely aligned with the structure of the workplace, however, in the current dynamic environment, this is no longer necessarily the case.[24]

Situational Awareness: An Example

Being situationally aware means that you have a firm understanding of the internal politics and external environment facing any organization: Who are the players, who holds the power, and what must be done to move a potential idea, product, or strategy forward?[25] It is about having sufficient emotional intelligence to understand the personalities of those in charge and how they will potentially respond to change. It comes from understanding the underlying incentive structure by identifying who will benefit and who might be harmed within a new set of circumstances. Most importantly, it is about understanding one's own position in the organization, what can realistically be accomplished, and how alliances might form to ensure success.

There is no universal theoretical construct that magically transforms someone into being situationally aware. It is context-specific and therefore is more suited to an experiential approach. That being said, it is possible to embed the appropriate cues within existing course structures to develop this skill and eventually turn it into a capability.

The first step toward integrating situational awareness within a traditional course structure is to identify key touchpoints where context can be enhanced, and the student can be situated within a set of circumstances that embody some sense of realism. This might happen by using complementary course materials, broadening class discussion, or through the inclusion of an active learning component where students might engage in role playing.[26]

The next step is to match course content to the various identified touchpoints. This can be as simple as selecting cases that more easily lend themselves to the introduction of situations with potentially impactful outcomes.[27] Finding or creating additional content that places the student in a richer and more robust context could be combined with existing cases, simulations, or projects. Alternatively, it may involve placing constraints on actions or variables that reflect context and using these limitations to challenge students to navigate the best path given a particular set of circumstances.

Changing the content in a course can lay the foundation for skill development and the eventual transformation of those skills into capabilities. This change can be enhanced and accelerated by involving an industry professional in the classroom environment. Bringing in an industry professional as a guest speaker who can talk about their own experience related to a particular soft skill/capability can help to create a closer connection and deeper understanding of how to apply skills within an organizational process.

By their senior year, many students have learned how to follow a syllabus, successfully navigate a series of assignments, and perform relative to class standards. To better prepare them for a work environment, industry professionals can be invited in to evaluate final presentations or written assignments so that student achievement depends on professional expectations as well as academic ones. Professionals who are more willing to become involved as part of a course might assume the role of project manager and share their experience and tacit knowledge to enhance a simulation or consulting project. Understanding the needs of a consulting client and meeting their expectations is more of an art than a science, and students benefit from the insight and guidance of a working professional.

Notes

1. Roose (2020, p. 71).
2. Education, like many social entities, requires training (Bourdieu & Passeron, 1977).
3. The benefit of incorporating life into academia is elaborated in Rogoff (1990) and Rogoff et al. (2016).
4. How universities are responding to AI such as ChatGPT is discussed in Huang (2023).
5. A survey undertaken by Deloitte offers interesting insights (Hupfer, 2020).
6. World Economic Forum (2020).
7. World Economic Forum (2020). Also see PwC (2017).
8. Coursera (2022).
9. Dewey (1963), Rogoff (1990), and Rogoff et al. (2016).
10. Dewey (1963), Rogoff (1990), and Rogoff et al. (2016).

11. Verbal communication is just one item that is usually found on every list of those skills desired by employers. The growing importance of soft skills is discussed in Deming (2017).

    In addition to a number of other websites, Indeed.com, a major job website, has its own list of 11 Work Readiness Skills (Indeed Editorial Team, 2022).
12. The importance of storytelling for leaders is discussed in more depth in Denning (2011).

    The importance of storytelling in communicating novel ideas can be found in Falchetti et al. (2022).
13. Advertising provides a great example of the power of a strong narrative. See, for example, Kang et al. (2020).
14. Fryer (2003).
15. Bruner (1991) and Hammack (2008).
16. More information about the EconJourney project can be found in Niman et al. (2018).
17. More about the hero's journey can be found in Campbell (1973). The broader use of the idea is elaborated on in Vogler (2007).
18. Bischof (2022).

    The "dark" side of remote work is discussed in Janin (2022).
19. An interesting study undertaken by McKinsey & Company looks at reasons why it is so difficult to attract and retain talent (Dowling & Schaninger, 2021).
20. Of particular concern to employers, if workers don't get that flexibility from their current employer, they are not hesitant to find one that will (Bindley & Cutter, 2022).
21. Bindley (2022).
22. Bindley and Cutter (2022).
23. Smith (2022) and, Parker and Horowitz (2022).
24. The traditional workplace emphasized showing up to a physical space (the office) at a predefined time (e.g., 9–5, Monday–Friday), with employees hired to perform a specific task and assessed based on how well they got the job done.
25. The military was one of the first to recognize situational awareness as an important capability for fighter pilots. It was used by fighter pilots to assess flying conditions, formulate responses to potential threats, and map out future courses of action. It later became a standard tool in the area of health and safety. Within a business organization, being situationally aware can help determine what you should be doing, how it is going to be received, and what sort of follow-up will be required to ensure you have made an impact. Much of the academic work is based on Endsley (1995).

26. Reacting to the Past is an engaged learning pedagogy based on role-playing games. More information about the approach can be found in Reacting Consortium (2023).
27. Just as textbooks have responded to learning goals, we might expect to see case authors build more soft skills development into their materials. This is similar to what we might call the goalification of the publishing industry.

References

Bindley, K. (2022, March 4). Tech companies are reopening their offices, but tech work has changed forever. *Wall Street Journal.* Retrieved March 21, 2023, from https://www.wsj.com/articles/tech-companies-reopen-their-offices-facebook-google-11646365155?mod=hp_lead_pos4

Bindley, K., & Cutter, C. (2022, January 25). Workers care more about flexible hours than remote work. *Wall Street Journal.* Retrieved March 21, 2023, from https://www.wsj.com/articles/workers-care-more-about-flexible-hours-than-remote-work-11643112004?mod=article_inline

Bischof, J. (2022, May 29). Hybrid competence is the newest soft skill with an outsize impact on your career. Here's how you can work it into your resume. *Insider.* Retrieved March 21, 2023, from https://www.businessinsider.com/hybrid-competence-is-the-newest-soft-skill-for-your-resume-2022-5

Bourdieu, P., & Passeron, J. C. (1977). *Reproduction in education, society, and culture.* (R. Nice, trans.). Sage.

Bruner, J. (1991). The narrative construction of reality. *Critical Inquiry, 18*(1), 1–21.

Campbell, J. (1973). *The hero with a thousand faces* (1. Princeton/Bollingen paperback print., 3. print). University Press.

Coursera. (2022). Global skills report. *Coursera.* Retrieved March 21, 2023, from https://pages.coursera-for-business.org/rs/748-MIV-116/images/Coursera-Global-Skills-Report-2022.pdf

Deming, D. J. (2017). The growing importance of social skills in the labor market*. *The Quarterly Journal of Economics, 132*(4), 1593–1640. https://doi.org/10.1093/qje/qjx022

Denning, S. (2011). *The leader's guide to storytelling: Mastering the art and discipline of business narrative* (Revised and updated ed.). Jossey-Bass.

Dewey, J. (1963). *Experience and education.* Collier Books.

Dowling, B., & Schaninger, B. (2021). *The great attrition or the great attraction? The choice is yours.* McKinsey & Company. Retrieved March 21, 2023, from https://www.mckinsey.com/featured-insights/mckinsey-live/webinars/the-great-attrition-or-the-great-attraction-what-will-it-be-for-you

Endsley, M. R. (1995). Toward a theory of situation awareness in dynamic systems. *Human Factors: The Journal of the Human Factors and Ergonomics Society, 37*(1), 32–64. https://doi.org/10.1518/001872095779049543

Falchetti, D., Cattani, G., & Ferriani, S. (2022). Start with "Why," but only if you have to: The strategic framing of novel ideas across different audiences. *Strategic Management Journal, 43*(1), 130–159. https://doi.org/10.1002/smj.3329

Fryer, B. (2003, June). Storytelling that moves people. *Harvard Business Review*. Retrieved March 21, 2023, from https://hbr.org/2003/06/storytelling-that-moves-people

Hammack, P. L. (2008). Narrative and the cultural psychology of identity. *Personality and Social Psychology Review, 12*(3), 222–247. https://doi.org/10.1177/1088868308316892

Huang, K. (2023, January 26). Alarmed by A.I. Chatbots, universities start revamping how they teach. *The New York Times*. Retrieved March 21, 2023, from https://www.nytimes.com/2023/01/16/technology/chatgpt-artificial-intelligence-universities.html

Hupfer, S. (2020, March 3). Talent and workforce effects in the age of AI. *Deloitte*. Retrieved March 21, 2023, from https://www2.deloitte.com/us/en/insights/focus/cognitive-technologies/ai-adoption-in-the-workforce.html

Indeed Editorial Team. (2022, June 24). 11 work readiness skills. *Indeed*. Retrieved March 21, 2023, from https://www.indeed.com/career-advice/career-development/work-readiness

Janin, A. (2022, February 20). Thanks to remote work, many in Gen Z may never work in an office. Will it matter? *The Wall Street Journal*. Retrieved March 21, 2023, from https://www.wsj.com/articles/remote-lets-generation-z-work-without-any-office-will-matter-11645220523?mod=hp_lead_pos7

Kang, J., Hong, S., & Hubbard, G. T. (2020). The role of storytelling in advertising: Consumer emotion, narrative engagement level, and word-of-mouth intention. *Journal of Consumer Behaviour, 19*(1), 47–56. https://doi.org/10.1002/cb.1793

Niman, N. B., Furnagiev, S., & Lemos, S. (2018). Developing the journey process: A novel approach to teaching undergraduate economics. *Journal of Economics and Finance Education, 17*, 96–113.

Parker, K., & Horowitz, J. M. (2022, March 9). *Majority of workers who quit a job in 2021 cite low pay, no opportunities for advancement, feeling disrespected*. Pew Research Center. Retrieved March 23, 2022, from https://www.pewresearch.org/fact-tank/2022/03/09/majority-of-workers-who-quit-a-job-in-2021-cite-low-pay-no-opportunities-for-advancement-feeling-disrespected/

PwC. (2017). Workforce of the future: The competing forces shaping 2030. *PwC*. Retrieved March 21, 2023, from https://www.pwc.com/gx/en/services/people-organisation/publications/workforce-of-the-future.html

Reacting Consortium. (2023). Reacting to the past. *Reacting Consortium*. Retrieved March 23, 2023, from https://reactingconsortium.org/

Rogoff, B. (1990). *Apprenticeship in thinking: Cognitive development in social context*. Oxford University Press.

Rogoff, B., Callanan, M., Gutiérrez, K. D., & Erickson, F. (2016). The organization of informal learning. *Review of Research in Education, 40*(1), 356–401. https://doi.org/10.3102/0091732X16680994

Roose, K. (2020). *Futureproof: 9 rules for humans in the age of automation*. Random House.

Smith, M. (2022, January 14). Professor who predicted 'The Great Resignation' shares the 3 trends that will dominate work in 2022. *CNBC*. Retrieved March 23, 2023, from https://www.cnbc.com/2022/01/14/the-great-resignation-expert-shares-the-biggest-work-trends-of-2022.html

Vogler, C. (2007). *The writer's journey: Mythic structure for writers* (3rd ed.). Michael Wiese Productions.

World Economic Forum. (2020). The future of jobs report. *World Economic Forum*. Retrieved March 21, 2023, from https://www3.weforum.org/docs/WEF_Future_of_Jobs_2020.pdf

Self-Discovery and Curriculum

Survey after survey demonstrates that students enroll at a college or university to get a "better job."[1] The standard metric to determine how well higher education is living up to that promise is a comparison in terms of lifetime earnings between those holding a bachelor's degree and others who have never enrolled or completed a degree.[2] A different perspective is offered by those who have an opportunity to reflect back on their life where they place less importance on the earnings premium associated with an undergraduate degree.[3] In a study done by Merrill Lynch Wealth Management (a part of Bank of America Corporation) titled *Leaving a Legacy: A lasting gift to loved ones*, Americans 55 and older were asked to look back on their lives and on what they believed constitutes a life well lived. At the top of the list *was having family and friends that love me* (94%), coming in second was m*aking a positive impact on society* (75%), and in a distant third was *being successful in my career* (27%). With respect to higher education, most notable was the metric for *accumulating a lot of wealth*, important to only 10% of respondents.[4]

The ability to make a positive impact on society is often tied to one's job. In fact, researchers at McKinsey & Company discovered that "approximately 70 percent of people say they define their purpose through work." Thus, they believe that it is good business for a company to help their employees find and live their purpose at work. In doing so, they find that employees will "do better and are more likely to want to stay, as well as more likely to want to go above and beyond."[5]

N. B. Niman, J. R. Chagnon, *The Work-Ready Graduate*,
https://doi.org/10.1007/978-3-031-33910-3_4

Higher education could make a similar business case. Institutions able to demonstrate that they do a better job of helping their students find a sense of purpose could use this as a source of competitive advantage. Students might be more likely to enroll, and stay to complete a degree if they believe they are on a path toward making a real difference. More is required, however, than stoking the passions of an entering student and helping them find some purpose in their life.[6] Discovering what is of interest, what one likes, or what brings a sense of joy is only the first step to graduates making a positive impact.[7] They must also be given the tools and experiences needed to hone their abilities so that they are prepared to act, have access to a structured set of experiences, and aided in navigating the myriad of possibilities. Discovering one's true place is a process that begins in college but may take a lifetime. For those who choose to attend a college or university, the curriculum provides perhaps the best opportunity to get started.

Self-Discovery

What do you want to be when you grow up? This is a question we are all asked repeatedly throughout our youth. Similarly, when a student enters college, they are inevitably asked a similar question about their major and what they want to do when they graduate.[8] For majors with a clear pathway to a career, it may be a straightforward question, but for those in majors without a clear pathway to a career it becomes more challenging to make, defend, or explain their choices.[9]

If the goal is to find purposeful work that has an impact and provides a sense of pride (and money), the process of self-discovery cannot terminate in an academic major but must jointly end with a better understanding of how one might realize purpose outside of academia.[10] Failing to develop requisite capabilities will lead to an endless sense of frustration if there is no way to achieve a laudable goal. Learning from a work-ready perspective marries the acquisition of knowledge with the development of capabilities thereby making it possible to both dream *and* develop the means to bring those dreams to fruition. Students need not only to be exposed to a diversity of ideas. They must also be empowered to put those ideas into practice. Since most of this will likely take place in the workplace, becoming empowered to act requires the corresponding development of work-ready capabilities.

This line of thinking is what underlies the concept of a T-shaped graduate[11] A T-shaped graduate is one who has a broad base of knowledge/skills (the top of the T) along with deep knowledge/skills in one area (the bottom of the T). The concept of a T-shaped graduate aligns nicely with the traditional college curriculum. A general education program provides a broad base of knowledge (the top of the T), while the disciplinary knowledge found in a major provides the depth of understanding in one area (the bottom of the T).[12] Throw in a mix of skills such as communication, collaboration, problem solving, and critical thinking and it is no wonder that many believe that higher education offers a great deal of value.[13]

General Education

Every accredited university includes a general education program.[14] The program is designed around a collection of courses that provide a breadth of knowledge and understanding that helps to develop a more well-rounded graduate with interests that extend beyond the major. For students who have not decided on a major or are looking for a change in major, these courses can provide an opportunity to discover a new set of interests and potential career opportunities.[15]

Accrediting bodies do not proscribe particular courses or entire curricula, but rather set parameters that guide curriculum development at individual campuses. Thus, the New England Commission on Higher Education (NECHE) provides direction in the sparsest terms. For the NECHE, a general education program must be coherent, substantive, and reflect an institution's mission and values. The general education requirement must ensure "adequate breadth for all degree-seeking students by showing a balanced regard for what are traditionally referred to as the arts and humanities, the sciences including mathematics, and the social sciences." Course offerings should include these three areas as well as how the areas relate to each other. All must take place within a footprint that includes at least the equivalent of 40 semester credits in a bachelor's degree program.[16]

Constructing a work-ready general education program need not run contrary to the parameters set out by an accrediting body. Rather, it speaks more directly to how these courses are designed and delivered. In an ideal world, a general education program would not only provide adequate breadth but also help a student find what is the best fit for them in terms of the type of work they enjoy doing.

Take, for example, a course such as Introduction to Business. It has all the hallmarks of a general education course. It provides a survey of what, at many universities, is the most popular major. It provides an overview of the functional areas of business and, in a perfect world, would help a student determine if 1] business is the right major for them and 2] which area of business is the most interesting and merits further study.

For those courses designed around one of the standard textbooks, the experience can be less than helpful in generating interest in a particular area, let alone the entire field of business. Speaking from our experience at Paul College, the faculty who were responsible for delivering the course determined that when it was taught in a traditional format, students were disengaged from the material and focused more on what to memorize, how to pass the next quiz, and whether they actually needed to attend class. Rather than generating interest in the study of business, many students questioned whether it made sense to take additional business courses.

In redesigning the course, Neil, the Associate Dean at the time, along with the new instructors brought in to teach the course shifted the focus from an exercise in learning about the functional areas of business to how fundamental business principles might be *applied* in a meaningful context. The course was built around the premise that the student inherited a business, and was designed to walk them through a structured decision-making process that took them through each functional area of the business. Hence, business principles were taught with a purpose, and the students were asked to use those principles to work their way through a semester-long scenario that ultimately determined whether the business would succeed or fail.[17] By showing how these foundational principles could be applied in a meaningful context, student satisfaction rose dramatically, and professors in subsequent courses found the students to be better prepared for more intensive study in a particular area.

What works in an Introduction to Business course could certainly work in many areas of study. By shifting the focus of the course to include how knowledge is applied in a variety of contexts or situations, students gain a better understanding of why they might study a particular discipline. In terms of creating a work-ready graduate, understanding how knowledge can be applied, rather than learning in the abstract, makes it easier for students to envision what they might do with what they have learned, thus identifying potential career paths or purpose.[18]

Reimagining General Education

At the beginning of one's educational journey, skill acquisition forms the foundation for the subsequent development of a work-ready scaffold. It is not about career choices (i.e., what you can do with a particular major). It is about the types of work that someone might do either with a particular major or in a specific industry. In this discovery phase, students benefit from learning how they might go about doing something and the skills that are required, so that they can focus on selecting the appropriate courses that will contribute toward the subsequent development of those skills.[19]

Looking at the general education program offered at the University of New Hampshire, for example, every student is required to take a course with a laboratory component. It is not that a large number of students will become scientists who work in a lab, but rather, the faculty who determine the curriculum believe that experience in the laboratory is essential for learning the scientific method. It is important that students grasp how science is done regardless of whether they choose to pursue a career in science.[20]

Something similar should apply to the development of work-ready capabilities. General education should help students understand the different types of work they are likely to encounter after graduation and obtain a better understanding of what skills will be needed so they can engage in the types of work they actual enjoy. Once a student discovers what they enjoy doing, it becomes easier to narrow down how they might apply those skills. The potential of general education for developing a work-ready graduate is that it can showcase different approaches and ways of doing things in the hope of sparking interest in a student and the corresponding development of skills that would position them for successful work post graduation.[21]

An expanded general education program designed for the development of work-ready capabilities would include the following elements:

- Learning *and* developmental goals
- Skills on par with Ideas
- Meaningful applications

Developmental goals focus on the ability to do something such as communicate clearly, think creatively, or solve problems effectively.[22] It is easy to contend (and many have done just that) that developmental goals are a natural outgrowth of the learning process. It is not clear, however, that when the development of such capabilities is merely a byproduct of a learning process, the job will be well done. For example, it would be similarly easy to argue that because students can critically analyze a body of work, they have become critical thinkers.[23] However, it is something else entirely when students are given multiple opportunities to put their core knowledge into practice and think critically about how to do something, solve a problem, or how to complete a task with guidance and feedback to improve how they approach constructing a solution.

Developmental goals focus on the transformation of soft skills into human capabilities that position a student for professional success. These are capabilities that develop over time, as skills are employed multiple times in a variety of contexts over the traditional four-year time span. From the perspective of prospective employers, they are as important as, if not more important than, mastering a specific body of knowledge.

Context is important when turning skills into capabilities. Employers not only want to know that a prospective employee has successfully applied knowledge to an existing set of circumstances but also want to gain a sense of whether that person has the ability to use those skills in a variety of situations. It is the ability to problem solve when the unexpected occurs that is highly valued by many employers.

Arguably, students are better served by learning about different types of work they might encounter to determine what they like to do most. For example, whether they like to solve complex problems using mathematics, or the degree to which they like working with people. Alternatively, they may be less interested in what they do and are more concerned about whether the work itself is aligned with their sense of purpose.

Expanding a general education program requires a shift from thinking in terms of offering students a large collection of applications that demonstrate how a particular concept might be applied within the context of an academic major, to focusing on how one might go about doing what is required to accomplish a particular task outside of the confines of a particular academic discipline. By elevating how you might do something rather than specific knowledge content, students gain a greater understanding of what is required to accomplish a task and whether engaging in that type of work is something they might like to do.

Key-Shaped Graduates

From the perspective of preparing a work-ready graduate, the question is not just who do you want to be, but rather, what kind of things pique one's curiosity and might generate a sense of satisfaction. Do you like to work alone or as part of a team? Do you enjoy working with numbers or people? Do you want work that requires creativity and imagination, or would you prefer following someone else's prescribed path? It is about discovering the type of work a student might enjoy doing rather than what area of knowledge best captures their interest.

From the perspective of recruiters who hire based on whether a prospective employee is a good fit, experience and the associated capabilities developed as a result of that experience can be more important than job-specific knowledge.[24] For example, many companies in the area of finance look for "quant jocks" rather than finance majors because they need candidates that can perform calculations that involve a higher level of mathematics and hence often look to STEM majors from the sciences. STEM majors have the appropriate mathematical backgrounds and experience applying those same principles to solve complex problems. It is easier for that graduate to pick up the terminology used in finance than it is to take an existing finance major with a modest math background and have them do advanced quantitative work.

This raises the question of whether there is an equivalent concept to the T-Shaped graduate that could capture a mix of experiences and capabilities that can showcase a graduate's work-readiness. In a world that has become more complex, and where solutions depend more on working across disciplinary boundaries, the idea of a *key-shaped graduate* has emerged. A key-shaped graduate is one who has knowledge in multiple areas of varying degrees capable of handling complex problems that transcend a particular area of knowledge.[25] Within this conception of a desirable graduate, the spine of the key serves the same function as the top of the T by representing general areas of knowledge and skills that can be applied to almost any set of circumstances. The bottom of the T is replaced by multiple pins that represent knowledge and skills from more than one discipline developed to various degrees just as the pins of a key consist of different lengths.

Rather than thinking in terms of knowledge and skills, we can use the key to represent experiences and capabilities. From this perspective, the spine of the key represents general capabilities valuable regardless of a specific job function, with more specialized skills that have been put into practice forming the various bits along the key.

Business analytics can serve as an example of such an approach. Business analytics is a multidisciplinary approach applied by businesses to take advantage of the availability of large quantities of data to construct strategies and solutions for complex problems (Fig. 1). Business analytics draws from academic disciplines such as computer science, mathematics, and some of the functional areas of business.

Along the top of the key are examples of general capabilities that are particularly well suited for a career in business analytics. Situational awareness in this case would be the ability to identify what data is relevant and how it would best be analyzed and displayed. Storytelling is a general capability that speaks to how the analysis would be described and pitched to interested parties. Agile is a project management/development framework that adheres to the motto of failing fast to succeed sooner. The basic idea is to release a "minimum viable product" relatively quickly, so it becomes possible to incorporate feedback sooner instead of waiting to release something that is perfect.

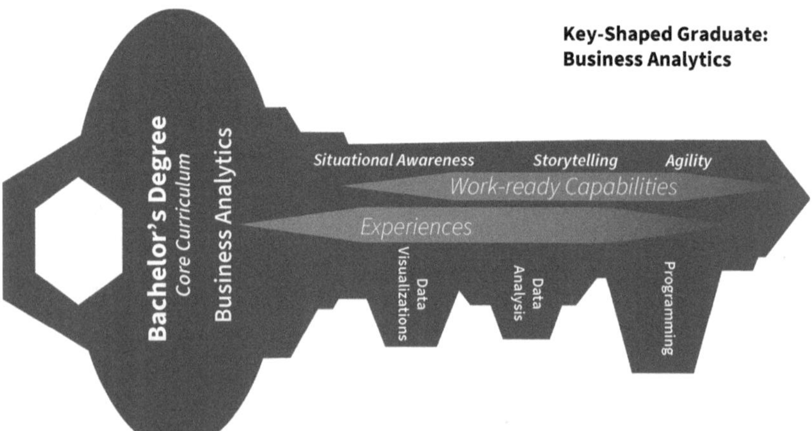

Fig. 1 An example of a key-shaped graduate for a Business Analytics major. Experiences for a Business Analytics major may include programming, data analytics, and data visualizations. Corresponding work-ready capabilities that the student may develop may be in Agile, storytelling, and situational awareness

Each bit along the spine represents an experience that helped to develop a skill used in business analytics. Here, a candidate generally needs to be proficient in at least one programming language (often R or Python). In addition, they must be able to transform raw data into a usable data set and often apply some statistical package for analyzing it. Finally, to tell the story properly, data visualizations are used to communicate to an audience of executives, customers, or members of a team. A candidate who can point to an experience where they were able to put each skill into practice is in a stronger position to make the case that they are qualified for a particular job.

Experiential Learning

Experiential learning provides perhaps the best opportunity for students to put their skills into practice as part of a broader effort to develop work-ready capabilities.[26] Experiential learning is often thought of as "learning by doing."[27] In experiential business education, students actively engage with a business professional, problem, or set of circumstances to achieve some tangible objective. It is learning in which the focus is more on the process than on the memorization of an abstract set of principles. In doing so, students develop the professional skills and capabilities sought by employers and which contribute to professional success.

Experiential learning can take a number of different forms. Some examples include:

- **Cases**—Cases are narratives that capture a real situation and invite analysis in terms of what to do or how to solve a problem. Courses are discussion-based, and cases are used to add an element of realism to the learning process. Teachable moments emerge from class discussion that is moderated by the instructor.
- **Simulations**—Simulations are highly structured learning experiences that attempt to closely mirror a real business environment. Students are provided with levers that they can modify to see the impact of changes in key variables. By placing students in an artificial context that approximates a set of real circumstances, students gain a bird's eye view of the consequences of their actions.
- **Consulting Projects**—Project-based learning is often organized around student teams that work collaboratively on a problem (in business education, this is usually for a real business enterprise). Under the supervision of a faculty member, a student team has the

opportunity to apply what they have learned in a meaningful context. When projects are properly designed, students develop desirable soft skills as they learn to manage the needs and expectations of a client by working through steps that include defining the scope of work, parceling out tasks, and performing the work needed to reach a successful conclusion.

- Internships—Internships have become synonymous with experiential learning. They give the student an opportunity to become part of a functioning business organization and to see, first-hand, how principles can be applied within a real context. For many students, the internship has become more than just a high-impact learning experience. It is an opportunity for employers and students to evaluate the quality of fit and whether it makes sense to tender (and accept) a more permanent job offering.
- Co-Op Programs—Cooperative education programs combine classroom learning with hands-on work experience with a local employer. Students are offered an opportunity to put their knowledge into practice through a credit-bearing structured learning experience. As these last longer than a traditional internship, students have an opportunity to tackle projects of a longer duration that require more advanced responsibilities.
- **Apprenticeships**—Traditionally associated with vocational education, apprenticeships provide hands-on learning opportunities under the supervision of a mentor. They are typically paid positions that lead directly to a job within a chosen field.

Cases

One of the longest-running debates within business education exists between the proponents of the scientific method and the defenders of the case method. Adherents of the scientific method point to the value of robust theories that can be generalized and applied across a spectrum of problems that managers might encounter. Those who promote the use of cases point to the advantages of using practical examples that provide important context for decisions a manager might encounter over the course of their career. It is an instructional method that increases the level of student engagement, provides an opportunity for students to share their own personal experiences, and places the instructor more in the role of facilitator than the proverbial "sage on the stage."

Critics of the case method point to the fact that the cases themselves are the product of the inherent biases of their authors. The case method has students thinking about what they might have done differently within a context that was most likely relevant for a different time, set of decision-makers, and business environment.[28] In addition, criticism is levied that it is not useful for developing technical skills and its effectiveness is dependent on the ability of the instructor to facilitate an engaging dialogue. Moreover, it does little beyond possibly advancing presentation skills to develop those soft skills that have become increasingly important to prospective employers.[29]

From our perspective, an authentic experience that has students interacting with real players is crucial to gain exposure to the social and institutional cues that are helpful for sound decision-making within a specific context. Moreover, while a business school professor might be very proficient with the underlying theoretical constructs, they may have no, or limited, experience in applying those principles in real-life situations.[30] In other words, while professors may have a wealth of explicit knowledge, they may also be limited in the informal knowledge that is needed to develop the situational awareness required to make sound decisions in a real context.[31]

Simulations

Because of the inherent limitation of cases and how they are delivered, there is growing interest in the use of simulations.[32] In a well-designed simulation, the student has an opportunity to experience a fabricated environment that challenges their understanding of core curriculum concepts and provides them with data or a set of circumstances that require the application of those concepts to reach a decision. The simulated environment would be fully capable of processing that information and revealing an outcome in a relatively short period of time. Through multiple engagements with the simulation, students can refine their choice criteria, learn from their decisions, and identify why some variables have a larger impact and under what set of circumstances.[33]

Of course, all of this comes at a considerable expense. The more closely the simulation approximates the "real" world, the more expensive it is to develop.[34] The more abstract the simulation, the fewer the variables or potential deviations from the correct answer the student will encounter.

As such, there is a fairly strong tradeoff between the cost of development and the amount of realism one might expect.

The use of simulations, as with cases, is at the discretion of the instructor, and their success depends on how they are implemented in a course. They can be very effective in helping a student understand the relationship between key variables to demonstrate the usefulness of a core theoretical concept. What is missing is the insider knowledge that only comes from previous experience, and if the faculty member has limited professional experience or that experience happened many years previously, the learning experience may not be very robust.

The same holds true for the team that developed the simulation. A simulation is only as good as the expertise that is used to develop the scenario and algorithm that processes the data to generate an outcome. This can add unintentional limitations in the decision framework that can bias outcomes.[35]

Consulting Projects

Another option that has grown in popularity is corporate consulting projects.[36] Depending on the complexity of the project, it may be integrated into an existing course to provide a sense of realism to the course material; it may be the sole activity/focus of a specially designed course, or happen outside the course structure and take place in the form of a student organization activity.[37] Working on a consulting project provides students an opportunity to see what works (or does not work) in a real company environment on an actual project. It affords an opportunity to gain feedback from company executives, which provides some sense of what the student might expect once they enter the professional workforce.[38]

Unless the school is willing to outsource the problem and rely on a vendor to supply projects, it requires a substantial investment in a support structure designed to make contact with the local business community and actively solicit projects that can be matched to courses in the curriculum. Sometimes it is possible to leverage existing relationships with companies that come to recruit a school's graduates or provide internships for continuing students. Most likely, it will involve developing deeper relationships with executives within a company that go beyond the hiring function.

Projects need to be carefully vetted. Often, a prospective client does not know what they want or will change their mind after the project has started. Sometimes they respond to calls or emails immediately, and other times they might go missing in action for an extended period of time. As a result, despite the best laid plans, projects fail to materialize or fall apart after a few weeks, leaving students stranded without a consulting opportunity.

For those that pan out, a semester-long consulting project can teach valuable soft skills that will be useful regardless of the type of career to be pursued. Client management, working collaboratively as part of a team, responding to feedback, problem solving, and presenting the final product in the best way affords multiple opportunities to polish those nascent skills that businesses find to be most useful. In addition, there is an opportunity to develop hard skills based on the scope of work for the project. It may require developing a marketing or business strategy, constructing a report, providing content for a website, or putting together a financial analysis. With a faculty advisor who possesses extensive experience working on consulting projects and can help their students navigate the ins and outs of a particular situation, a consulting project can create a powerful and memorable learning experience.

Internships

It has become commonplace to outsource the practice of business to partners who provide their students with internships. The internship ostensibly allows for an applied experience that helps students develop a better understanding of how generalized business concepts can be put into practice.[39] The challenge of this approach is that there is often a lack of consistency between internship experiences, and many internships are out of reach for under-resourced students.[40]

Internships certainly score high on the authenticity scale. They are generally hosted at an external business location and overseen by an individual employed by the company. A well-designed internship would have that person serve in the role of professional mentor for the student in order to enhance the learning process. The intern would begin the opportunity as a legitimate peripheral participant who is assigned meaningful projects and is invited to participate in meetings so they can observe the social and institutional cues essential for transitioning into a corporate environment.[41]

It is the legitimacy of participation that often determines the success or failure of an internship. Is the intern given worthwhile tasks to perform? Is their contribution acknowledged, appreciated, and ultimately incorporated in real work production? Are they given access to the reasons why a problem exists and why it is being solved one way relative to another? Have they been afforded the opportunity to gain an awareness of what constitutes real accomplishments and how to navigate the intricacies of the organization and the involved personalities? Successful internships accomplish all of this and more. By outsourcing the process, however, it becomes difficult to assess the efficacy of each and every opportunity.

Many interns find themselves working alone or on the periphery within a company. Since each of their coworkers has a set of responsibilities that are often not closely aligned with the internship, frequently there is limited opportunity to participate in a community of practice where skills are developed, and ideas are refined through mutual help and understanding. Without the ability to work closely with others, many internships offer a limited opportunity for professional development. Moreover, if it is indeed true that practice makes progress, it is difficult to see how, in the course of three months, sufficient opportunities exist to bridge the gap between the generalized business education that takes place in the core curriculum and the development of those skills, tools, and experiences coveted by employers.

Co-Op Programs

When thinking about co-op programs, Northeastern University immediately comes to mind. Working with over 3100 employers across 131 countries, Northeastern students alternate between their studies in traditional course work and working in the field full time for an employer.[42] Students on the job are essentially full-time employees and are expected to perform at a level commensurate with other staff.[43] While working for an employer, students have an opportunity to put their skills into practice, identify potential career pathways, make useful industry connections, and bring that understanding back into the classroom to create a more robust learning experience.

In many ways, a well-managed co-op experience can help with the development of skills as well as put them into practice. Given the amount of time the student spends in a co-op, there is ample opportunity to turn those skills into capabilities. This is perhaps one of the primary reasons why Northeastern business graduates are so highly sought after by employers and why employers choose to participate in the program.[44] They are able to hire a graduate who has already demonstrated that they are a good fit and have gotten a head start on developing a specific set of capabilities that are particularly well suited to the company.

Developing a network of co-op opportunities, however, is complex and requires a significant commitment of resources. Although this is not an insurmountable hurdle, it explains in part why so few universities have adopted the co-op model. Location is also a factor: colleges and universities that are located in major metropolitan areas with a high concentration of businesses would find it much easier to create a co-op program than those located in more rural areas where opportunities are limited.

Apprenticeship Programs

With increasing interest in the need to develop work-ready graduates, higher education has started programs that go beyond the traditional internship. Jamie Merisotis, President and CEO of the Lumina Foundation, identifies (in a provocative post) that business schools in particular should view apprenticeships (and not internships) as a missed opportunity.[45] He points to the lack of inclusion often associated with internships and their inadequate integration in a student's academic program. Recognizing that some form of "real" experience is essential to the development of work-ready skills, he asks whether apprenticeships that are closely aligned with academic programs can provide both the experience and the credentials needed for future success in the workforce.

Higher education is no stranger to the apprentice model. It is a common method for training the next generation of doctoral students. However, most students will not go on to do original research, earn a PhD, or become a professor, so the skills developed may not easily translate to the workplace. Working effectively in a team rather than independently under the supervision of a faculty member is just one example. In many work situations, it is not about coming up with an original contribution, rather, it is about being able to take the strategy created by senior management and implement it to achieve an established set of goals. This involves applying capabilities to a set of business and not academic challenges. Thus, a faculty member whose only experience has been in the generation of new knowledge may not possess the requisite experience needed to mentor a student whose future path has them entering the workforce.

Matters related to scale aside, apprenticeships are better suited for students who have a definite career or industry in their sights. The purpose of traditional apprenticeships is for the apprentice to step into a specific role at the culmination of their apprenticeship experience.[46] Most apprenticeships include a significant investment of time shadowing a person and learning their particular approach and methodology. In this way, it may not be a good fit for students earlier in their undergraduate experience or for those who are still in a discovery phase directed toward finding a sense of purpose or what they enjoy doing.

Capabilities Across the Curriculum

For those universities that are already familiar with writing across the curriculum, it would not be too much of a stretch to expand the program to add elements that are essential for developing a work-ready graduate.[47] A Capabilities Across the Curriculum program would ensure that the skill development occurring within individual courses leads to a set of capabilities that will prepare a graduate to handle future and current challenges.

Skills are developed through repetition and transformed into capabilities when they are put into practice. From the perspective of curriculum development, this involves identifying touchpoints across multiple courses. Making a presentation in a single course is a great start, but the typical student will not feel comfortable enough, or have sufficient experience, to gain a sense of what works and what does not for a particular audience. With multiple touchpoints, students have an opportunity to develop their presentation skills over time. More importantly, by developing presentations over different topics, delivering to multiple audiences, and having their work assessed by different instructors, students will develop a more nuanced understanding of what is required to make an effective presentation.[48]

Unsurprisingly, many games share the same basic structure. The player makes choices, and those choices have consequences that affect outcomes and ultimately whether the game is won or lost. As part of the journey toward victory, challenges become progressively more difficult, the choices become more complicated, and a collection of small wins provides the motivation needed to keep moving forward. As the game unfolds, play improves, confidence grows, and with that increased sense of power, victory begins to appear within grasp. It is this sense of making progress toward a well-defined goal that keeps the player engaged and trying their best.

In terms of developing capabilities across the curriculum, we can imagine a similar progression taking place. Variables such as length, complexity, or audience can help shape the development of capabilities across an undergraduate career. For example, lower division courses might have students writing assignments that are short in length, that are designed to utilize only a basic understanding of the underlying concepts, and that are machine graded to manage the large numbers of students typically enrolled in introductory courses. As a student moves through the curriculum, assignments might grow in length, become more complex in design and ambition, and shift from being machine graded to peer graded, then evaluated by the instructor, and finally industry professionals.

To ensure the development of a work-ready graduate, a capabilities map that shows various touchpoints and how the capability has been molded and shaped over the course of the student's academic career can provide guidance to students, while supplying employers with confidence that any achievements earned along the way are more than just an empty promise. Creating a capabilities map can also provide accrediting bodies with the information they need to evaluate the efficacy of a curriculum. Further, it allows opportunities for faculty to engage in continuous improvement by focusing their attention on what they are doing and how they might do it better.

Notes

1. The Higher Education Research Institute (HERI) at UCLA publishes the results of an annual survey they conduct of incoming students. In their 2019 survey, the number one reason for deciding to go to college was to get a better job (83.5%) (Stolzenberg et al., 2020, p. 42).
2. Ma et al. (2019).
3. The Social Security Administration has carried out their own analysis (Social Security Administration, 2015) at: https://www.ssa.gov/policy/docs/research-summaries/education-earnings.html. A more nuanced look is provided by the Center for Education and the Workforce (Carnevale et al., 2021):
4. Merrill (2021).
5. Dhingra and Schaniger (2021).
6. "If employed graduates feel their college prepared them well for life outside of it, the odds that they are engaged at work rise nearly three times. Experiences in college that contribute to feeling prepared for life after college, such as internships or jobs where students are able to apply what they are learning in the classroom, active involvement in extracurricular activities and organizations, and working on a project that took a semester or more to complete are part of this preparation" (Gallup and Purdue University, 2014, p. 9).

7. "More college graduates are thriving in purpose well-being than any other element of well-being. These graduates like what they do every day and get to learn or do something interesting on a daily basis, leading more than half of them (54%) to be thriving in this area. Other Gallup research shows that people with purpose/well-being are more than twice as likely to be thriving in their lives overall" (Gallup and Purdue University, 2014, p. 15).

   For a theoretical exploration of educational experiences that contribute to fulfillment see Dewey (1963), Freire (1973), and Walton and Cohen (2011).
8. According to the US Department of Education, about 30% of undergraduates with a declared major changed their major at least once within three years of enrollment (Leu, 2017).

   A survey by Best Colleges looks across generations at the reasons for changing majors (Staff Writers, 2022).

   More detailed analyses can be found in Eide and Waehrer, (1998), Galotti (1999), Galotti et al. (2006), and Wright (2018).
9. In a study undertaken by Ellucian, almost two-thirds felt overwhelmed by the process of selecting a major and one in three students was unsure which major aligns with their chosen career path (Ellucian, 2019, p. 5). This agrees with a more theoretical examination of social influences on our choices by Bourdieu and Passeron (1977).
10. The convergence of evidence from a variety of scholarly efforts suggests that there are three needs with respect to finding purposeful work: self-determination, competence, and interpersonal relatedness (Deci & Ryan, 1985, 2000).
11. Bierema (2019), Jackson et al. (2022), and Martin and Rees (2019).
12. In making their case that learning needs to be linked to work through career-relevant instruction, Taylor and Haras contend: "The value of non-professional majors has not been represented to employers the way that professional majors have… The issue is that liberal arts are often contextualized within the confines of academia and have yet to fully embrace their relevance in the workplace, and in language that speaks to employers (and students)" (Taylor & Haras, 2020, p. 2).

    See again, Eliot (1898).
13. A liberal education for the twenty-first century mandates the acceleration of integrative, high-impact learning opportunities that engage every student in solving unscripted, real-world problems across all types of institutions, within the context of the workforce, not apart from it. Lynn Pasquerella, President of the Association of American Colleges and Universities, reports on the work the organization is doing in support of the liberal arts in her 2019 Harvard Business Review article (Pasquerella, 2019).

A longer exposition can be found in American Association of Colleges and Universities (2020).

Finally, for a theoretical perspective see Eliot (1898). Charles Eliot, president of Harvard University for 40 years and respected educational theorist espousing the merits of a liberal arts education, contended that higher learning in the US needed to be "broadened, deepened, and invigorated."

14. Brint et al. (2009) introduces four general education models.
15. Trends in general education are discussed in Section II of the AAC&U and Hanover Research report (American Association of Colleges and Universities and Hanover Research, 2022).
16. New England Commission of Higher Education (2021).
17. "Students, as they are increasingly posed with problems relating to themselves in the world and with the world, will feel increasingly challenged and obliged to respond to the challenge. Because they apprehend the challenge as interrelated to other problems within a total context, not as a theoretical question, the resulting comprehension tends to be increasingly critical and thus constantly less alienated" (Freire, 1968, p. 68). See also Rogoff (1990).
18. Dewey (1906, 1963), Prince (2004), and Rogoff (1990).
19. Skills, and not just knowledge, need to be intentionally taught.
20. Wells (2008).

    For a theoretical perspective on the importance of an expansive liberal education see Eliot (1898).
21. Education should not be separated from the identities and personal interests of the students, lest it become an alienating and unmotivating entity; in offering educational experiences that align with student interests, an institution is providing a number of avenues for students to pursue meaningful work that interests them (Bourdieu, 1987; Dewey, 1963; Eliot, 1898; Freire, 1968; Freire, 1973).
22. Wells (2008) and Rogoff et al. (2016).
23. Freire (1973).
24. Many companies hire based on fit, which often means the candidate is the type of person you would want to have a beer with. Interesting lessons about how to hire can be found in McCord (2018).

    One of the concerns associated with hiring for fit is that it perpetuates cultural biases. See, for example, Tulshyan (2022).
25. The idea behind key-shaped graduates can be found in Wilkinson (2021).
26. Kolb (1984). Criticism of experiential learning with respect to management education is surveyed in Kayes (2002).
27. Dewey (1906, 1963), Rogoff (1990), and Wells (2008).
28. Some of the challenges associated with the case method are found in Jack (2018).

29. As more and more job activities become automated, soft skills, which cannot yet be replicated by machines, have become more important to employers (Lau, 2021).
30. Of course, this is less of an issue for MBA programs that require their students to have at least five years of work experience. In that set of circumstances, the students are able to bring relevant experience into the classroom that might offset any lack of real experience on the part of the professor. An interesting story that captures industry vs. academic environments can be found in Osborn (2018).

    The advantages of working in a non-academic environment are chronicled in Lohr (2016).
31. Sternberg et al. (1993).
32. Vlachopoulos and Makri (2017).
33. Laverie et al. (2022) discuss the effectiveness of simulations in marketing courses.
34. Hippe et al. (2020) and Maloney and Haines (2016).
35. Bias may emerge in a manner that is similar to the development and adoption of textbooks. Due to the large upfront development costs that can only be recouped if there is a large number of adopters, publishers/developers may try to create a simulation that appeals to the broadest audience possible. By appealing to the least offensive outcome, the simulation may be so generic that there is little to be learned upon successful completion. In addition, machine learned models exhibit bias, often because of implicit biases in the developer or due to biases in the datasets used to train them (Motavalli & Nestel, 2016).
36. Grossman (2002) and Heriot et al. (2008).
37. Grossman (2002).
38. Grossman (2002) and Heriot et al. (2008).
39. Some of the key findings from a Strada Education Network study of internships found that: (1) students with paid internships tend to get paid more after graduation; (2) students with work-based learning experiences report greater career satisfaction after graduation; (3) paid internships lead to greater confidence (Torpey-Saboe et al., 2022).
40. Unfortunately, another finding from that same Strada report is that black and Latino students, women, low-income students, and first-generation students are less likely to experience a paid internship. Students located in rural communities also find it challenging to navigate (and afford) the logistics associated with a paid internship (Torpey-Saboe et al., 2022; Ezarik, 2022).
41. The idea of legitimate peripheral participants is developed in Lave and Wenger (1991).
42. Northeastern University (2023).

43. Cooperative education was developed at the University of Cincinnati in 1906. A brief discussion of the history and benefits associated with cooperative education can be found in Cedercreutz and Cates (2010).
44. Northeastern reports that 90% of their graduates are employed full time or enrolled in graduate school within nine months of graduation. Fifty percent of students receive a job offer from their co-op employer and 89% of graduates are doing full-time work in a field related to their major (Northeastern University, 2023).
45. See Merisotis (2021).

    The case for apprenticeships is presented in Decker (2019).
46. The number of internships is growing. There are about $800,000 internships and while college enrollments have declined by about 15% over the past decade, the number of apprenticeships has increased by more than 50% (Belkin, 2023).
47. More information about writing across the curriculum can be found in Palmquist et al. (2020).
48. As noted by Knight and Yorke (2003, p. 4), "The student learning that makes for strong claims to employability comes from years, not semesters; through programmes, not modules; and in environments, not classes."

References

American Association of Colleges and Universities. (2020). *What liberal education looks like: What it is, who it's for, and where it happens*. American Association of Colleges and Universities. Retrieved March 21, 2023, from https://secure.aacu.org/imis/ItemDetail?iProductCode=E-WHATLELL

American Association of Colleges and Universities and Hanover Research. (2022). *On the same page? Administration and faculty views on what shapes college learning and student success*. American Association of Colleges and Universities. https://dgmg81phhvh63.cloudfront.net/content/user-photos/Research/PDFs/OntheSamePage_FINAL_2-15-22_pdftoprint.pdf

Belkin, D. (2023, March 16). More students are turning away from college and toward apprenticeships. *The Wall Street Journal*. Retrieved March 23, 2023, from https://www.wsj.com/articles/more-students-are-turning-away-from-college-and-toward-apprenticeships-15f3a05d?page=1

Bierema, L. L. (2019). Enhancing employability through developing t-shaped professionals. *New Directions for Adult and Continuing Education, 2019*(163), 67–81. https://doi.org/10.1002/ace.20342

Bourdieu, P. (1987). *Distinction: A social critique of the judgment of taste*. Harvard University Press.

Bourdieu, P., & Passeron, J. C. (1977). *Reproduction in education, society, and culture*. (Richard Nice, trans.). Sage.

Brint, S., Proctor, K., Murphy, S. P., Turk-Bicakci, L., & Hanneman, R. A. (2009). General Education Models: Continuity and Change in the U.S. Undergraduate Curriculum 1975–2000. *The Journal of Higher Education, 80*(6), 605–642 https://doi.org/10.1353/jhe.0.0071

Carnevale, A. P., Cheah, B., & Wenzinger, E. (2021). *The college payoff: More education doesn't always mean more earnings.* Center on Education and the Workforce, Georgetown University.

Cedercreutz, K., & Cates, C. (2010). Cooperative education at the university of Cincinnati: A strategic asset in evolution. *Peer Review, 12*(4), 20–23.

Deci, E. L., & Ryan, R. M. (1985). *Intrinsic motivation and self-determination in human behavior.* Springer US. https://doi.org/10.1007/978-1-4899-2271-7

Deci, E. L., & Ryan, R. M. (2000). The "what" and "why" of goal pursuits: Human needs and the self-determination of behavior. *Psychological Inquiry, 11*(4), 227–268. https://doi.org/10.1207/S15327965PLI1104_01

Decker, D. (2019). Student perceptions of higher education and apprenticeship alignment. *Education Sciences, 9*(2), 86. https://doi.org/10.3390/educsci9020086

Dewey, J. (1906). The experimental theory of knowledge. *Mind Association, 15*(59), 293–307.

Dewey, J. (1963). *Experience and education.* Collier Books.

Dhingra, N., & Schaniger, B. (2021). The search for purpose at work. *The McKinsey Podcast,* McKinsey & Company. Retrieved March 23, 2023, from https://www.mckinsey.com/capabilities/people-and-organizational-performance/our-insights/the-search-for-purpose-at-work

Eide, E., & Waehrer, G. (1998). The role of the option value of college attendance in college major choice. *Economics of Education Review, 17*(1), 73–82. https://doi.org/10.1016/S0272-7757(97)00004-6

Eliot, C. W. (1898). *Educational reform: Essays and addresses.* The Century Co.

Ellucian. (2019). Course correction: Helping students find and follow a path to success. *Ellucian.* Retrieved March 23, 2023, https://www.ellucian.com/assets/en//2019-student-success-survey-results.pdf

Ezarik, M. (2022, October 24). Hurdles to navigate for in-person internship commutes. *Inside Higher Ed.* Retrieved March 23, 2023, from https://www.insidehighered.com/news/2022/10/24/student-internship-transportation-issues-and-ideas-infographic?utm_medium=email&_hsmi=232397%E2%80%A6

Freire, P. (1968). *Pedagogy of the oppressed.* Bloomsbury Press.

Freire, P. (1973). *Education for critical consciousness.* The Seabury Press.

Gallup and Purdue University. (2014). *Great jobs great lives: The 2014 Gallup-Purdue Index report.* Gallup, Inc. Retrieved March 23, 2023, from https://www.gallup.com/services/176768/2014-gallup-purdue-index-report.aspx

Galotti, K. M. (1999). Making a "major" real-life decision: College students choosing an academic major. *Journal of Educational Psychology, 91*, 379–387. https://doi.org/10.1037/0022-0663.91.2.379

Galotti, K. M., Ciner, E., Altenbaumer, H. E., Geerts, H. J., Rupp, A., & Woulfe, J. (2006). Decision-making styles in a real-life decision: Choosing a college major. *Personality and Individual Differences, 41*, 629–639. https://doi.org/10.1016/j.paid.2006.03.003

Grossman, T. A. (2002). Student consulting projects benefit faculty and industry. *Interfaces, 32*(2), 42–48. https://doi.org/10.1287/inte.32.2.42.66

Heriot, K. C., Cook, R., Jones, R. C., & Simpson, L. (2008). The use of student consulting projects as an active learning pedagogy: A case study in a production/operations management course. *Decision Sciences Journal of Innovative Education, 6*(2), 463–481. https://doi.org/10.1111/j.1540-4609.2008.00186.x

Hippe, D. S., Umoren, R. A., McGee, A., Bucher, S. L., & Bresnahan, B. W. (2020). A targeted systematic review of cost analyses for implementation of simulation-based education in healthcare. *SAGE Open Med, 19*(8). https://doi.org/10.1177/2050312120913451

Jack, A. (2018, October 29). Why Harvard's case studies are under fire. *Financial Times.* Retrieved March 23, 2023, from https://www.ft.com/content/0b1aeb22-d765-11e8-a854-33d6f82e62f8

Jackson, D., Shan, H., & Meek, S. (2022). Enhancing graduates' enterprise capabilities through work-integrated learning in co-working spaces. *Higher Education, 84*(1), 101–120. https://doi.org/10.1007/s10734-021-00756-x

Kayes, D. C. (2002). Experiential learning and its critics: Preserving the role of experience in management learning and education. *Academy of Management Learning & Education, 1*(2), 137–149. https://doi.org/10.5465/amle.2002.8509336

Knight, P. T., & Yorke, M. (2003). Employability and good learning in higher education. *Teaching in Higher Education, 8*(1), 3–16. https://doi.org/10.1080/1356251032000052294

Kolb, D. A. (1984). *Experiential learning: Experience as the source of learning and development.* Prentice-Hall.

Lau, Y. (2021, January 20). Soft skills are essential to the future of work. *Forbes.* Retrieved March 23, 2023, from https://www.forbes.com/sites/forbeshumanresourcescouncil/2021/01/20/soft-skills-are-essential-to-the-future-of-work/?sh=8de78aa13416

Lave, J., & Wenger, E. (1991). *Situated learning: Legitimate peripheral participation.* Cambridge University Press.

Laverie, D. A., Hass, A., & Mitchell, C. (2022). Experiential learning: A study of simulations as a pedagogical tool. *Marketing Education Review, 32*(1), 3–17. https://doi.org/10.1080/10528008.2020.1843360

Leu, K. (2017). *Data point: Beginning college students who change their major within 3 years of enrollment.* National Center for Education Statistics. Retrieved March 21, 2023, from https://nces.ed.gov/pubsearch/pubsinfo.asp?pubid=2018434

Lohr, S. (2016, September 3). Goodbye, ivory tower. Hello, silicon valley candy store. *The New York Times.* Retrieved March 23, 2023, from https://www.nytimes.com/2016/09/04/technology/goodbye-ivory-tower-hello-silicon-valley-candy-store.html

Ma, J., Pender, M., & Welch, M. (2019). *Education pays 2019: The benefit of higher education for individuals and society.* College Board. Retrieved March 23, 2023, from https://research.collegeboard.org/media/pdf/education-pays-2019-full-report.pdf

Maloney, S., & Haines, T. (2016). Issues of cost-benefit and cost-effectiveness for simulation in health professions education. *Advances in Simulation, 1*(13). https://doi.org/10.1186/s41077-016-0020-3

Martin, R., & Rees, M. (2019). Student insights: Developing T-shaped professionals through work-integrated learning. *International Journal of Work-Integrated Learning, Special Issue, 20*(4), 365–374.

McCord, P. (2018). How to hire: Chances are you're doing it all wrong. *Harvard Business Review.* Retrieved March 23, 2023, from https://hbr.org/2018/01/how-to-hire

Merisotis, J. (2021, March 2). *Why apprenticeships are a missed opportunity.* Association to Advance Collegiate Schools of Business. Retrieved March 23, 2023, from https://www.aacsb.edu/insights/articles/2021/03/why-apprenticeships-are-a-missed-opportunity

Merrill. (2021). *Leaving a legacy: A lasting gift to loved ones.* Bank of America Corporation. Retrieved March 23, 2023, from https://images.em.bankofamerica.com/HOST-01-19-2701/ML_Legacy_Study.pdf

Motavalli, A., & Nestel, D. (2016). Complexity in simulation-based education: exploring the role of hindsight bias. *Advances in Simulation, 1*(3). https://doi.org/10.1186/s41077-015-0005-

New England Commission of Higher Education. (2021). *Standards for accreditation.* New England Commission of Higher Education. Retrieved March 23, 2023, from https://www.neche.org/resources/standards-for-accreditation

Northeastern University. (2023). *Experiential learning.* Northeastern University. Retrieved March 23, 2023, from https://experiential-learning.northeastern.edu/co-op/

Osborn, C. (2018, February 8). Trading the tenure track for tech. *Inside Higher Ed.* Retrieved March 23, 2023, from https://www.insidehighered.com/advice/2018/02/08/tenure-track-professor-explains-why-she-left-academe-join-tech-company-opinion

Palmquist, M., Childers, P., Maimon, E., Mullin, J., Rice, R., Russell, A., & Russell, D. R. (2020). Fifty years of wac: Where have we been? Where are we going? *Across the Disciplines, 17*(3), 5–45. https://doi.org/10.37514/ATD-J.2020.17.3.01

Pasquerella, L. (2019, September 19). Yes, employers do value liberal arts degrees. *Harvard Business Review.* Retrieved March 23, 2023, from https://hbr.org/2019/09/yes-employers-do-value-liberal-arts-degrees

Prince, M. (2004). Does active learning work? A review of the research. *Journal of Engineering Education, 93*(9), 223–231. https://doi.org/10.1002/j.2168-9830.2004.tb00809.x

Rogoff, B. (1990). *Apprenticeship in thinking: Cognitive development in social context.* Oxford University Press.

Rogoff, B., Callanan, M., Gutiérrez, K. D., & Erickson, F. (2016). The organization of informal learning. *Review of Research in Education, 40*(1), 356–401. https://doi.org/10.3102/0091732X16680994

Social Security Administration. (2015). *Education and lifetime earnings.* Social Security Administration. Retrieved March 23, 2023, from https://www.ssa.gov/policy/docs/research-summaries/education-earnings.html

Staff Writers. (2022, March 20). New survey finds most college grads would change majors. *Best Colleges.* Retrieved March 23, 2023, from https://www.bestcolleges.com/blog/college-graduate-majors-survey/

Sternberg, R. J., Wagner, R. K., & Okagaki, L. (1993). Practical intelligence: The nature and role of tacit knowledge in work and at school. In *Mechanisms of everyday cognition* (pp. 205–227). Lawrence Erlbaum Associates, Inc.

Stolzenberg, E. B., Aragon, M. C., Romo, E., Couch, V., McLennan, D., Eagan, M. K., & Kang, N. (2020). *The American freshman: National norms fall 2019.* Higher Education Research Institute, UCLA. Retrieved March 21, 2023, from https://www.scribd.com/document/510883541/The-American-Freshman-2019#

Taylor, S. C., & Haras, C. (2020). *Beyond classroom borders: Linking learning and work through career-relevant instruction.* American Council on Education. https://www.acenet.edu/Documents/Beyond-Classroom-Borders.pdf

Torpey-Saboe, N., Leigh, E. W., & Clayton, D. (2022). *The power of work-based learning.* Strada Educational Network. Retrieved March 23, 2023, from https://stradaeducation.org/wp-content/uploads/2022/06/031522_PV-report.pdf

Tulshyan, R. (2022, March 15). *Don't hire for culture fit.* Society for Human Resource Management. Retrieved March 23, 2023, from https://www.shrm.org/executive/resources/articles/pages/dont-hire-for-culture-fit-tulshyan.aspx

Vlachopoulos, D., & Makri, A. (2017). The effect of games and simulations on higher education: A systematic literature review. *International Journal of Educational Technology in Higher Education, 14*(22). https://doi.org/10.1186/s41239-017-0062-1

Walton, G. M., & Cohen, G. L. (2011). Sharing motivation. In D. Dunning (Ed.), *Social motivation* (pp. 79–101). Psychology Press.

Wells, G. (2008). Learning to use scientific concepts. *Cultural Studies of Science Education, 3*(2), 329–350. https://doi.org/10.1007/s11422-008-9100-6

Wilkinson, D. (2021). *New research: The shift between T-shaped and Key-shaped employees.* Oxcogntia LLC. Retrieved March 23, 2023, from https://oxford-review.com/shift-between-t-key-shaped-people/

Wright, C. (2018). *Choose wisely: A study of college major choice and major switching behavior.* RAND Corporation. https://doi.org/10.7249/RGSD414

Connections and Signals

In a provocative opinion piece, Ryan Roslansky and Byron Auguste (CEOs of LinkedIn and Opportunity@Work, respectively) observe that "The labor market has long been one of the opaquest markets in the world, burdened by the inefficient and unequal ways we match talent and opportunity."[1] Noting that many under-resourced groups do not have an opportunity to earn the "right" degree from the "right" school, they contend that employers are starting to look beyond a college education and a bachelor's degree as a requirement for employment. Roslansky and Auguste believe that a one-time intensive period of study provides a modest (at best) signal in an era where technological change requires that everyone continuously expand their skills. It represents one more perspective supporting the idea that the ability to take learned skills and apply them to new and previously unimagined situations (what we have been calling capabilities) has become the new holy grail for prospective employers.

Identifying the potential of a particular candidate by assessing their capabilities presents a whole new set of challenges for recruiters. In its report on the graduating class of 2022, ZipRecruiter notes that "93% of employers say soft skills play a critical role in their decision about whom they want to hire."[2] Unfortunately, soft skills are not only difficult to develop and assess, they are also challenging to communicate to prospective employers.[3]

N. B. Niman, J. R. Chagnon, *The Work-Ready Graduate*,
https://doi.org/10.1007/978-3-031-33910-3_5

This perhaps explains why networking has become even more important in today's labor market. In a startling statistic, as many as 85% of job vacancies are filled through networking.[4] Even more eye opening is the reality embedded in LinkedIn data that shows that where you grow up, go to school, and work can give a person a 12-fold advantage in gaining access to an employment opportunity.[5]

Unfortunately, many undergraduates do not build a professional network that could assist, when the time comes, in helping them acquire that first job.[6] It takes time to identify useful potential contacts and develop a common set of interests/experiences that would lead someone to make an important connection. This might explain some of the desire for alternate credentials. A more targeted approach to conveying what one has learned and can do potentially mitigates the need for a well-developed professional network.[7]

Connections

Certainly higher education is aware of the importance of professional networks in placing graduates. Nearly every university offers job fairs, networking events, opportunities to connect with alumni, and the ability to schedule interviews with recruiters.[8] These events and opportunities, however, require that a student be prepared to make the most of the experience. They require more than just an updated resume. The student needs to be able to make conversation, talk about themselves (having identified what might be of most interest to a prospective employer), demonstrate some knowledge about an industry, job category, or specific company, and follow up after the initial contact is made.

Since a person can only make a first impression once, students need to be prepared when one arises. Often, skills need to effectively network or interview are relegated to career services. That being said, many students don't use these services or wait until their final year to take advantage of them.[9] By then, it is often too late. Preparing to become work-ready is not something that can be accomplished a few months before graduation. It needs to be started as soon as a student walks on to campus.

A common mistake is thinking that career-readiness is the same as becoming work-ready. When the conversation is framed in terms of career readiness, it connotes going out and pursuing a particular job. In contrast, being work-ready is about laying the foundation for entering the workforce. It is not job specific; rather, it is more about general professional preparation.

Unfortunately, many students believe they need to have a specific career in mind to begin preparing for life after graduation. It is the difference between *I want a job* and *I want to become ready so that I can pursue a career option once I know what I want to do.*

The reason this is important is that many students arrive on campus not knowing what they want to major in and end up changing their mind at least once before they graduate.[10] It is difficult to imagine a career without having a major. Many students think that a career is something that follows the selection of a major and along with that, they need to reach more advanced courses before they are able to get a sense of potential career paths. As a result, the preliminary work needed to effectively develop and take advantage of a professional network is not done, and by the time a student realizes the need, it is difficult to do anything meaningful about it.

It should therefore come as no surprise that all of this talk about careers would be off-putting to a student who is still in that self-discovery phase of their undergraduate experience and more focused on fitting in socially, becoming more self-sufficient, and achieving academic success in what is likely a challenging curriculum.[11] Throw in the need to know what you want to do with the rest of your life (or at least the first step after graduation), and it can be more than many students can handle comfortably.

The solution is to dissociate the immediate need for professional preparation from the future concerns associated with selecting a career. For students who begin from day one to lay a solid foundation for becoming work-ready and subsequently develop an area of interest, constructing a professional network may be the natural next step in their progression.[12] An internship or job opportunity can emerge organically rather than as the result of a job fair or posting on an electronic job board. Work-readiness must become an integral part of the undergraduate experience in a way that is untethered from career-specific preparedness (despite the obvious connections). It is about framing the conversation in a way that leads to behaviors where work-readiness becomes as natural as reading, writing, or arithmetic.[13]

Initiating Relationships

Building a professional network is an ongoing investment. Relationships must be nurtured if they are to grow into something that might pay off down the road with a career opportunity. Students need to overcome their fears of asking for help or sharing their aspirations, feel comfortable interacting with working professionals, and view these contacts as useful resources.[14] Students have heard the adage 'It is more about who you know than what you know.' They need to realize not only that this is true, but that they need both, capability and connection, to get noticed. Institutions need to think creatively about how to bring working professionals into contact with students in a substantive way, where they can develop a professional relationship with an industry professional who might recommend a student or leverage their network to help.

Universities that have a mission to serve the public good often have a speaker's bureau designed to promote faculty and their research.[15] This is a list of experts who are available to speak to the local community about interesting topics. It is a form of outreach that is designed to promote goodwill and demonstrate some of the ways that the work of the faculty is having a positive impact on society. Many of these institutions, however, struggle with utilizing alumni databases and other community lists in a concerted way for a students' professional development. A similar bureau could be established to leverage the relationships with alumni or friends of the university who are willing to engage in particular ways with students as guest speakers, panelists, mentors, and so on. The information may already exist, but it may be siloed within academic departments or non-academic units, thereby decreasing accessibility and reach. Investing in supportive resources, such as engagement coordinators or offices, is worthwhile and can help supercharge the building of professional relationships.

Bringing working professionals to campus and having them speak about what is required to step into a particular role can reinforce the motivation to complete a course of study preparation for life after graduation. Many of these interactions may also keep students at arm's length and therefore subsequent follow-up and professional habits need to be encouraged or barriers need to be lowered. It is common to couple events with networking, which can be intimidating for students who have little experience.[16] Developing purpose in attending the networking event can lead to more fruitful outcomes, such as making a few new connections through LinkedIn with a personalized follow-up message to the connection, finding at least one connection in a field or organization of interest, or asking a connection to conduct an informational interview (at a later time) about what they do or challenges they faced in transitioning to the professional world.[17] Meaningful opportunities must be cultivated in existing networks to open up the potential for connecting with working professionals posessing similar interests.

If the opportunity is geared toward students at the early stages of their academic journey, they would gain more from a general discussion of work-readiness supported by a conversation about what is possible upon completion of a particular field of study. Many students in majors with a less direct and obvious career path might benefit from a broader discussion of what is possible or, more importantly, steps that they can take regardless of major to prepare themselves for entry into the labor market. More students will likely participate if they are welcomed specifically because they are unsure of what they want to do after graduation.

Another approach is to leverage academic clubs and campus organizations. They may offer the best opportunity for bringing working professionals to campus because numerous students have already opted to join a group, and many of these groups already interact with alumni or industry professionals. Additionally, they may be able to offer more opportunity for connection by being more student-focused (than a community-wide or college-wide event), offering less formal or more candid exchanges, and inviting participants to meet face-to-face. With the work of an engagement coordinator, they could identify working professionals who might come and speak but could also potentially offer their professional expertise to help the group develop new or enhance existing programming.

For example, students might organize an investment club where interested students meet to talk about financial markets and track an idealized portfolio that serves as a vehicle to track individual investments and the overall economy. By bringing in working professionals from the investment community, students can gain access to their expertise and, in the process, learn about what capabilities are valuable for building a career in the financial services industry. A robust program that includes participation by high-profile alumni/investment professionals affords the potential for conferring status on the organization, which makes it easier to recruit new members and enhance the opportunities available to members.

Specialized Programming

Many universities are creating mentorship programs as a way to both provide students with professional guidance and open the door to their professional networks.[18] Through one-on-one coaching, it is believed that students will be able to identify potential careers and become better prepared to enter the workforce when they graduate. As noted by Julia Freeland and Richard Price in their piece "Alumni Networks Reimaged," many students fail to take advantage of these opportunities. Furthermore, without a supporting infrastructure of some sort that sustains these relationships in an ongoing and substantive way, not much is effectively accomplished.[19]

A similar view is promoted in the 2022 e-book *The Learner First Approach*, published by PeopleGrove. It effectively makes the case that the success of a mentorship program lies in the amount of social capital that can be developed through a robust experience. The basis for success is found in the strength of the institutional commitment to the creation of applied learning projects that afford a unique opportunity for generating work-integrated opportunities that are relationship-rich and help to build connections likely to open career doors.[20]

Competitions are a great example of specialized programming that can bring together students and mentors. At Paul College, the Holloway Competition is an innovation to market competition that has students paired with an advisor (often a faculty member) who works with them to develop a business proposal that is presented to panels of working professionals in the hope of securing up to $10,000 in seed funding. Multiple opportunities exist to interact with working professionals in obtaining additional assistance, helpful advice, or, at later stages, possible connections outside the university that can help turn their idea into reality.

Community service, or service-learning projects, are another example of how students can work with members of the local community to accomplish a project with purpose. Working at a regional non-profit is a great way to develop work-ready capabilities under the tutelage of community leaders who may share their life experiences and can provide opportunities for students to practice both networking and work-ready skills.

Signals

An introduction and recommendation from a credible source (a person working in the industry) may be the best entry point to a desirable position at a company, but cultivating those contacts may represent a formidable challenge for some.[21] This is why most students must rely on a variety of signals to communicate whether they possess the requisite capabilities to effectively do a particular job that goes beyond the traditional resume and transcript.[22]

This perhaps explains the interest in alternative credentials, badges, or portfolios as a signaling strategy to communicate one's readiness to step into a particular position. For some, a collection of alternate credentials and badges is viewed as a substitute for a traditional bachelor's degree.[23] For others, it is a way for students in majors that do not offer a direct career path or are associated with a marketable set of skills to develop a competency valued by employers that might place the holder in a more advantageous position when pursuing a particular employment opportunity.[24]

Alternative Credentials

To get accepted to the university of their choice, many high school students try to build a record of academic achievement and a list of extracurricular activities that showcase the characteristics and qualifications they believe will give them a competitive edge. A similar learned response characterizes the last year or two of an undergraduate's career as they look to assemble a comparable record of accomplishment in preparation to graduate and enter the workforce. Often this manifests itself in the belief by some that they would be better served by two majors instead of one, or the addition of a minor, or specific courses that enables them to demonstrate knowledge that sets them apart from other graduates who are vying for similar positions.[25]

This might in part explain the growing interest in alternate credentials that target particular skills or areas of knowledge (generally surrounding technology) that employers find particularly appealing. For some, this takes the form of a certification that is earned with the completion of a set of lessons and a final examination that signals that the individual has acquired the requisite knowledge to perform a task or job function. It provides an alternate filtering device for employers to gauge interest, knowledge, and work ethic when evaluating potential candidates for a position. It also ensures a steady supply of trained workers that can provide a reserve pool of potential employees who can fill a growing need when business is expanding at little cost to the company.[26]

In many ways, this appears to be the ideal relationship. Companies know what they need and can ensure that they get what they want by creating their own training curriculum. Higher education can continue to pursue what it perceives to be its mission and can marshal an acceptable response to anxious parents or students who are concerned about their return on investment by trumpeting various industry partnerships without having to divert their own resources to professional development. Why not allow companies such as Google, HubSpot, and Amazon Web Services to make the investment in professional training and leverage it to reap many of the rewards to the benefit of both?[27]

The challenge with industry-developed alternative credentials is that they often are designed to meet the needs of a specific company rather than generalized knowledge that is easily transferable to a variety of situations or circumstances. They are more about training than educating, and while they foster skill development, they don't emphasize turning those skills into capabilities. Alternative credentials, then, serve as a double-edged sword: they may help position a student as a more compelling graduate than those from other institutions, but the more heavily an institution touts the value of those credentials, the more it is making the case that a student can achieve professional success without the traditional bachelor's degree.

Badging

Badges can be used as a visual representation of qualifications and therefore offer the potential for being a powerful signaling device capable of communicating, in part, whether a graduate is qualified for a particular position.[28] In contrast to an alternate credential that certifies the completion of additional work that supplements a traditional curriculum, badges are often used to highlight aspects of an existing curriculum that might potentially signal the acquisition of work-ready skills.

In addition to communicating positive attributes, badges can be a source of motivation[29] by making possible relative comparisons between members of a cohort, applicant pool, or peer group. They make it easy for an individual to gain a feeling of relative superiority if they have earned more badges than the next person or if they demonstrate a degree of difficulty that makes it tough for others to achieve. Badges confer status and in doing so promote self-esteem.[30]

All of this is only true, however, if the badges represent something meaningful. Take, for example, running a race or playing a game where there is a definite start and finish in which accomplishment can be numerically measured. The winner can proclaim their time was the fastest, and comparisons can not only be made in terms of those who ran the race but also between all of the races that have been run that year at that distance.

Here, the trophy, winning time, or ribbon that might be awarded is backed by an objective standard (time) that can be used to make relative comparisons that qualify the winner for other competitions. Unfortunately, matters become a great deal murkier when the same qualifying system is applied to work-readiness. Take, for example, earning a qualification from one of the major tech companies. Becoming certified in Google Ad Words, for example, might signal an interest in the subject and the willingness to invest some time and effort in learning that particular skill, but what the badge or certification cannot easily communicate is whether that skill, or the knowledge associated with it, is developed to the point where it can effectively be put into practice.[31]

Watching a series of videos and passing an exam may make a potential candidate more familiar with the requirements of a particular job, and the candidate with the badge or certification may have a head start over others, but this does not necessarily mean they can actually employ Google Ad Words or some other technology successfully within an organization. Where being able to run a specific distance within a particular time is a good proxy for conditioning or natural talent and ability, the Google certificate represents a much weaker signal in terms of qualifications or ability.

A similar skepticism might exist for the runner who has only won a single race or achieved a particular time just once in their career. It is the ability to demonstrate winning results over an extended period of time that provides the clearest and strongest signal. By competing in multiple races, the runner is putting their talent and ability "into practice" and is building a record of achievement that can establish their position relative to other competitors at the same distance. Because it is less clear how a badge demonstrating work-ready skills was achieved, it is an imperfect signal reflecting what a potential job candidate can accomplish. Moreover, with a lack of standards, it becomes more difficult to make relative comparisons.[32] Thus, badges, to a large degree, signal an interest in a particular area but are less effective as a means for evaluating a candidate's capabilities.

Badging is often a victim of its own success. As interest in badges grows, there is an incentive to turn anything and everything into a badge. As a result, the proliferation of badges itself contributes to additional noise that makes it challenging to evaluate the underlying skills that may or may not exist with a candidate.[33] Badges therefore represent, at best, a flawed substitute for experience.

e-Portfolios

An e-portfolio can serve as a great way to showcase what a student has accomplished over the course of their undergraduate experience. It can communicate a student's career-readiness by putting on display the work they have accomplished. If assembled in an effective manner, it can also communicate a story that documents the progress made over time through the course of their studies.[34] The more directly the portfolio can show examples of work similar to what would be required in a particular job, the more directly it can speak to one's qualifications and potential for success. In the case of digital marketing, for example, showcasing a website, series of blog posts, email marketing campaign, or a similar type of work product can help a recruiter determine the quality of work and whether a candidate might be a good fit for a particular position.

Where there is no direct connection between the candidate's work product and the tasks associated with a specific job, a portfolio becomes a less effective signal of a candidate's suitability for a position. In this case, the recruiter is more interested in what a person is capable of doing rather than what they have previously accomplished. Those attributes that are most important might consist of factors such as how well the candidate can work with clients, adapt to changing circumstances, or fit within the culture of their organization. This might be more reflective of how a candidate presents themselves rather than what they have done.

A Communications Strategy

Regardless of whether it is an alternative credential, badge, or portfolio, with respect to work readiness, the challenge is how to communicate a set of capabilities that are not obvious. When potential employers are looking for intangibles such as confidence, work ethic, and the ability to get things done, the institution, as well as its graduates, must craft narratives that speak directly to the development of human capabilities that accompany the completion of an academic degree.

Constructing a narrative is a potent tool for sensemaking,[35] and can serve as a powerful promotional tool capable of sending a stronger and clearer signal to potential employers.[36] Because potential employers want insight into whether the graduate is a good fit and possesses what it will take to thrive in their work environment, they will most likely enlist behavior-based interviewing. The responses to these questions hinge on the ability to articulate a strong personal narrative.

The development of capabilities and corresponding confidence are more about the process than the final outcome. The same holds true for the information gathered during a behavior-based interview. In both cases, the valuable signals stem from the process one employs to arrive at the outcome. Work-ready signals reveal the capability of applying knowledge and skills to navigate various situations and to work through challenges.

A narrative, of course, can only have an impact if a door opens and creates an opportunity to share that narrative with someone of importance or consequence. This is why it is important to have students engage with working professionals from the start. These connections are developed over time long before the interview process begins. In fact, they can inform what is discussed and how a candidate is evaluated by a potential employer. The combination of a narrative and a strong personal connection has the potential to shift the interview from the gathering of information to an opportunity to validate a preexisting narrative. Likewise, earlier investments in becoming work-ready will pay dividends in regard to demonstrating and signaling the value of the candidate, as well as securing a good fit for both the student/prospective employee and the employer.

Notes

1. Roslansky and Auguste (2022).
2. ZipRecruiter (2022).
3. Handshake (2023) offers suggestions on how graduates might communicate soft skills to employers. They recommend constructing a narrative and using the STAR approach.
4. Why Business Networking Matters (Finances Online, 2023).
5. Why networks matter is discussed in stark terms by Garlinghouse (2019).
6. Students wait until just before they graduate to do important networking and job search. A provocative piece trying to answer why students are not taking advantage of career services can be found in Fadulu (2018).
7. One challenge is that many applicant tracking systems do not recognize alternate credentials: https://www.shrm.org/hr-today/news/hr-magazine/summer2022/pages/alternative-credentials-help-increase-talent-pool-.aspx.
8. The evolution of career services to connected communities is described in Dey and Cruzvergara (2014).
9. A 2017 survey by Strada-Gallup (Strada Education Network & Gallup, 2017a) found that nearly four in ten students have never visited their career services office or used online career resources (pp. 15–21). This is the case

despite evidence that visiting career services is highly beneficial to career success post graduation (Busteed, 2020; Colorado State University Institutional Research Planning and Effectiveness, 2018).

10. Networks are not only important for gaining employment after graduation, they also play a large role in the selection of a major. See Strada Educational Network and Gallup (2017b).
11. Fischman and Gardner (2022).
12. The challenges associated with becoming work-ready are exacerbated by those subtle influences created by one's peer group. For first- and second-year students who are either still searching for a major or are ensconced in a series of foundational courses whose value might not be immediately apparent, social considerations tend to dominate the daily choices made by the typical undergraduate. Very few friends are attending networking events or are focused on professional preparation, so these do not garner the level of importance they perhaps should. As juniors and seniors, students become more concerned about getting a job and have relevant experiences that make going to a networking event less intimidating—so they are more likely to attend.
13. Tversky and Kahneman (1981).
14. See, for example, Kim et al. (2022).
15. Land-grant universities were authorized under the Morrill Acts of 1862 and 1890. They provided a funding mechanism for the delivery of and equitable access to agriculture and technical education (Alabama A&M University, 2023).
16. In one study that tracked the behavior of 100 businesspeople at a mixer, Ingram and Morris (2007) discovered that it was more of an opportunity to catch up with past contacts rather than make new ones.
17. In 2022, LinkedIn had over 900 million users, 49 million who use the platform to search for jobs, and eight people who are hired every minute (Aslam, 2023).
18. Unfortunately, many mentorship programs are focused on their success in terms of rating academic performance and improving student retention rather than preparation for entering the workforce. An overview of peer mentoring can be found in Terrion and Leonard (2007). The effectiveness of faculty mentoring of students is discussed in Campbell and Campbell (1997).
19. Fisher and Price (2021).

    The effectiveness of alumni networks has been called into question (Auter & Marken, 2019).
20. PeopleGrove (2022).

21. Referrals have been found to increase the likelihood of being hired, negotiate a higher starting salary, and have longer tenure at a firm (Brown et al., 2014).
22. See Caplan (2018).
23. The importance of educational credentials is discussed in Gallagher (2018).
24. Interest in alternative credentials from an institutional perspective is discussed in Fong et al. (2022).
25. According to Del Rossi and Hersch (2016), students who combine a business and STEM major earn a premium over single majors. However, combining a liberal arts major with STEM or business fields does not increase earnings.
26. For a comprehensive look at those skills needed to be competitive in a region or industry, see Coursera (2022).

    Emsi, now known as Lightcast, provides their own skills assessment in a report entitled Resilient Skills (Coffey et al., 2020).
27. Stoll (2020).
28. See, for example, Zucker and Hicks (2019).
29. For a better understanding of the differences between intrinsic and extrinsic motivation, see Deci and Ryan (1985, 2000), Ryan and Deci (2000), and Walton and Cohen (2011).
30. See Immorlica et al. (2015).
31. An excellent review of the literature on signals and filters in the labor market can be found in Bills (2003). It serves as a cautionary tale for those who believe that badges will shed more light than heat when it comes to sending the appropriate job market signals.
32. A lack of standards will hamper the ability of badges to send a clear signal of knowledge gained from a particular program of study. In this way higher education has an advantage through the accreditation process.
33. Is it possible to have too many badges, in essence to become a jack of all trades, master of none? Jodie Cook in *Forbes* magazine makes the argument that the bigger mistake is not to try new things and, in turn, never discover what you really want to do or who you want to become (Cook, 2021).
34. Carter (2021).
35. Cunliffe and Coupland (2012).
36. See, for example, Schwab and Malleret (2022).

    For a theoretical exploration of the merit of the narrative see Bruner (1991) and Hammack (2008). Educational theorists and psychologists have long understood the value of the narrative as a way individuals order their life and make sense of their identities. With respect to potential employers, narrative tools could be powerful indicators. Also, in the words of Daniel Kahneman (2011), we all want to be the hero of our own story (p. 11).

References

Alabama A&M University. (2023). *Morrill act of 1890*. Alabama A&M University. Retrieved March 21, 2023, from https://www.aamu.edu/about/our-history/morril-act-1890.html

Aslam, S. (2023, February 8). 90 LinkedIn statistics you need to know in 2023. *Omnicore*. Retrieved March 21, 2023, from https://www.omnicoreagency.com/linkedin-statistics/

Auter, Z., & Marken, S. (2019, January 15). *Alumni networks less helpful than advertised*. Gallup, Inc. Retrieved March 21, 2023, from https://news.gallup.com/opinion/gallup/245822/alumni-networks-less-helpful-advertised.aspx

Bills, D. B. (2003). Credentials, signals, and screens: Explaining the relationship between schooling and job assignment. *Review of Educational Research, 73*(4), 441–469. https://doi.org/10.3102/00346543073004441

Brown, M., Setren, E., & Topa, G. (2014). *IZA DP No. 8175: Do informal referrals lead to better matches? Evidence from a firm's employee referral system*. IZA Institute of Labor Economics. Retrieved March 23, 2023, from https://www.iza.org/publications/dp/8175/do-informal-referrals-lead-to-better-matches-evidence-from-a-firms-employee-referral-system

Bruner, J. (1991). The narrative construction of reality. *Critical Inquiry, 18*(1), 1–21.

Busteed, B. (2020, December 21). Career services will define the next big boom in college enrollment. *Forbes*. Retrieved March 21, 2023, from https://www.forbes.com/sites/brandonbusteed/2020/12/21/career-services-will-define-the-next-big-boom-in-college-enrollment/?sh=75aac22145e7

Campbell, T. A., & Campbell, D. E. (1997). Faculty/student mentor program: Effects on academic performance and retention. *Research in Higher Education, 38*, 727–742. https://doi.org/10.1023/A:1024911904627

Caplan, B. D. (2018). *The case against education: Why the education system is a waste of time and money*. Princeton University Press.

Carter, S. (2021). ePortfolios as a platform for evidencing employability and building professional identity: A literature review. *International Journal of Work-Integrated Learning, 22*(4), 463–474.

Coffey, C., Burrow, G., Sentz, R., Kirschner, K., & Saleh, Y. (2020). Resilient skills: The survivor skills that the class of Covid-19 should pursue. *Emsi*. Retrieved March 23, 2023, from https://www.economicmodeling.com/wp-content/uploads/2020/08/Emsi_Resilient-Skills_Full-Report.pdf

Colorado State University Institutional Research, Planning and Effectiveness. (2018). *Career services usage and student success*. Colorado State University. https://career.colostate.edu/wp-content/uploads/2022/07/Student-Success-and-Career-Services-Usage.pdf

Cook, J. (2021, May 13). Why being a jack of all trades is essential for success. *Forbes*. Retrieved March 23, 2023, from https://www.forbes.com/sites/jodiecook/2021/05/13/why-being-a-jack-of-all-trades-is-essential-for-success/?sh=3496bb6e1c45

Coursera. (2022). Global Skills Index. *Coursera*. Retrieved March 21, 2023, from https://pages.coursera-for-business.org/rs/748-MIV-116/images/gsi2020_final.pdf

Cunliffe, A., & Coupland, C. (2012). From hero to villain to hero: Making experience sensible through embodied narrative sensemaking. *Human Relations, 65*(1), 63–88. https://doi.org/10.1177/0018726711424321

Deci, E. L., & Ryan, R. M. (1985). *Intrinsic motivation and self-determination in human behavior*. Springer US. https://doi.org/10.1007/978-1-4899-2271-7

Deci, E. L., & Ryan, R. M. (2000). The "what" and "why" of goal pursuits: Human needs and the self-determination of behavior. *Psychological Inquiry, 11*(4), 227–268. https://doi.org/10.1207/S15327965PLI1104_01

Del Rossi, A. F., & Hersch, J. (2016). The private and social benefits of double majors. *Journal of Benefit-Cost Analysis, 7*(2), 292–325. https://doi.org/10.1017/bca.2016.14

Dey, F., & Cruzvergara, C. Y. (2014). Evolution of career services in higher education: Evolution of career services in higher education. *New Directions for Student Services, 2014*(148), 5–18. https://doi.org/10.1002/ss.20105

Fadulu, L. (2018, January 20). Why aren't college students using career services? *The Atlantic*. Retrieved March 23, 2023, from https://www.theatlantic.com/education/archive/2018/01/why-arent-college-students-using-career-services/551051/

Finances Online. (2023). 45 significant business networking statistics: 2023 conversion rates & challenges. *Finances Online*. Retrieved March 24, 2023, from https://financesonline.com/business-networking-statistics/

Fischman, W., & Gardner, H. (2022). *The real world of college: What higher education is and what it can be*. The MIT Press.

Fisher, J., & Price, R. (2021). *Alumni networks reimagined: Innovations expanding alumni connections to improve postsecondary pathways*. Christensen Institute. Retrieved March 23, 2023, from https://www.christenseninstitute.org/wp-content/uploads/2021/01/Alumni_Networks.pdf

Fong, J., Ahluwalia, A., & Etter, B. (2022). Shifting Paradigms: Understanding Institutional Perspectives on Microcredentialing. Modern Campus & UPCEA. chrome-extension://efaidnbmnnnibpcajpcglclefindmkaj/https://moderncampus.com/pdfs/shifting-paradigms-understanding-institutional-perspectives-on-microcredentialing.pdf

Gallagher, S. R. (2018). *Educational credentials come of age: A survey on the use and value of educational credentials in hiring*. Northeastern University Center for the Future of Higher Education and Talent Strategy. Retrieved March 23,

2023, from https://cps.northeastern.edu/wp-content/uploads/2021/03/Educational_Credentials_Come_of_Age_2018.pdf

Garlinghouse, M. (2019, September 26). *Closing the network gap*. LinkedIn Corporation. Retrieved March 23, 2023, from https://blog.linkedin.com/2019/september/26/closing-the-network-gap

Hammack, P. L. (2008). Narrative and the cultural psychology of identity. *Personality and Social Psychology Review, 12*(3), 222–247. https://doi.org/10.1177/1088868308316892

Handshake. (2023). *How to show off your soft skills to employers—with samples*. Handshake. Retrieved March 23, 2023, from https://joinhandshake.com/blog/students/how-to-show-off-your-soft-skills-to-employers-with-samples/

Immorlica, N., Stoddard, G., & Syrgkanis, V. (2015). Social status and badge design. *Proceedings of the 24th International Conference on World Wide Web*, 473–483. https://doi.org/10.1145/2736277.2741664

Ingram, P., & Morris, M. W. (2007). Do People Mix at Mixers? Structure Homophily and the "Life of the Party". *Administrative Science Quarterly, 52*(4), 558–585. https://doi.org/10.2189/asqu.52.4.558

Kahneman, D. (2011). *Thinking, fast and slow* (1st ed.). Farrar, Straus and Giroux.

Kim, J., Oh, J., & Rajaguru, V. (2022). Job-seeking anxiety and job preparation behavior of undergraduate students. *Healthcare, 10*(2), 288. https://doi.org/10.3390/healthcare10020288

PeopleGrove (2022). The 2021-2022 PeopleGrove Social Capital Impact Report. PeopleGrove. chrome-extension://efaidnbmnnnibpcajpcglclefindmkaj/https://resources.peoplegrove.com/hubfs/Benchmark_21-22_Print_July22.pdf

Roslansky, R., & Auguste, B. (2022, October 13). Opinion: It's time for employers to stop caring so much about college degrees. *CNN*. Retrieved March 23, 2023, from https://www.cnn.com/2022/10/13/perspectives/college-degrees-careers-roslansky-auguste/index.html

Ryan, R. M., & Deci, E. L. (2000). Self-determination theory and the facilitation of intrinsic motivation, social development, and well-being. *American Psychologist, 55*(1), 68–78. https://doi.org/10.1037/0003-066X.55.1.68

Schwab, K., & Malleret, T. (2022, April 8). *The power of narrative*. NautilusNext, Inc. Retrieved March 23, 2023, from https://nautil.us/the-power-of-narrative-238456/

Stoll, J. D. (2020, November 9). This degree is brought to you by Amazon. *The Wall Street Journal*. Retrieved March 23, 2023, from https://www.wsj.com/articles/this-college-degree-is-brought-to-you-by-amazon-11604941263

Strada Educational Network and Gallup. (2017a). *2017 college student survey: A nationally represented survey of currently enrolled students*. Gallup, Inc. Retrieved March 21, 2023, from https://news.gallup.com/reports/225161/2017-strada-gallup-college-student-survey.aspx

Strada Educational Network and Gallup. (2017b). *Major influence: Where students get valued advice on what to study in college*. Gallup, Inc. Retrieved March 23, 2023, from https://news.gallup.com/reports/269081/strada-gallup-major-influence-where-students-get-valued-advice-report.aspx?utm_source=Strada_Reports_Confirmation_Email&utm_medium=email&utm_campaign=Confirmation_Email_Dec2019&utm_content=Download_the_Report_Link_8

Terrion, J. L., & Leonard, D. (2007). A taxonomy of the characteristics of student peer mentors in higher education: Findings from a literature review. *Mentoring & Tutoring: Partnership in Learning, 15*(2), 149–164. https://doi.org/10.1080/13611260601086311

Tversky, A., & Kahneman, D. (1981). The framing of decisions and the psychology of choice. *Science, 211*(4481), 453–458. https://doi.org/10.1126/science.7455683

Walton, G. M., & Cohen, G. L. (2011). Sharing motivation. In D. Dunning (Ed.), *Social motivation* (pp. 79–101). Psychology Press.

ZipRecruiter. (2022). *The class of 2022: The job market outlook for grads*. ZipRecruiter, Inc. https://www.ziprecruiter.com/grad-report

Zucker, L., & Hicks, T. (2019). Alternative assessments, unintended consequences: The promise and peril of digital badges. *Transformations: The Journal of Inclusive Scholarship and Pedagogy, 29*(1), 113–123. https://doi.org/10.1353/tnf.2019.0008

EdTech to the Rescue?

What a difference ten years makes. Ten years ago, MOOCs (massively open online courses) were all the rage, and followers of Clayton Christensen thought this would lead to a major disruption of higher education.[1] Today, the mantel has been taken up by prognosticators such as Scott Galloway, a lecturer in marketing at the NYU Stern School of Business.[2] While some small institutions have either merged or gone out of business and many universities have been more welcoming of remote learning, higher education has remained largely unchanged.[3]

What happened? What the leading advocates of disruption seemed to have forgotten is that the university experience is more than just a collection of courses. Students (and their parents) are still willing to pay for a residential collegiate experience. While getting away from mom and dad is part of it, finding out who you are and what you want and learning how to get it extends far beyond what happens in the average classroom.

Rather than looking for a wholesale rethinking of higher education, EdTech has morphed into a collection of services that are designed to supplement and, in some cases, enhance components that contribute to university education. At its core, the vast majority of EdTech products leverage the ability to store large amounts of data, facilitate the making of connections between various stakeholders, educators, and the broader information universe, and incorporate smart technologies to help develop a deeper understanding of what is important. It goes beyond remote and

N. B. Niman, J. R. Chagnon, *The Work-Ready Graduate*,
https://doi.org/10.1007/978-3-031-33910-3_6

personalized learning to include collaboration between students, faculty, employers, and alumni in new and unique ways.[4]

The products offered by EdTech companies have a strong appeal for those students who find the time or cost of a four-year bachelor's degree to be prohibitive. EdTech products are also appealing to colleges or universities that do not have the time or resources to internally develop some of the functions that have now become a requirement to stay competitive in a declining market. For these reasons, there is a great deal of interest in EdTech from traditional brick and mortar institutions. According to PitchBook, EdTech (including K-12 and higher education) represented a $220 billion opportunity in 2020 with a CAGR (compound annual growth rate) of 16.3%.[5] To put these numbers in perspective, IBISWorld estimates that colleges and universities in the US had total revenues of $565.7 billion in 2021, and the industry is projected to only grow at an annual rate of 1.8% over the next five years.[6]

To understand how EdTech is penetrating the higher education market, we can revisit the six unrealized opportunities of the university experience identified in our earlier chapter highlighting those "Unrealized Opportunities". The important question we will explore is whether EdTech is providing supportive solutions that make substantial progress toward producing work-ready graduates or whether it is merely scratching the surface.

Human Capabilities

For a time, the potential of EdTech was thought to reside in the ability to connect students with "best in class" faculty so that any and every student would have access to true leaders in the field or master instructors who have demonstrated an exceptional ability to explain complex ideas to students of differing ability levels.[7] In addition, where some universities might be limited in the depth and breadth of courses they could offer, students enrolled in their degree programs could access a broad array of courses that would expand learning opportunities. In this way, the university experience could remain local, but students might go beyond the limits of an individual institution to access world-class education.

Rather than embracing the new model, students found that remote learning posed a series of challenges. Sitting through one online (and often recorded) session after another turned out to be a great deal more fatiguing than anyone thought. The informal learning that takes place by hanging out with classmates or a professor was eclipsed by isolated learning with contact only by appointment and mediated by technology. Even something as simple as making a new friend with common interests turned from casual to contrived.

Since few were interested in what companies such as Coursera, Udacity, or EdX were offering, these companies chose to pivot in an effort to find an audience for their online courses.[8] They have taken the lessons learned from the Massively Open Online Course (MOOC) space and spent a great deal of effort creating educational pathways to in-demand careers based on current trends in the economy. Career seekers can take an individual course or participate in an entire curriculum comprising multiple courses that concludes with a certificate, credential, or truncated degree. Such a micro-credential can speak to the intention, interest, and willingness to advance along a particular career path and serve as a strong signal to current or prospective employers. These new credentials could offer an alternative to a traditional degree with the added benefit of requiring a smaller investment in both time *and* money.[9]

The challenge with this approach is that many online curricula presuppose that a person knows what they want or need. A student interested in e-commerce could, for example, look more closely at the Udacity nanodegree program in Digital Marketing. Within the curriculum, topics include subjects such as content strategy, social media, search engine optimization, email marketing, and Google Analytics. The content for the courses was created in collaboration with companies such as Facebook, Google, Hootsuite, HubSpot, Mailchimp, and Moz. Spanning three months, the program requires a commitment of 10 hours a week from start to finish. Within the curriculum, students work on projects such as crafting a social media post for three social platforms, evaluating a Facebook ad campaign, auditing a company's website, recommending improvements, or developing a marketing strategy. Personalized feedback is provided from a network of project reviewers, and answers to questions may be found in a proprietary wiki or by leveraging the power of the community in their student hub. All of this comes with human instructors who have previous work experience in digital marketing.[10]

This all sounds great if you are a professional working in digital marketing or transitioning to that industry by developing a new set of skills that would enable you to be a more competitive candidate. What someone takes away from an online program depends in part upon the individual and where they are in their professional development. A working professional who is looking to expand their skillset for a career path that was carefully chosen and at least partly developed will, however, have different needs than a college student who has limited experience in a work environment and who has difficulties selecting a major, let alone an entire career.[11] It is challenging to try to upskill or reskill someone who has limited skills in the first place or who has little to no context in terms of how skills may be applied. More importantly, we are talking about a population that in general is unsure of, and underexposed to, professional development. This has limited the ability of a program such as Coursera for Campus to penetrate brick and mortar institutions.

In one of the few studies that looks at MOOCs, Fiona Hollands and Aasiya Kazi found that the average age of the respondents enrolled in one of the specializations created by MOOC providers was 36. Sixty-seven percent held at least a bachelor's degree. The most popular expected benefit was to "Improve my performance in my current job" (42%). All of this suggests that the market for specialized and career-driven online offerings is adult learners who have already earned a bachelor's degree.[12]

Of particular interest was that only 40% expected to earn the credential at the end, and completion rates followed those of other MOOCs, below 15%.[13] Low completion rates have been a problem for online courses since their inception.[14] Online course providers hypothesized that a credential might serve as a strong signaling device to potential employers and lead to better opportunities or higher levels of compensation. Hoping that prospective employers would place more value on a credential than a single course, students would pay for the credential and, in turn, be more willing to stick around to complete the required course work.

Bundling courses into credentials does not seem to be the answer to a problem plaguing this segment of the EdTech sector. While the programs are designed to further career development by awarding some form of credential, consumers of these services appear to be more interested in filling an immediate need and, once that need has been satisfied, abandoning what remains.[15] As a result, the "only pay for what you need" approach is more about skill development than about building a set of capabilities that provide a longer return on investment.

Self-Discovery

Regardless of whether human capabilities are provided by brick and mortar colleges and universities or EdTech, the development of a work-ready graduate begins with a discovery process that helps traditional students establish a sense of who they are and what they want to do. Many undergraduate students do not have a clue about whether they want to be a data analyst, scientist, architect, or product manager. They might not be interested in data at all. Many do not know what type of company they would like to work for, let alone what path is best suited for them. Moreover, most recent college graduates lack the soft skills that companies covet.

Focus2Career is an example of a tech-based product designed to help students learn about themselves and their interests, values, and current skills. The platform's structured set of questions is designed to guide a discovery process that helps a student identify potential careers and recommend which majors provide the best foundation for pursuing a particular path.

Some of these platforms can also help students understand the steps they might take to increase their chances for success as they travel along a particular career path. VMock, another EdTech company in this space, uses artificial intelligence to help students improve their résumés. Their Career Fit module evaluates how well a student's career profile matches individual job characteristics and assists in the development of an action plan that increases the probability of landing a particular job upon graduation.

All of this can be helpful, but again, it is important to note that career-readiness is not the same thing as work-readiness. EdTech solutions that promote career-readiness typically reside within student services. Work-readiness, as it addresses the development of human capabilities, is firmly rooted in professional experiences. If EdTech is to become an important player in the work-ready space, it must help in creating stronger connections in the development of those capabilities that transcend a particular discipline. A more comprehensive approach needs to be fashioned that incorporates the entire student experience so that careers are tied to more than just majors and capabilities are the outgrowth of a structured set of experiences.

Curriculum

For the longest time, the state-of-the-art in digital learning seemed to be nothing more than the release of conventional textbooks such as e-books or their digital homework platforms that did away with print-based study guides. What began as a means to increase textbook adoptions fundamentally transformed the market to its current state where the textbook has become ancillary to the digital learning platform.

All this changed with the incorporation of artificial intelligence and the development of adaptive learning technologies. One of the earliest pioneers was Knewton, a company formed in 2008. The company's original business model was based on partnerships with traditional publishers. Rather than trying to compete head on, Knewton licensed its technology to major textbook publishers such as Pearson.[16] Knewton's adaptive learning technology (Alta) was a groundbreaking development that truly made personalized learning possible for the first time. Alta enabled traditional textbook companies to develop digital platforms that could provide personalized solutions based on a student's demonstrated proficiency levels. By tracking student performance as they worked through a list of assignments, the technology could identify where the student was struggling to master a specific concept or its application and make recommendations for further reading, additional problems to solve, or resources based on their own weaknesses.

This was all in an effort to help remediate the issues standing in the way of developing a desired level of proficiency, thereby creating a personalized learning opportunity that is unique to that individual student. In addition, the technology also contained learning analytics features that enabled an instructor to predict when a student might need additional assistance before the student disengages or to identify learning patterns across an entire class to identify topics that requires additional time or resources to ensure that everyone has developed an acceptable level of mastery.[17]

The challenge for personalized approaches is that learning becomes an individual experience that leads to large variations in outcomes.[18] They tailor learning to the specific needs of a person at a particular place and time relative to the material to be mastered. The software, as a product of the work of professors rather than working professionals, misses those important social and professional cues that lead to success in a particular workplace. It also misses the value of the informal learning that takes place when working as part of a team or developing relationships within an organization. Nor does it necessarily help with the ability to put knowledge into practice, or the development of the confidence and emotional stability needed to challenge oneself and take a risk—all components of what it means to become work-ready.

The solution to some of these drawbacks can be found in the tech platforms being offered by companies such as Riipen or Parker Dewey that incorporate project-based learning. Project-based learning is just one possibility within a growing movement to infuse existing curricula with experiential learning opportunities. For these EdTech companies, it takes the form of embedding experiential learning opportunities within the context of an existing course.[19]

This is an opportunity that universities such as Arizona State find particularly attractive because of the ability to scale it across an entire institution.[20] Alternatively, project-based learning is being promoted by companies such as HubSpot, which is partnering with Parker Dewey to develop micro-internships targeted at university students who are seeking careers in digital marketing.

These companies offer a fully integrated solution that enables professors to embed real projects into existing courses. It is a relatively low-cost means for inserting authenticity and relevance directly into the curriculum without requiring substantial revision. Riipen, for example, accomplishes this by providing a technology platform that stores, monitors, and tracks student progress. It can be thought of as an applied project management tool that easily allows a faculty member to assign students to a project, verify their contribution, and report outcomes. It solves a real problem for many faculty members who rely on textbooks, problem sets, and test banks for the delivery of their courses where the application of knowledge is often done in the abstract and more focused on the ability to demonstrate that one has mastered the concepts rather than place them into practice.

Where publishers have tied their learning management systems to their own textbooks and more generic versions such as Blackboard, Canvas, or Moodle are tied to individual courses, Riipen's system is tied to projects. By managing projects that can extend across an entire curriculum, it more easily enables students to construct portfolios that can help showcase their work to potential employers. Riipen also provides a matchmaking service that utilizes an extensive network of vetted companies that can provide projects that fit well within existing course structures. These projects, initiated either by a professor who is looking for a project for their course or a company that has a project and is looking for an academic partner, are advertised on the technology platform where both sides of the match can receive guidance from Riipen employees overseeing the matchmaking process.

From the perspective of developing a work-ready graduate, the impact can be felt far beyond an individual project or portfolio designed to display a set of accomplishments. Textbooks, for example, are conceived and vetted by professors through an extensive testing and review process. The assignments are as current and useful as the professors who imagine, comment on, and use them. It should be noted, however, that one consequence of this review process is the broad acceptance of what constitutes the most important concepts that should be included in what is determined to be the core of a particular academic discipline.

Riipen follows a similar model, but the projects engage working professionals rather than academics. These projects offer the potential to be more relevant because they incorporate real problems and tasks rather than the hypotheticals created by professors. The projects are evaluated based on what clients rather than faculty think is important. This creates a library of projects that are more current and authentic.

The challenge this presents is that the projects themselves must still fit within the framework of a course that was created by an academic who, for the most part, has a set of learning goals that are more informed by the needs of an accrediting body, graduate school, or past tradition than the current workplace. Certain content must be covered and mastered for a student to be deemed professionally competent or prepared for advanced study. This sets up an inherent conflict between the needs of the major, socialization in the field, and what is perhaps desired in the employment market.

Connections

In the professional business world, many of the skills required to successfully perform a job are acquired by experience—what is essentially learning by doing.[21] Experience is often the best teacher, but it is a process that includes a great deal of trial and error with a number of successes and failures along the way.

To foster skill development, many companies have adopted a two-track approach. Major investments are made in job training programs designed to facilitate the acquisition of new skills.[22] The second track incorporates mentorship to accelerate the process. New hires are assigned a mentor who can help them navigate the organization, clarify what competencies need to be developed in the current business environment, and gain an inside look at what needs to be done or how to do it. In combination, these dual tracks work together to develop a working professional and assist in their development.

Unfortunately, such a professional development program does not exist in higher education. Many faculty members have limited professional experience, so the focus is, for the most part, directed toward that foundational knowledge that rests at the core of most curricula. Filling the gap between the acquisition of knowledge and the skills required to put that knowledge into practice has not generally been the focus of many academic majors. In response, many colleges and universities have created mentorship programs where industry professionals are matched with students who have similar interests and career aspirations. The main idea is that through one-on-one coaching, these students become better prepared to enter the workforce and gain a head start in becoming career-ready.

Matching people and interests is one of the things that EdTech does best, and companies such as PeopleGrove have crafted a solution designed to bring together alumni and students to foster career development. PeopleGrove enables universities to construct walled gardens that, in contrast to other services such as LinkedIn, enable institutions to develop customized solutions that incorporate their unique identity and the interests of current students and alumni. It enables a university to trade on affinity and loyalty to create a group of mentors available exclusively to their student body. It provides students with a natural opening to a group of motivated professionals who are there to connect.

Utilizing such a platform truly adheres to the adage that you only get as much as you put in. For students and alumni to come together, there has to be a compelling reason that extends beyond the fact that each attended the same institution. Someone needs to start the conversation, but then it must be kept going to bring interested parties to the platform. Once there, if the relationship is to contribute toward the development of a work-ready graduate, it must extend beyond professional networking, the identification of potential career pathways, or introduction to someone who can open a door and get that first interview.

The development of a set of work-ready capabilities, however, goes beyond a simple networking opportunity. Mentors and mentees within a company share a common context, understanding of personalities, and idiosyncratic characteristics that uniquely define a particular company or work situation. Because of this shared foundation, a mentor can play a large role in accelerating professional development and helping to expand on a given set of capabilities that influenced the initial hiring decision. The problem that EdTech has not been able to solve up to this point is how to take advantage of a mentorship relationship that is more than informational or an extension of one's professional network.

Signals

For the student who has progressed during their undergraduate years—found a major that matches their interests and used that core knowledge, skills, and experiences to develop a set of capabilities that would be of value to a potential employer—one challenge remains: How will a potential employer know that this student would be an exceptional candidate for their open position? It is all about sending the appropriate signal. For many, the focus turns to the résumé, that one-page document that lists where you went to school, your major, grade point average, relevant experience, any credentials earned and skills you might have picked up along the way.

To try to cut through the noise that makes it difficult for a potential employer to determine if a graduate is truly work-ready, EdTech has begun the skillification of the curriculum along with the creation of skillibi.[23] The concept underlying skillification is a simple one. Scour all of the job listings from popular employment sites, compile a list of skills and keywords being requested, and create a giant database that matches skills with professions to create a series of career pathways. Then, scan an entire campus's course listings and syllabi to pull out learning objectives, mentions of specific skills, or software packages used and mash them together to compile a curriculum profile and then add a dash of artificial intelligence to skim a student's transcript and pull out a list of "skills" that they have presumably developed. Finally, compare the skills asked for in the list of job openings and the list of skills derived from an analysis of the student's course work and their résumé to perform a gap analysis. The analysis compares the skills desired with those acquired to identify career matches, or for those with specific ambitions, to help them understand what else they need to do to meet the qualifications for a specific career.

Companies such as Lightcast and VMock believe that this is the solution needed to help students position themselves to achieve career success. It is a high-tech version of a matching game where words suggest skills (whether real or imagined) that add to the mix of signals that communicate the suitability of a candidate for a specific job opportunity.[24]

What skillification is hoping to achieve for course work, companies such as Suitable are trying to do with extracurricular activities. Recognizing that participating in everything a university has to offer can also help in making a student work or career-ready, companies such as Suitable offer the capability to construct cocurricular transcripts that can communicate to a prospective employer what a student has accomplished outside the classroom, which makes them particularly suitable for a particular employment opportunity.

Regardless of whether we are looking at what happens inside or outside the classroom, EdTech's solution takes a checklist approach that is designed to make employers more aware of what a student might have learned from a particular course, program of study, or selected extracurricular opportunity. Whether this signal just adds to the noise or provides an accurate statement of a student's capability in the workplace depends on whether satisfying a course requirement truly reflects the development of a specific level of proficiency that qualifies one for a particular employment opportunity.

For example, identifying a presentation requirement on a syllabus does not necessarily mean that upon completion of a course, the student has become an excellent presenter. Many skills are only developed when accompanied by some instruction covering best practices and refined through feedback and repetition. The skillification of course syllabi can identify points in the curriculum where a student might have an opportunity to be exposed to a particular skillset, but there is no guarantee that those skills were developed in a deliberate and thoughtful way.

Is EdTech the Answer?

The products offered by EdTech companies have a strong appeal for students who find the time or cost of a four-year bachelor's degree to be prohibitive. In addition, EdTech products are appealing to colleges or universities that do not have the time or resources to internally develop some of the functions that have now become a requirement to stay competitive in a declining market or are drawn to the allure of a possible turnkey solution.

For universities that define themselves as research institutions, the main focus has always been on the creation and dissemination of knowledge. In response to this mission, EdTech has created a number of products that assist in the mastery of core knowledge to ensure the academic success of the student. Acknowledging that every student who earns a bachelor's degree is not going to advance to graduate school, and in response to questions surrounding the value of a four-year degree, many colleges and universities have invested heavily in career-readiness—assisting their students in identifying a career, a major, and at the end, a first job. But career-readiness is not the same as work-readiness. To become work-ready, students need to not only learn core concepts but also be able to put them into practice. If we are truly interested in developing a work-ready graduate, higher education needs to fashion a new set of responses to existing challenges. This leads to a fundamental conflict between the need/desire to scale and a more resource-intensive personalized approach tailored to today's undergraduate population that has little direction, truncated social skills, and a great deal of anxiety about their place in the world.

Notes

1. Clay Christensen was a long-time Harvard Business School professor who rose to prominence with his ideas about how technology affords the potential to create major disruptions in familiar industries. For more information about how higher education is not immune to those same disruptive forces, see Christensen and Eyring (2011).

   The return of 'Ed-Tech Mania' is back with a cautionary tale (Reich, 2020).
2. Scott Galloway has created his own EdTech company at: http://section4.com. For more information on his prediction about the coming dominance of EdTech, see Walsh (2020).
3. Increased student acceptance and support for remote learning is discussed in Ubell (2022).

   An evaluation of the effectiveness of online learning is discussed in Marcus (2022).
4. See Joint Information Systems Committee (JISC) and Emerge Education (2020) for more information.
5. Visit PitchBook (2020) for more details.
6. See Le (2023) for more data.
7. The early history of MOOCS is detailed in Daniel (2012).
8. See Stober (2015) for more on this topic.
9. Rivas et al. (2020) found that employers prefer a traditional degree to a MOOC credential. The work reveals that micro credentials are not viewed as adequate replacements for traditional degrees.
10. The curriculum can be found on Udacity's website (Udacity, 2023).
11. In fact, 51% of college students are unsure of their career path, according to Ellucian (2019).
12. Holland and Kazi (2018, p. 6).
13. For more details, see Hollands and Kazi (2018, p. 9).
14. For more information, see Reich and Ruipéz-Valiente (2019).
15. Amy Ahearn states that "the two organizations where I've built online courses—we've found that many MOOC users sign up, download the read-

ings and workbooks, watch a select number of the videos, and even take key insights back to their team or work—but never complete and upload all of the assignments. Our users self-report these behaviors in postcourse surveys and qualitative interviews. They explain that they either come to MOOCs with specific learning goals that they selectively pursue or are simply not motivated to earn a certificate." For more, see Ahearn (2018).

16. Pearson terminated its relationship with Knewton in 2017 to focus on the development of its own adaptive learning technology. The company was then sold in 2019 to Wiley at a bargain basement price.
17. All of this can promote the mastery of a defined body of knowledge. However, this does not necessarily translate into the development of work-ready capabilities. With further development, these platforms might be adapted to support the development of work-ready capabilities, but this is a priority that would need to be identified as being important to an individual professor, program of study, or possibly an accrediting body. Textbook publishers have woken up to the importance of accreditation and have broadened their platforms to make it easy to insert learning goals and track how those goals are achieved through the various readings, exercises, or assessments chosen by the professor.
18. See Roberts (2016) for an expanded view on this topic.
19. In a recent survey undertaken by the AAC&U and Hanover Research (Finley, 2009), the ability to place ideas into practice was identified as a competency highly valued by employers. Also see Salisbury and Kraft (2020).
20. See Johnson (2021) to read the Arizona State University press release.
21. Learning by Doing harkens all the way back to John Dewey. See Dewey (1963).
22. The size of the market for workplace training in North America was $165.3 billion. For more related facts, see Statista (2022).
23. For more on this topic, see Verougstrataete et al. (2021).
24. For a nonspecific example, review Coffey et al. (2020).

References

Ahearn, A. (2018, November 28). Stop asking about completion rates: Better questions to ask about MOOCs in 2019. *EdSurge*. Retrieved March 21, 2023, from https://www.edsurge.com/news/2018-11-28-stop-asking-about-completion-rates-better-questions-to-ask-about-moocs-in-2019

Christensen, C. M., & Eyring, H. J. (2011). *The innovative university: Changing the DNA of higher education from the inside out* (1st ed.). Jossey-Bass.

Coffey, C., Burrow, G., Sentz, R., Kirschner, K., & Saleh, Y. (2020). Resilient skills: The survivor skills that the class of Covid-19 should pursue. *Emsi*.

Retrieved March 23, 2023, from https://www.economicmodeling.com/wp-content/uploads/2020/08/Emsi_Resilient-Skills_Full-Report.pdf

Daniel, J. (2012). Making sense of MOOCs: Musings in a maze of myth, paradox and possibility. *Journal of Interactive Media in Education, 2012*(3), 18. https://doi.org/10.5334/2012-18

Dewey, J. (1963). *Experience and education*. Collier Books.

Ellucian. (2019). Course correction: Helping students find and follow a path to success. *Ellucian*. Retrieved March 23, 2023, from https://www.ellucian.com/assets/en//2019-student-success-survey-results.pdf

Finley, A. (2009). *How college contributes to workforce success*. Association of American Colleges and Universities. Retrieved March 24, 2023, from https://dgmg81phhvh63.cloudfront.net/content/user-photos/Research/PDFs/AACUEmployerReport2021.pdf

Hollands, F., & Kazi, A. (2018). *Benefits and costs of MOOC-based alternative credentials*. Center For Benefit-Cost Studies of Education. Retrieved March 24, 2023, from https://www.academia.edu/37862783/Benefits_and_Costs_of_MOOC_Based_Alternative_Credentials_2018_

JISC and Emerge Education. (2020). The future of employer-university collaboration—A vision for 2030. *JISC & Emerge Education*. https://beta.jisc.ac.uk/reports/the-future-of-employer-university-collaboration-a-vision-for-2030

Johnson, E. (2021, August 11). ASU goes big with work-based learning 'marketplace'. *WorkShift*. Retrieved March 24, 2023, from https://workshift.opencampusmedia.org/asu-goes-big-with-work-based-learning-marketplace/

Le, T. (2023). Industry Report 61131A College and Universities in the US. *Ibisworld*.

Marcus, J. (2022, October 6). With online learning. 'Let's take a breath and see what worked and didn't work'. *The New York Times*. Retrieved March 24, 2023, from https://www.nytimes.com/2022/10/06/education/learning/online-learning-higher-education.html

PitchBook. (2020). *Vertical Snapshot: EdTech*. PitchBook.

Reich, J. (2020, September 14). *Ed-Tech Mania is Back: Utopia-minded tech gurus promise they'll solve all of academe's problems. They won't*. The Chronical of Higher Education. Retrieved March 24, 2023, from https://www.chronicle.com/article/ed-tech-mania-is-back

Reich, J., & Ruipéz-Valiente, J. A. (2019). The MOOC pivot: What happened to disruptive transformation of education? *Science, 363*(6423), 130–131. https://doi.org/10.11126/science.aav7958

Rivas, M. J., Baker, R. B., & Evans, B. J. (2020). Do MOOCs make you more marketable? An experimental analysis of the value of MOOCs relative to traditional credentials and experience. *AERA Open, 6*(4), 233285842097357. https://doi.org/10.1177/2332858420973577

Roberts, J. W. (2016). *Experiential education in the college context: What it is, how it works, and why it matters*. Routledge.

Salisbury, A., & Kraft, K. (2020). Unlocking career potential: An analysis of the career navigation & guidance product landscape. *Entangled Solutions*. Retrieved March 24, 2023, from https://www.equitablefutures.org/wp-content/uploads/2020/05/Entangled-Unlocking-Career-Nav-Deck-Overview_Apr2020_vFINAL.pdf

Statista. (2022). Total training expenditures in the United States from 2012 to 2022 (in billion U.S. dollars). *Statista*.

Stober, D. (2015, October 15). MOOCs haven't lived up to the hopes and the hype, Stanford participants say. *Stanford News*. Retrieved March 24, 2023, from https://news.stanford.edu/2015/10/15/moocs-no-panacea-101515/

Ubell, R. (2022, December 20). Why college students turned from being down on remote learning to mostly in favor of it. *EdSurge*. Retrieved March 24, 2023, from https://www.edsurge.com/news/2022-12-20-why-college-students-turned-from-being-down-on-remote-learning-to-mostly-in-avor-of-it

Udacity. (2023). How to become a digital marketer. *Udacity*. Retrieved March 24, 2023, from https://www.udacity.com/course/digital-marketing-nano degree%2D%2Dnd018

Verougstrataete, R., Safranski, A., & Peasley, A. (2021). Skills required. *Lightcast*. Retrieved March 24, 2023, from https://www.datocms-assets.com/62658/1669779239-skills-required-ebook_lightcast.pdf

Walsh, J. D. (2020, May 11) The coming disruption: Scott Galloway predicts a handful of elite cyborg universities will soon monopolize higher education. *New York Magazine*. Retrieved March 24, 2023, from https://nymag.com/intelligencer/2020/05/scott-galloway-future-of-college.html

PART II

Capitalizing on the Unrealized Potential

Practice-Based Learning

Practice-based learning builds on the groundwork laid by other forms of experiential learning and further situates the learning dynamic within a contextualized experience.[1] The emphasis is on a learner-centric approach where students engage with industry professionals with an intentional and targeted set of learning and development goals. Process-based, these guided experiences seek to leverage the tacit knowledge of a practitioner that, when combined with carefully designed activities, creates a robust learning experience. This design aims to accelerate the development of work-ready capabilities by giving the students opportunities to gain insights as they learn by doing.

Practice-based learning seeks to recreate many of the benefits associated with externally generated high-impact experiences in a controlled campus setting.[2] Rather than focusing on the mastery of a body of knowledge or a set of principles, practice-based learning concentrates on the *development* of the individual learner to further their professional acumen through the application of desired soft skills with an opportunity to put them into practice within a collection of diverse and authentic situations. Students are encouraged to make connections to the real world by utilizing the previous experience of a working professional who guides the learning process.[3]

What distinguishes practice-based learning from project-based learning is the guided portion of the experience.[4] Learning by doing for a working professional generally means following a process that they have designed,

N. B. Niman, J. R. Chagnon, *The Work-Ready Graduate*,
https://doi.org/10.1007/978-3-031-33910-3_7

is proprietary to a current/previous employer, or follows a standard industry methodology.[5] Students learn by actively engaging with that process to create a final deliverable. This closely mirrors processes they are likely to encounter in a real organization or professional environment. Taught using an experience-based semi-structured learning process, students are presented with an opportunity that helps them explore the value associated with doing something in a particular way.

Practice-based learning is as much about how one gets there (the journey) as achieving a final result that meets a set of expectations. It is an approach that focuses on more than just the ability to meet today's challenges. It also prepares the learner by challenging them to consider how they might apply knowledge and skills to a changing set of conditions.

ISA^2

The hallmark of practice-based learning is what we call ISA^2 (informal, situated, active, and applied). It eschews formal instruction for a guided process that takes advantage of the knowledge and experience of a working industry professional. The carefully designed learning experience attempts to replicate, as closely as possible, the types of tasks and processes that are found in a real business environment. Students actively engage with a project, client, or problem, where they are focusing more on the how than the why of doing something. It is designed in a manner that encourages students to apply their core knowledge to gain a greater understanding for how those principles are used in an authentic business setting.

The goal is not to tell students the best way to do something. Instead, it is a process that allows students a degree of agency in discovering a pathway forward in a low-risk environment to perform taks within a reasonable period of time.[6] To gain a better understanding of the approach, we can look at each element individually using examples of BiP courses we have designed and offered as part of the curriculum at the University of New Hampshire.[7]

Informal

Learning is associated more with a guided experience than formal instruction. An industry professional draws from their work history as they guide a group of students through an intentionally designed learning experience. Students are expected to actively participate and in part, influence how learning unfolds within a preconceived and flexible set of learning goals. The importance of pairing students with professionals stems from the meaningful activities that are incorporated in the course design.[8] It provides an opportunity for students to take advantage of the tacit knowledge possessed by the working professional that comes from years of direct experience.[9]

In the learning experience *The B-Side of Music*, students work with a veteran of the music industry with his own music label. Collaborating with local bands across a variety of genres, students are challenged to develop a plan designed to launch an actual band's career. Working together, they further develop work-ready capabilities by creating a touring schedule, generating interest from the music-loving public, constructing a merchandising plan, and setting the parameters for a recording contract. After an initial experience that empowers students to bring what they know to the table, students are re-tasked with a series of steps in a process that culminates in a plan presented to their band. The student teams receive feedback, as well as an opportunity to share their thought process where they can ask questions in what becomes a cooperative learning environment.[10]

Situated

Drawing from early apprenticeship models, Jean Lave and Etienne Wenger believe that knowledge needs to be presented in an authentic context because learning is inherently social and involves building relationships with proficient practitioners.[11] What people learn, see, and do is situated in their role as a member of a community. In other words, learning is a function of doing within a particular context and culture.[12] The traditional learning experience is heightened by real projects sourced from actual organizations, and can make a substantial contribution toward the development of work-ready capabilities. Placing concepts into an authentic context and having students solve a problem can help them understand how to apply important concepts in a meaningful way.

In *The Business of Podcasting*, students work with a long-established podcaster in the industry. With the industry professional's guidance, students develop their own podcasts and work in teams to create individual episodes. The class collaborates on a central theme, teams work to produce their own content for an individual show, and together they develop and execute a marketing plan designed to attract listeners. All of this occurs within the parameters of a corresponding revenue model created to sustain the endeavor.

Active

As discussed in the chapter "Human Capabilities," it is difficult to develop work-ready capabilities when learning by listening. A lecture can be an effective tool for disseminating core knowledge, but to truly understand how to do something, there is no substitute for experience.[13] By asking students to accomplish a task or deliverable, they must actively participate by using the skills needed to engage in brainstorming/ideation, collaboration, project management, or persuasive communication. Exercising these abilities will subsequently impact their ability to function on the job after graduation by teaching students how to effectively become doers.[14]

For example, in *How to Spin Up Mobile Apps*, we designed an interactive experience by constructing a scenario where management has made the decision to create a mobile app and placed the student on a four-person team tasked with developing one. Teams followed a development process that was similar to what they would likely encounter in a corporate environment. They developed use cases for various stakeholder/user groups, constructed a prototype, tested user experience, and responded to feedback and consumer testing to refine the product. The goal was not for students to passively learn about the development process or become subject matter experts. Instead, students were given enough exposure to standard industry tools and design processes that they could collaborate as a team and take the necessary steps to bring an idea (a mobile app in this case) to market.

Applied

Great attention is directed toward the application of important ideas, behaviors, and skills. The goal is to give students an opportunity to apply a concept in a real business situation guided by working professionals who utilize these concepts on a regular basis. It is more about connecting theory to practice by having students work through an actual process that reflects current practices in an industry than developing a deeper understanding of the underlying principles.

In the course *Building an Inspired Personal Brand*, students use their understanding of marketing principles along with a structured process to assist them in building their own personal brand. Under the guidance of a brand marketing professional (who works with a number of professional athletes to develop their own brand), students are guided through a multistep process that culminates in the creation of a brand book capable of delivering a consistent personal brand across different channels that reflects a corresponding brand purpose.

The Power of Guided Experiences

Turning skills into capabilities is not just about how to do something. It also encompasses the ability to think for oneself in a given situation.[15] It is about knowing when a particular element is useful and should be applied in a given situation.

Take, for example, a tool such as Excel. There are a large number of online courses, certifications, or self-paced tutorials available for teaching someone the mechanics of the advanced features available in the software program. Any of them provide a great reference for how a function works and offer exercises that are designed to help develop a level of mastery worthy of earning a badge or a credential. However, what is missing from many of these learning experiences are insights into when, how, and where a particular feature should be employed to solve a business issue. A problem exists as these lessons are often without the assistance of a working professional to help guide the learning process for a typical undergraduate with limited work experience.[16]

The advantage of developing a carefully designed experience, which allows flexibility and encourages students to come up with their own solution under the guidance of an industry professional is that students can gain needed coaching while they learn from their progress or mistakes. By embedding experienced-based feedback into every step of the process, students can make multiple adjustments as they grapple with a project and bring it to final completion.[17] The goal is not to earn a grade but rather to develop a deeper realization of how to progress toward reaching a particular goal.

By focusing on the process rather than the outcome, it is possible to shape the learning process in a way that lends itself to the development of work-ready capabilities. For example, we created a learning experience called *Urban Redevelopment* with the Director of Economic Development for a small city in the state of New Hampshire. A property in the downtown area that was marked for redevelopment was the context for the course experience. The basic design consisted of students working in teams, but also as part of a collaborative class effort where each group was assigned responsibility for constructing one section of a development proposal that would be pitched to the city manager at the end of the course.

The experience created a unique opportunity for the students to learn how each section (following common industry practices) needed to work in concert with the others to construct a complete and coherent proposal. As a result, not only did the students need to work well with the other members of their group but the groups themselves needed to learn how to work together. Only by working closely together could a seamless proposal emerge with the individual elements tightly aligned within a structured set of parameters. Thus, for example, the team evaluating what might be the best economic opportunity for the property must make sure that the site is suitable for that proposed use and that the current zoning is consistent with the potential site plan. In this way, students need to ensure that their team's contribution is consistent with the overall development proposal. Once this group of teams has created a development concept, the next collection of groups must then evaluate the economic feasibility of the idea. The cost of the project in terms of construction and the financing required to make it a reality must be balanced against the stream of potential revenues that ultimately determines the viability of the project.

By the end of the experience, each individual part of the proposal must seamlessly work together as students gain experience at a micro level by contributing their part and then at a more macro level to ensure that each component fits together into a coherent proposal. To further add a dose of reality to the experience, a random factor was added to the mix requiring a response from each of the teams before finalizing their contribution to the finished proposal. Examples include a change in interest rates, a lender abandoning the project, a spike in building costs, a change in zoning, and the approval of a similar project just down the street. The goal of a last-minute change is for the students to experience first-hand the need to be flexible and develop an informed response to something unexpected.

The promise of what we are calling a guided experience is that students have an opportunity to collaborate with an industry professional who has them working through a process that is designed to reach a definitive conclusion. This is a process where students both take action and advantage of the experience of the industry professional who serves as a guide to keep matters on track and provide an insider perspective that adds clarity to what needs to be done.

In this case, while most of the students will not go on to a career in real estate development, the capabilities that they are developing are transferable to other processes that are commonly used to solve problems, work to achieve a collective goal/project, and collaborate on interdisciplinary teams. Context breathes life into the process by which capabilities are developed while providing a way to demonstrate those same capabilities through a relevant narrative that might be shared at a job interview. In addition, it provides students with insight and appreciation of local economic development as well as the real estate industry.

Turning Skills Into Work-Ready Capabilities

As discussed in an earlier chapter, to develop a set of work-ready capabilities, a student must have more than one opportunity to apply/repeat a skill.[18] They also need an opportunity to place those skills into practice under the guidance of someone who can speak to the particular skill and offer feedback and insight into how it is used in an authentic business setting. It can be a more powerful experience when a skill/capability is made explicit and integrated into the course design rather than as an afterthought or byproduct that may or may not be achieved.

The work-ready capabilities we focus on in our learning experiences include the following:

Situational Awareness—Being Attentive to One's Surroundings

In the *Productization and Market Segmentation* course, students learn how a large-format printing company specializing in signage for sports facilities grew from a small startup to a dominant player in the market with revenues in the hundreds of millions of dollars. Students work on developing new revenue opportunities for the company and, at the end, pitch their ideas to senior management.

Storytelling—Crafting a Compelling Narrative

In *Data Storytelling*, students are provided with large data sets and learn the art of connecting the dots and constructing a story that showcases insights derived from the data. Students then present their stories to motivate managers to take action in order to further a particular strategy or set of goals.

Collaboration—Working Collectively to Advance a Shared Purpose

Let's Make a Deal is a course we designed where multi-functional teams work together to create a hypothetical loan package for a medium-sized business. Putting together a deal requires teams to work on a segment and, in the end, collaborate to create a funding proposal presented to senior management.

Initiative—Knowing When and How to Take Action

Business Networking and Social Selling is a course where students utilize social media to promote themselves and various products through connections made on several platforms. Students learn how to establish advantageous relationships and then leverage those connections as professional assets.

Adaptability—Responding to Changing Conditions and Circumstances

In the course *Reducing Cyber Risks*, a sample network is constructed and a malware attack is simulated. In the process, students gain a better understanding of what makes a network vulnerable and construct with the NIST cybersecurity framework, the steps that can be taken to protect an organization.

Business in Practice

We have embraced practice-based learning in our Business in Practice Program (BiP) offered at the Peter T. Paul College of Business and Economics. BiP has extended experiential learning beyond internships, study abroad, and corporate projects.

Instead of relying on a collection of self-directed opportunities for students or only offering high-impact experiential opportunities to a select few (approximately 12% of Paul College's students), we created a program for all Business Administration students that comprises guided experiences led by industry professionals, and is carefully crafted around well-defined learning and developmental goals.[19] Within the program, students are required to take four two-credit courses as part of their degree program, one in each intelligence category: social, analytical, competitive, and professional. Class size is usually kept around 24 students. These work-ready intelligence courses are designed to "sit on top" of the existing curriculum and serve as a bridge between business practice and the foundational knowledge taught in the core curriculum.

BiP learning experiences are designed around the passion, interests, and work history of the industry professional, who serves more as a guide or facilitator than an instructor. Courses are offered in-person, synchronously remote, or in a hybrid combination. Each course employs active learning within an environment where students can take risks, learn from failure, ask candid questions, and build a rich portfolio of experiences and skills. In other words, they enable our students to see first-hand how business principles are applied to achieve real-world outcomes in classes designed to give them a head start with those tools, techniques, and skills that are desired most by today's employers. In doing so, we have been able to provide our students with the opportunity to see how the theoretical constructs they have learned as part of the core curriculum can be put into practice.

More than just a collection of courses, the program is designed to foster meaningful relationships between the business and university communities. Communities that contribute to the professional success of our students, whether it is learning a useful skill, forming a better understanding of how work is accomplished, or making a connection that leads to that first job. In doing so, we have built a nexus that brings together students, departments, alumni, and the business community.

By participating in learning experiences that are both relevant to business and situated in practice, our students are in a better position to know what they like and what needs to be done to pursue a particular career or work in a particular field. Centered around a current skill, process, or methodology that modern businesses value, Business in Practice instructors bring the context, culture, values, and competencies they gained in their professional careers distilled into a two-credit course and a unique learning experience.[20]

The Role of Practice-Based Learning

Practice-based learning takes the idea of a journey seriously and emphasizes process over outcome. It is based on the premise that if a purposefully crafted set of steps is designed, an impactful learning experience will unfold with the development of work-ready capabilities soon to follow.

Outcomes may be a standard measure when the matter under consideration is the acquisition of discipline-based knowledge. A student could not have completed the major, passed the course, and satisfied their degree requirements if they did not possess the requisite knowledge. When we are talking about the acquisition of skills and the development of capabilities, outcomes send a less powerful signal. How well a student can size up a situation, work with others, and solve complex problems does not necessarily stem from completing a program of study. That is not to say that student portfolios, transcripts, or other evidence of accomplishments hold no value. The point is more nuanced than that: if we are to develop a work-ready graduate, the intentional development of soft skills and the curriculum that provides opportunities for those skills to become capabilities are both paramount. Thus, the development of discipline-based knowledge and work-ready capabilities need to move together simultaneously to ensure that a graduate possesses both discipline-based knowledge *and* the skills needed to take that knowledge and effectively put it into practice.

The challenge for higher education is how best to create a strategy that integrates authentic experiences into the curriculum in a meaningful way. More is required than an unconnected smattering of events or networking opportunities. The development of work-ready capabilities requires a carefully thought-out, structured set of experiences where students have an opportunity to place their skills into practice that will embody a narrative that they can share with potential employers.

Notes

1. Kolb's experiential learning theory (ELT) continues to be one of the most influential theories of management learning and serves as the basis of many experiential learning analyses. Kolb (1984); Freedman and Stumpf (1980); Holman et al. (1997); Kayes (2002); and McMullan and Cahoon (1979) contrast and compare criticisms of practice-based/experiential learning.
2. High-impact learning experiences are deep approaches to learning that go beyond traditional curricular and classroom practices and content; exam-

ples include participating in learning communities, service learning, study abroad programs, student-faculty research, and senior culminating experiences (Brownell & Swaner, 2009, 2010; Kuh & Schneider, 2008).

According to Kuh, "Deep approaches to learning are important because students who use these approaches tend to earn higher grades and retain, integrate, and transfer information at higher rates" (p. 14). The impact of these approaches is greater when colleges and faculty take the time to design these experiences carefully, paying attention to each piece of planning and implementation. Designing these activities with an eye to each campus's own culture and goals will increase the likelihood of strong educational outcomes for all students.

3. Dewey (1902, 1906, 1963) and Vygotsky (1978).

   One of the foremost philosophical constructivists is John Dewey. Constructivist theory is the idea that learners construct new knowledge and understanding through the process of integrating novel concepts with prior knowledge and experiences.

   Lev Vygotsky, a leading thinker in developmental psychology, similarly argues that mental and cognitive abilities are not so much biologically determined as shaped through interactions with the social and cultural environments around us.

4. Projects may or may not be guided. In contrast, when projects are a component of practice-based learning, they are *always* guided (Brown & Campione, 1994; Freire, 1968; Kolb, 1984).

   Guided learning experiences stand in direct contrast to what critical educational theorist Paulo Freire calls the "Banking Model" of education in which teachers are the bankers of education, depositing information into their students and expecting it to remain (Freire, 1968). In guided educational experiences, teachers provide guidance and prompts, allowing students to go through their own individual processes of learning, rather than expecting students to memorize decontextualized information in a standardized manner.

5. Dewey (1963) and Rogoff (1990).
6. Bourdieu (1987) and Freire (1973).
7. We have taken the idea of learning by doing to heart and over the last four years have developed 70+ courses in collaboration with working professionals. All of the examples involve courses we have developed. They are actual courses that have been offered, and as a result, we can speak from actual experience based on student feedback and instructor reactions.
8. Rogoff (1990) and Rogoff et al. (2016). Informal learning differs across distinct settings but with important commonalities distinguishing informal learning from formal learning. Informal learning is nondidactic, is embedded in meaningful activity, builds on the learner's initiative, interest, or

choice (rather than resulting from external demands or requirements), and does not involve assessment external to the activity.

9. The idea of tacit knowledge is generally attributed to the work of Michael Polanyi, who observes that "we know more than we can tell" (Polanyi, 1966). For David Autor, this creates what he calls Polanyi's paradox, which has major repercussions for what types of employment will be replaced by automation. To explain tacit knowledge, Autor uses the following example:

    > When we break an egg over the edge of a mixing bowl, identify a distinct species of birds based only on a fleeting glimpse, write a persuasive paragraph, or develop a hypothesis to explain a poorly understood phenomenon, we are engaging in tasks that we only tacitly understand how to perform. Following Polanyi's observation, the tasks that have proved most vexing to automate are those demanding flexibility, judgment, and common sense—skills that we understand only tacitly. (Autor, 2014, p. 8)

10. Cooperative and peer learning are highly beneficial and should arguably be incorporated into all learning experiences because they mimic how we, as socialized and cultural beings, learn from day one outside of the classroom (Bourdieu, 1977; Dewey, 1902; Rogoff et al., 2016; Vygotsky, 1978).
11. Situated learning emphasizes the idea that much of what is learned is specific to the situation in which it is learned. For further exploration of situated learning, and its proponents and critics, see Anderson et al. (1996); Brown et al. (1989); Greeno et al. (1992); Lave (1986); Lave and Wenger (1991); and Slavin (1990).

    > ...learning involves the whole person; it implies not only a relation to specific activities, but a relation to social communities—it implies becoming a full participant, a member, a kind of person. In this view, learning only partly—and often incidentally—implies becoming able to be involved in new activities, to perform new tasks and functions, to master new understandings. Activities, tasks, functions, and understandings do not exist in isolation; they are part of broader systems of relations in which they have meaning. These systems of relations arise out of and are reproduced and developed within social communities, which are in part systems of relations among persons. (Lave & Wenger, 1991, p. 53)

12. Freire (1968). In *Pedagogy of the Oppressed*, highly influential educational theorist Paolo Freire introduces what he terms as the "banking model" of education. Banking education follows the *transmission model* of education, which views education as knowledge that is transmitted from teacher to student; it emphasizes teacher-centric learning where students are passive

absorbers of information and in which the purpose of learning is memorization of facts.

13. Dewey (1902, 1906) and Freire (1968).

    > Students, as they are increasingly posed with problems relating to themselves in the world and with the world, will feel increasingly challenged and obliged to respond to the challenge. Because they apprehend the challenge as interrelated to other problems within a total context, not as a theoretical question, the resulting comprehension tends to be increasingly critical and thus constantly less alienated. (Freire, 1968, p. 68)

14. Dewey (1937) and Freire (1968, 1973).

    > Knowledge emerges only through invention and reinvention, through the restless, impatient, continuing, hopeful inquiry [wo]men pursue in the world, with the world, and with each other. (Freire, 1973, p. 58)

15. Dewey (1963), Rogoff (1990), and Rogoff et al. (2016).
16. The importance of feedback in a clinical setting is discussed in Clynes and Raftery (2008).
17. Barber et al. (2008), Dewey (1906), and Yang et al. (2016).
18. When we looked at high-impact, experiential learning opportunities that existed within the college, but outside of the BiP program, we found that they only served about 12% of the student population. Looking at the criteria for these experiences, almost all required or based selection on high academic (GPA) performance. We additionally found instances where the same students were offered/held these opportunities.
19. The courses are taught as topics courses so they can be quickly developed, delivered, modified, and abandoned when they are no longer relevant. We currently offer approximately 70+ BiP courses a year in collaboration with 50–60 industry professionals contracted as the adjunct faculty.

References

Anderson, J. R., Reder, L. M., & Simon, H. A. (1996). Situated learning and education. *Educational Researcher, 25*(4), 5–11. https://doi.org/10.3102/0013189X025004005

Autor, D. (2014). *Polanyi's paradox and the shape of employment growth* (No. w20485; p. w20485). National Bureau of Economic Research. https://doi.org/10.3386/w20485

Barber, S. J., Rajaram, S., & Marsh, E. J. (2008). Fact learning: How information accuracy, delay, and repeated testing change retention and retrieval experience. *Memory, 16*, 934–946. https://doi.org/10.1080/09658210802360603

Bourdieu, P. (1977). *Outline of a theory of practice.* Cambridge University Press.

Bourdieu, P. (1987). *Distinction: A social critique of the judgment of taste.* Harvard University Press.
Brown, A. L., & Campione, J. C. (1994). Guided discovery in a community of learners. In K. McGilly (Ed.), *Classroom lessons: Integrating cognitive theory and classroom practice* (chap. 9) (pp. 229–270). MIT Press.
Brown, J. S., Collins, A., & Duguid, P. (1989). Situated cognition and the culture of learning. *Educational Researcher, 18*(1), 32–42. https://doi.org/10.3102/0013189X018001032
Brownell, J., & Swaner, L. (2009). High-impact practices: Applying the learning outcomes literature to the development of successful campus programs. *Peer Review, 11*(2), 26.
Brownell, J., & Swaner, L. (2010). *Five high-impact practices: Research on learning outcomes, completion and quality.* Association of American Colleges and Universities. Retrieved March 24, 2023, from https://www.aacu.org/publication/five-high-impact-practices-research-on-learning-outcomes-completion-and-quality
Clynes, M. P., & Raftery, S. E. C. (2008). Feedback: An essential element of student learning in clinical practice. *Nurse Education in Practice, 8*(6), 405–411. https://doi.org/10.1016/j.nepr.2008.02.003
Dewey, J. (1902). *The child and the curriculum and the school and society.* The University of Chicago Press.
Dewey, J. (1906). The experimental theory of knowledge. *Mind Association, 15*(59), 293–307.
Dewey, J. (1937). Education and social change. *Bulletin of the American Association of University Professors, 23*(6), 472–474.
Dewey, J. (1963). *Experience and education.* Collier Books.
Freedman, R. D., & Stumpf, S. A. (1980). Learning style theory: Less than meets the eye. *The Academy of Management Review, 5*(3), 445–447. https://doi.org/10.2307/257119
Freire, P. (1968). *Pedagogy of the oppressed.* Bloomsbury Press.
Freire, P. (1973). *Education for critical consciousness.* The Seabury Press.
Greeno, J. G., Smith, D. R., & Moore, J. L. (1992). Transfer of situated learning. In D. Detterman & R. J. Sternberg (Eds.), *Transfer on trial: Intelligence, cognition, and instruction* (pp. 99–167). Ablex.
Holman, D., Pavlica, K., & Thorpe, R. (1997). Rethinking Kolb's theory of experiential learning in management education: The contribution of social constructionism and activity theory. *Management Learning, 28*(2), 135–148. https://doi.org/10.1177/1350507697282003
Kayes, D. C. (2002). Experiential learning and its critics: Preserving the role of experience in management learning and education. *Academy of Management Learning & Education, 1*(2), 137–149. https://doi.org/10.5465/amle.2002.8509336

Kolb, D. A. (1984). *Experiential learning: Experience as the source of learning and development*. Prentice-Hall.

Kuh, G. D., & Schneider, C. G. (2008). High-impact educational practices: What they are, who has access to them, and why they matter. Association of American Colleges and Universities.

Lave, J. (1986). Experiments, tests, jobs and chores: How we learn to do what we do. In K. Borman & J. Reisman (Eds.), *Becoming a worker*. Norwood, NJ.

Lave, J., & Wenger, E. (1991). *Situated learning: Legitimate peripheral participation*. Cambridge University Press.

McMullan, W. E., & Cahoon, A. (1979). Integrating abstract conceptualizing with experiential learning. *The Academy of Management Review, 4*(3), 453–458. https://doi.org/10.2307/257203

Polanyi, M. (1966). *The tacit dimension*. Doubleday.

Rogoff, B. (1990). *Apprenticeship in thinking: Cognitive development in social context*. Oxford University Press.

Rogoff, B., Callanan, M., Gutiérrez, K. D., & Erickson, F. (2016). The organization of informal learning. *Review of Research in Education, 40*(1), 356–401. https://doi.org/10.3102/0091732X16680994

Slavin, R. E. (1990). *Cooperative learning: Theory, research and practice*. Prentice-Hall.

Vygotsky, L. S. (1978). *Mind in society: The development of higher psychological processes*. Harvard University Press.

Yang, J. J., Zhan, L. X., Wang, Y. Y., Du, X. Y., Zhou, W. X., Ning, X. L., et al. (2016). Effects of learning experience on forgetting rates of item and associative memories. *Learning & Memory, 23*, 365–378. https://doi.org/10.1101/lm.041210.115

Designing Learning Experiences

When it comes to developing a set of work-ready capabilities, it is not sufficient to expect that students will master a body of knowledge and hope that, as part of the process, they will also pick up the requisite skills that would later prepare them to actually put that knowledge into practice. Without explicitly bringing skills to the forefront and providing multiple opportunities to put them into practice, knowledge and applied skills will not converge into capabilities that will ultimately help advance a student's professional career.

When we think about course development, we need to take a different approach. From learning content the focus shifts to how those concepts and skills can be put into practice. In other words, learning by thinking *and* doing. The doing, however, is not about working through a set of exercises to develop a better understanding of the course material. Rather, it is about using the ideas contained in the course in a meaningful way to develop a deeper understanding of how knowledge turns into action and how actions assist in achieving a set of goals.

Ultimately, we are designing learning experiences, rather than a course. Experiences that encompass opportunities for students to drive the learning process as they apply knowledge and skills by doing something as part of an experiential design. From the perspective of Business in Practice, the focus is on developing a work-ready graduate who has the ability to contribute in a meaningful way to advance a purpose related to their professional future.

N. B. Niman, J. R. Chagnon, *The Work-Ready Graduate*,
https://doi.org/10.1007/978-3-031-33910-3_8

Building the course around a process used by a working professional challenges students to think about how they might actually go about doing a particular job. By placing that process front and center, students have a useful structure for understanding how the course will unfold, what is expected, and what they will need to accomplish to navigate and complete the course experience. Looking more closely at each step of the process focuses attention on the minimum amount of information required for students to do something—with the central idea being that by working through the process, they will learn the rest of what they need to know to complete it and achieve a well-defined goal at the end of the course.

Designing an Experiential Narrative: The STAR² Approach

All of our learning experiences employ the STAR² approach.[1] STAR (situation, task, action, result) is a common behavioral interview technique where a prospective candidate is asked a question about how they might respond to a given situation. This method challenges the candidate to answer with a concrete, personal account rather than a hypothetical of how one might navigate a situation. It provides an opportunity for the candidate to demonstrate the capabilities, thought process, and detailed steps employed in a specific situation. Some users of the approach add an additional R to include reflection—hence STAR².[2]

Just as STAR² is a useful tool for conducting a job interview, it also provides a useful framework for designing learning experiences where the focus is on developing skills and applying them in authentic situations that potentially resonate with prospective employers. By constructing experiences that lend themselves to the development of a strong narrative, both students and employers can more easily grasp the value of the experience and better understand how it might position the graduate to make a contribution to their organization.[3] In this way it serves as a strong signaling device able to send a more accurate message about a student's capabilities.

The approach serves first and foremost as a reminder that we are developing a learning experience with a focus on doing. Second, it helps keep the design process keep on track by serving as a framework for the principles underlying the ISA² approach to learning. Third, it provides the student with concrete examples of their skills, which can be communicated in a more effective narrative format. By following the STAR² approach, we can ensure a level of consistency and structure in the learning experiences we design, while still allowing for variation and experimentation. The STAR² method includes the following (Fig. 1):

- *Situation*—Situating the course idea within a context that is both current and relevant.
- *Task*—the process students will need to undertake in order to provide a deliverable at the end. Tasks may be individual or team-based relating to specific roles or responsibilities.
- *Action*—the individual steps a student takes to contribute to the task. The action demonstrates the current utilization of skills, behaviors, and knowledge.
- *Result*—the outcome of the individual's actions, in quantitative or qualitative measures.
- *Reflection*—an opportunity for the students to assess the result as it is related to their actions. It exemplifies the student's ability to make connections, consider feedback, and assess opportunities for improvement.

For the student who may have limited work experience, it becomes possible to showcase work-ready skills and capabilities, as well as to develop a confidence in their ability to transition to the professional world.[4] Each student finishing a Business in Practice course is equipped with a narrative that demonstrates their approach and contributions to an outcome designed to showcase what they have accomplished. This approach, which incorporates ISA², challenges students to be active and consider how they might apply their skills and knowledge to various situations.

An additional advantage is that it takes a learner centered approach that encourages active approaches and discourages the use of lecture as a form of instruction. For a working professional who has a great deal to share about what they do on a daily basis, there is a tendency to want to spend each class in full lecture mode.[5] This, however, is the least effective way to learn for many students.[6] The advantage of adopting the STAR² approach is that it forces the designer and working professional to think in terms of what students are going to be asked to do and how they will actively engage with the course material in a process that will lead to the further development of work-ready capabilities.

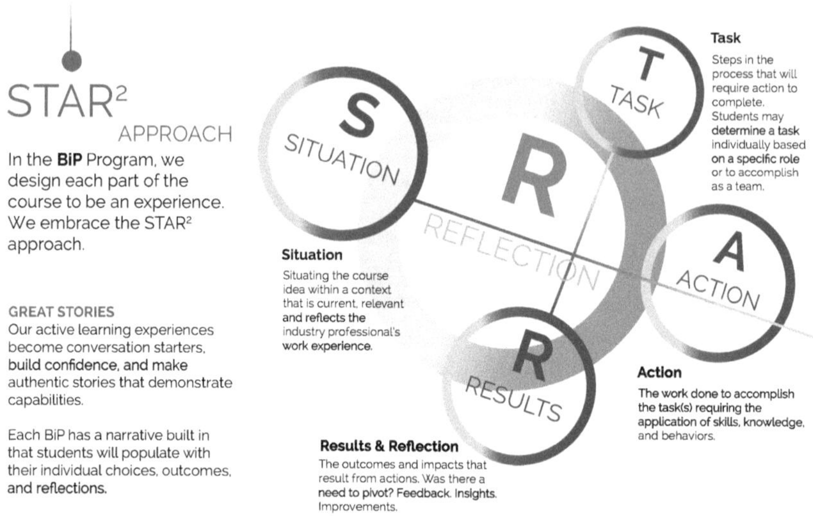

Fig. 1 The STAR² approach to experience design focuses on five key areas that provide organizational structure to transform the course content into an interactive, learner-focused experience. The five areas are (1) Situation, (2) Task, (3) Action, (4) Result, and (5) Reflection. This approach also provides a student with a method for demonstrating their capabilities in a structured narrative, as is reflective of the approach's original purpose in response to behavior-based interviewing (Niman and Chagnon, 2021)

Learning and Developmental Goals

Once the general framework has been set, it becomes possible to develop a set of learning *and* developmental goals. Because the dissemination of discipline-based knowledge is mostly the responsibility of the core curriculum, learning goals here are more focused on how to go about doing something within a specific context. Developmental goals include the explicit construction of a well-defined set of skills, and students need to have multiple opportunities to put those skills into practice.[7] We make sure that learning goals are aligned with the context that supports the course's narrative, and developmental goals are incorporated into the tasks and accomplished through the learner's actions.

Useful questions to consider when constructing the learning and developmental goals for a course include the following:

- What will you have your students do, and what should they take away from the experience?
- How will they accomplish their task(s) and what skills might they develop as a result?
- Will your students walk away with a greater awareness of something? If so, what is it?
- What will your students be able to do upon completion of the course that they could not previously accomplish?

These questions will help to identify the learning as well as the developmental goals for the course. The developmental goals are focused on skill development that either builds on previous experiences or creates a foundation for their further development.

Example 1: Technology Procurement

We offer a learning experience called *Tech Buying with Speed and Agility* offered by an alumnus who works as a technology procurement specialist for the Gartner Group. Students in the course work in teams and are guided through Gartner's proprietary process to deliver a tech purchasing strategy for a real client.[8]

Through weekly meetings with the client, students are able to develop a set of stakeholder use cases and requirements for a software solution, identify key vendors, make a purchase recommendation, and develop a negotiation strategy. Because of the industry professional's extensive experience with the procurement process, he is able to coach students so they can be more effective in client meetings, give feedback on the students' findings/proposals, and ensure the integrity of the work that is completed for the client. Students learn how to work with a client and those common problems that many organizations encounter, as well as how to follow through a structured process.

Given the design of the course, the corresponding learning and developmental goals include:

- Students should be able to understand the role of procurement in any organization.
- Students will develop a better understanding of the transformative nature of technology as it impacts business processes.
- Students will learn how to follow an established process and make a recommendation.

- Students will learn how to listen carefully to understand and respond to the needs of a client.
- Students will enhance their collaboration skills by supporting colleagues.

Example 2: Financial Narratives

A different variation illustrates the value of doing something multiple times so that students will have ample opportunity to learn from mistakes and carefully craft their final deliverable. This experience, called *Financial Narratives*, has the student learn the power of storytelling by having them work with real data to provide information or persuade potential investors to take an ownership position in a company. Working with real data, students craft a narrative and present their story through a set of carefully constructed slides. Taught over 14 weeks, the first third of the course has the students work on an informational slide deck. In the second third, teams are given the task of creating a persuasive deck. In the last third of the course, student teams are given a final opportunity to construct a narrative with new data, which is then presented to the entire class, and where the instructor and the class have an opportunity to ask questions and provide additional feedback.

The learning goals for this course include the following:

- Students will become more familiar with using financial and operational data.
- Students will learn how to use data to construct a narrative capable of supporting an informative or persuasive presentation.
- Students will develop enhanced presentation skills by utilizing a workshop-type structure to present their work multiple times where they can receive feedback in real time.
- Students will learn how to determine the most appropriate language, style, and layout for business presentations.
- Students will learn how to accept feedback constructively and use it to improve their work.

Example 3: Business Model Innovation

A third example, a course called *Business Model Innovation*, has students developing a business model canvas following an industry standard process. The working professional guiding the experience provides actual pitch decks from entrepreneurs looking for potential investors. Students, working in teams, take information traditionally found in a business plan and condense it into a concise model suitable for presentation to a venture capitalist. Students come away from the course with a greater understanding of the essential elements that ultimately determine whether or not a concept is likely to be funded as well as how to extract key pieces of information to communicate in a clear and concise manner.

The learning and developmental goals for this course include:

- Students will learn why the business model canvas is a useful tool.
- Students will learn how to simplify and present complex ideas.
- Students will learn how to use clear and concise language.
- Students will become better editors by determining what is essential and what content is of secondary importance.

Constructing the Learning Experience

The key to transforming a course into a learning experience is to create activities that are structured around a process where students have an opportunity to both learn by doing and take advantage of the unique knowledge and skillset of an experienced working professional. We speak in terms of learning experiences rather than courses because the most effective way for the working professional to disseminate their knowledge is by trying to, as closely as possible, replicate their experience in an organized environment. By having students assume a similar role or solve a problem that is familiar to the working professional, students can leverage a unique set of insights so they can then carry out what is required to effectively reach a solution.

The aim is to create opportunities that compare/contrast different possibilities to generate a deeper understanding. Highlighting differences and similarities in approach, constraints, or possibilities not only helps to develop a deeper understanding, but also encourages a student to form the ability to judge a particular situation and respond accordingly. This fosters the ability to think for oneself rather than merely following a set of directions. The structure of the learning experiences captures the nuances that exist between companies, industries, or roles within an organization. To truly unlock the experience of the working professional and to prepare students for their entry into the workforce, students need to be exposed to the multitude of variations that exist within a single decision problem.[9]

Structured properly, each team or student has something to bring to the conversation regardless of whether they are looking at the same business model, industry, or potential opportunity. Rarely do different teams or people work in exactly the same way and craft an identical solution to a multidimensional problem. A robust sharing of ideas can occur even when students are engaged in similar but, as immediately becomes apparent, not identical approaches. The working professional can provide additional insights by pointing out these subtle differences and drawing from their experience, thereby helping their students develop a lens to assess their options for action or reflect on their results.

Example 4: Immersive Executive Experiences

The richness of an experience can be enhanced by having different groups work on alternate facets of the same problem. This may take the form of different stages of the process or different applications of an identical process. Alternatively, the experience can be enhanced by seeing how different teams react to those random events that frequently occur and divert well-laid plans.

In the course on *Designing Immersive Executive Experiences*, teams work on creating special events for C-suite-level executives. Each team is developing a different event, which provides the opportunity to compare and contrast the approaches and goals across event types. At approximately two-thirds of the way through the course, each team is subjected to what we refer to as a roadblock where something unexpected occurs.[10] A keynote speaker becomes ill, the weather turns unhospitable, or the venue experiences some type of problem. The roadblock serves as a catalyst for students to be flexible/adaptable and develop a response that will be discussed with the rest of the class. The professional who is guiding the learning process by utilizing their own professional experience can ask critical questions, delve deeper into the thought process of the teams, or share best practices for consideration by the students.[11]

What makes this learning experience stand apart from a course in the core curriculum is that students not only learn by doing but also learn by engaging in an iterative process, which tests their performance and identifies areas of adjustment that they will have the opportunity to improve as they refine their work. The role of the working professional turned instructor is to guide the students in a discovery process that has them gleaning insights specific to their performance and holding students accountable to standards that they might encounter upon their entry into the working world.

To accomplish this, we rely heavily on a workshop approach where students share work in progress or report partial results as they take the next step toward reaching a deliverable at the end of a carefully structured process.[12] This gives the instructor multiple opportunities to share their experience so that students can incorporate those insights into their own work. It also provides an opportunity for meaningful peer-to-peer learning.[13] By sharing what they have done and creating an informal forum where others can comment on their progress, students gain insight through evaluating the work of others in an effort, not to pass judgment, but rather to share feedback, perspectives, and advance each other's efforts to accomplish a similar task. In this way, the classroom becomes an environment where insights are gained, work is redirected and strengthened, and efforts are targeted to maximize their effectiveness.

The Experience Arc

One of the advantages of the STAR^2 approach is that it initiates a conversation about the course narrative and how students are going to actively engage in the learning process. After the elements of STAR^2 are settled, we begin to map the STAR^2 experience to a narrative/experience arc. This visually assists us in ensuring there is an achievable progression over a defined time span. In addition, it sets up milestones for when students should achieve predefined objectives that will enable them to meet the final deliverable. Roadblock elements can be added as inflection points that call for reassessment and stimulate organic feedback and insights. Overall, the students should be progressing toward a purpose (deliverable) and on that journey, should come to points that call for action on their part.

To illustrate the experience arc and course development process, we will use an example that we designed in collaboration with a professional working in the strategic licensing field. The course was constructed to unfold over a seven-week span and called for students to work in a team structure mirroring a process utilized at the industry professional's organization.

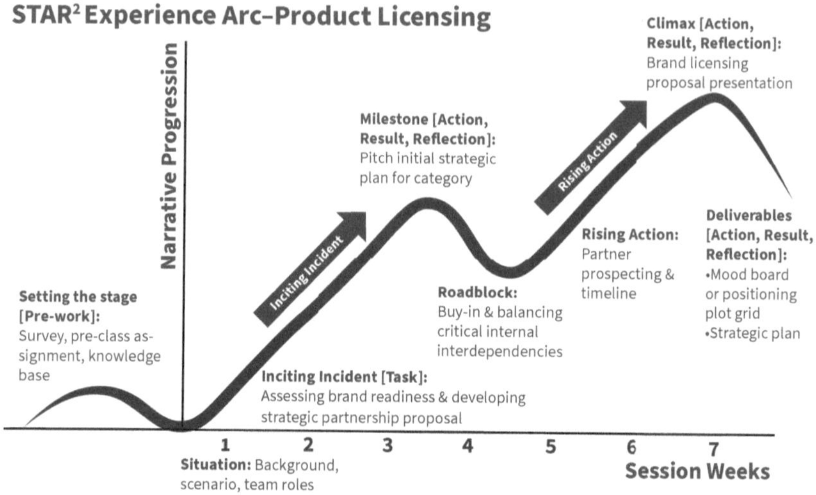

Fig. 2 The BiP STAR² experience arc illustrates the course narrative for a product licensing experience. Following the mechanics of a story arc, the progression of the course's STAR² elements is mapped as a coherent story. Students begin with foundational information and an Inciting Incident (Situation); they progress toward milestones (peaks of the graph) and roadblocks (valleys of the graph) and reach the culminating action (climax point), which is the strategic partnership proposal. In this course, the final deliverables occur after presentation and feedback, thus acting as a falling action and reflective stage of the overall experience

Example 5: Product Licensing

Through a mutual contact in the marketing department, the Vice President of Licensing and Strategic Initiatives at Vera Bradley (since retired) expressed interest in participating in our program.[14] She developed an interest in teaching after being involved in a course at the Ohio State University. With a wealth of knowledge and experience in product licensing, we had the raw material to develop a dynamic and valuable learning experience. What began with her suggestion to teach a course in product brand management (similar to what is offered in the core curriculum) turned into a Business in Practice course tailored to her individual passion and experience in product licensing.

Our goal as course designers was to take the process that she uses to develop a strategic licensing proposal for senior management and use that to help her students develop a better understanding of product licensing while fostering the development of those smart skills required to get the job done. Much of the design process involved taking what she does on a daily basis with her team and turning it into a multistep process that would fit within a seven-week footprint.[15]

The course narrative we created provided the scaffolding for the subsequent development of both learning and developmental goals. In this case, the learning goals include gaining a better understanding of the licensing process, how companies can extend their brand into new markets, and what is required to maintain and strengthen strategic alliances between companies. The corresponding developmental goals focused on role-driven collaboration, the creativity required to identify new strategic opportunities, and storytelling/persuasive communication.

To begin the development process, we applied our STAR^2 approach:

Situation—Vera Bradley is interested in expanding its brand into travel, home, and wellness. The goal of the course is to identify an opportunity within one of those categories that will enhance the growth and development of the Vera Bradley brand.

Task—Follow a strategic partnership and licensing process designed to create a proposal in support of a brand extension/expansion for consideration by senior management.

Action—Students will be working in teams of four where they are assigned industry-specific roles with corresponding responsibilities. Each week they will complete the steps that contribute to the development of the team's licensing proposal.

Result—A licensing proposal that is worthy of consideration by senior management at Vera Bradley.

Reflection—Student teams present their proposal to the class for feedback and have an opportunity to evaluate their own work before submitting their individual strategic plan and recommendation.

With the course narrative in hand, the next step is to map the course experience over the seven-week time span to ensure it contains progressive and achievable components. This is where the course experience arc aids in setting up the flow and structure of the course within the prescribed time frame. It assists in laying out the corresponding weekly tasks and actions that contribute to the formation of a climactic element that paves the way for the final deliverable.

A milestone is included in week three after foundational knowledge and engagement with the content, but early enough to gauge the progress of the students (and for the instructor to know if any teams need additional support). A roadblock is inserted as part of week four to create an inflection point that mirrors a common occurrence in the field. Here, students find that they must address internal concerns and generate buy-in for their proposal. In weeks five and six, students continue to progress along the arc as they see their proposals come together in anticipation of their collective presentation. In week seven, all teams deliver their presentations and students individually submit their other deliverables. Figure 2 illustrates the course experience arc over the seven-week term.

The weekly layout of the course is as follows:

Week 1: Product Licensing

Students learn what product licensing is, its strategic importance for a company, and the essential elements required to produce a licensing plan. It is also, for some, a first exposure to Vera Bradley as a company and a brand, and the economic opportunities created by licensing. Students are tasked with sharing potential licensing possibilities that align with the Vera Bradley brand. Working in teams of four, each student assumes a role (rotated each week): team lead, thought facilitator, note taker, or research lead.

Week 2: Assessing Brand Readiness

In this second week, teams choose a business model and approach that can be used in the chosen brand category expansion. They look for examples of brands that are currently leveraging their chosen business model and identify the key factors leading to success. Team members will form a consensus on their two best examples and prepare a presentation to be given to the rest of the class.

Week 3: Crafting the Strategic Plan

In week three, students are exposed to the elements that are part of any good strategic plan. This will provide the framework for the proposal they will present at the end of the course. Students are asked to select two subject areas related to a strategic plan and prepare supporting statements that buttress the licensing opportunity they have identified. They are asked to prepare one slide per component and come prepared to present and discuss their ideas with the rest of the class.

Week 4: Critical Interdependencies within the Organization
The viability of any strategic plan relies on the ability to gain support within the organization. In week four, teams are asked to rank the internal stakeholders most critical for the success of their chosen initiative and provide the supporting arguments that bolster their ranking. Each team will turn in their work prior to the next class and, with a different spokesperson, present their progress at the beginning of the next class.

Week 5: Key Attributes of a Prospective Partner
In week five, students are exposed to the criteria that should be considered when selecting a potential licensing partner. Teams are combined to provide for cross-pollination as groups of eight discuss, debate, and build a consensus that identifies three good prospects to approach when establishing a strategic partnership. Prospects and the rationale underlying their selection are turned in prior to the start of the next class and are presented for discussion and debate.

Week 6: Partner Prospecting: Approach and Timeline
Students return to their original teams to create a mood board for their chosen category to visually illustrate the aesthetic for the brand positioning they are trying to create. They are tasked with creating a positioning plot grid for their chosen category and will present their mood board in the next class.

Week 7: Ongoing Problem Management
In the final week of the course, students learn about the responsibilities of the licensor/licensee after the deal has been struck. Ongoing problem management is the key to a successful licensing agreement. They are also reminded about what is required for a successful final project. The final deliverable has each student working individually to turn in their plan designed to persuade senior management that they have identified a strategic licensing opportunity that meets the goals of the company.

For some students, this is their first exposure to the idea of product licensing and identifies a potential new career path. For every student, the course has developed a heightened awareness of the extent to which licensing is part of their everyday life. Context aside, it provides students with insight into a process that is used by many companies to identify and exploit a potential avenue for growth. It provides an opportunity for the working professional to communicate how they go about evaluating a prospect and prepare a report that is shared with senior management for potential action. The learning experience is not generated through a textbook, journal article, or news story. It consists of actions and responsibilities taken by the students and reinforced with insights from the practitioner that took years to acquire and refine through implementation in the field.

Work-readiness is achieved as students work through the tasks associated with the specific process. Students are asked to find what they need to complete a task, make decisions as a unit on the best path forward, and present their progress in a concise and impactful manner. Students are required to be good listeners as ideas are workshopped, feedback is received, and adjustments are made as the process unfolds. By working from prescribed roles, students get to experience the process from different perspectives and learn the different responsibilities that comprise a well-functioning team. All of this takes place under the guidance of an experienced professional who, through the workshop process, can provide insights that improve the work of all of the teams each week.

As we have illustrated, the collaboration and engagement of an industry professional is vital to the work-ready development of the student. In the next chapter, "Industry Professionals in the Classroom," we will delve deeper into how we incorporate industry professionals as partners in the learning process.

Notes

1. Boogaard (2022) and Gudmundsson (2022) explore the STAR method and its merit in job interviews.

   For a more in-depth examination of the power of narrative see Bruner (1991), Cunliffe and Coupland (2012), Denning (2011), and Hammack (2008).
2. Indeed Editorial Team (2022).
3. Exploring faculty perspectives on the career center, Schlesinger et al. (2021) observe, "Our participants described a skills gap, but it is in the students' inability to describe their own skills" (Schlesinger et al. 2021).
4. Rather than reduce students/potential employees to statistics, the $STAR^2$ approach makes room for the development of an individual's strengths and capabilities, successes and traits they are proud of, or elements of a student's identity that they can leverage with confidence. This is yet another example of the power of narrative (Bruner 1991; Cunliffe and Coupland 2012; Denning 2011; Hammack 2008).

5. In our experience observing our BiP instructors, the tendency to lecture occurs because they feel more comfortable in that format (especially when nervous). Many have experience presenting material but few with active learning techniques. In a survey of economics instructors that asked why they still lecture, a third expressed the ability to control the delivery and content, a third believes it is the most cost-effective way to deliver knowledge, and only a third incorporates more innovative teaching methods (Goffe and Kauper 2014).
6. To revisit the ineffectiveness of lecturing, see Dewey (1906), Freire (1968), Freire (1973), and Rogoff (1990).
7. In his column for *American Educator*, Willingham (2004) makes the point that sustained practice beyond the point of mastery is necessary for a new skill to become automatic or for new knowledge to become long-lasting.

   Voice and Stirton (2020) tested spaced repetition in an introductory physics course and discovered that allowing time to pass between each repetition (rather than last-minute cramming) led to scores that were a full classification higher.
8. In the first instance of the course, students helped Goosebay Sawmill & Lumber purchase a Point of Sale (POS) system. As a family-run business that has been operating for over 35 years in Chichester, NH, a shift from pencil and paper to a fully digital online system would open up whole new realm of possibilities for the business.
9. Engeström (2001) and Lee et al. (2014).
10. An unexpected element or challenge falls under what Clark and Bjork (2014) have identified as a "desirable difficulty," which, when used properly, can improve learning outcomes.
11. The importance of feedback as a tool to promote learning is discussed in Hattie and Yates (2014).
12. "By increasing the flow of knowledge, workshops assist in interaction and active participation boosting the skills and expertise of students" (Panigrahi 2023). Further, they contribute to alternative perspectives and ways of critical thinking; having a collaborative discussion helps to stimulate new ideas and acceptance of these ideas (Bourdieu 1987; Freire 1973).
13. Wenger (1999).
14. Vera Bradley, headquartered in Fort Wayne, Indiana, is a publicly traded company with revenues in 2020 of approximately $460 million. The company began in the handbag business and has subsequently expanded to include fashion and home accessories, office supplies, and patterned gifts, and in 2019 had 154 locations.
15. As a working industry executive, she lives in a small town approximately 30 minutes from the UNH campus and spends one week per month at company headquarters in Fort Wayne, Indiana. To accommodate busy professional schedules, we offer our courses in either a seven-week or 14-week format. The seven-week format best suited her work schedule.

References

Boogaard, K. (2022, July 1). The STAR Method: The secret to acing your next job interview. *The Muse*. Retrieved March 25, 2023, from https://www.themuse.com/advice/star-interview-method

Bourdieu, P. (1987). *Distinction: A social critique of the judgment of taste*. Harvard University Press.

Bruner, J. (1991). The narrative construction of reality. *Critical Inquiry, 18*(1), 1–21.

Clark, C. M., & Bjork, R. A. (2014). When and why introducing difficulties and errors can enhance instruction. In V. A. Benassi, C. E. Overson, & C. M. Hakala (Eds.), *Infusing psychological science into the curriculum*. American Psychological Association.

Cunliffe, A., & Coupland, C. (2012). From hero to villain to hero: Making experience sensible through embodied narrative sensemaking. *Human Relations, 65*(1), 63–88. https://doi.org/10.1177/0018726711424321

Denning, S. (2011). *The leader's guide to storytelling: Mastering the art and discipline of business narrative* (Revised and updated edition). Jossey-Bass.

Dewey, J. (1906). The experimental theory of knowledge. *Mind Association, 15*(59), 293–307.

Engeström, Y. (2001). Expansive learning at work: Toward an activity theoretical reconceptualization. *Journal of Education and Work, 14*(1), 133–156. https://doi.org/10.1080/13639080020028747

Freire, P. (1968). *Pedagogy of the oppressed*. Bloomsbury Press.

Freire, P. (1973). *Education for critical consciousness*. The Seabury Press.

Goffe, W. L., & Kauper, D. (2014). A survey of principles instructors: Why lecture prevails. *The Journal of Economic Education, 45*(4), 360–375. https://doi.org/10.1080/00220485.2014.946547

Gudmundsson, P. (2022, July 29). The STAR Method: How to ace a job interview. *U.S. News*. Retrieved March 25, 2023, from https://money.usnews.com/money/blogs/outside-voices-careers/articles/how-to-ace-the-star-interview-method

Hammack, P. L. (2008). Narrative and the cultural psychology of identity. *Personality and Social Psychology Review, 12*(3), 222–247. https://doi.org/10.1177/1088868308316892

Hattie, J. A. C., & Yates, G. C. R. (2014). Using feedback to promote learning. In I. V. A. Benassi, C. E. Overson, & C. M. Hakala (Eds.), *Infusing psychological science into the curriculum*. American Psychological Association.

Jon, Schlesinger, Caroline O'Shea, Jackie Blesso (2021). Undergraduate Student Career Development and Career Center Services: Faculty Perspectives. *The Career Development Quarterly, 69*(2), 145–157. https://doi.org/10.1002/cdq.v69.210.1002/cdq.12255

Indeed Editorial Team. (2022, December). How to use the STARR method in interview responses. *Indeed*. Retrieved March 25, 2023, from https://uk.indeed.com/career-advice/interviewing/starr-method

Lee, C. D., Vossoughi, S., Gutiérrez, K. D., Nasir, N. S., de Royston, M. M., & Rogoff, B. (2014). Learning as multi-dimensional psychological and cultural ecological spaces. In J. L. Polman, E. A. Kyza, D. K. O'Neill, I. Tabak, W. R. Penuel, A. S. Jurow, K. O'Connor, T. Lee, & L. D'Amico (Eds.), *Learning and becoming in practice: The International Conference of the Learning Sciences (ICLS)* (Vol. 3, pp. 1382–1387). International Society of the Learning Sciences.

Niman, N. B., & Chagnon, J. R. (2021). Redesigning the Future of Experiential Learning. *Journal of Higher Education Theory and Practice, 21*(8), 87–98.

Panigrahi, S. (2023). Importance of seminars and workshops for students in higher education. *Higher Education Review*. Retrieved March 25, 2023, from https://others.thehighereducationreview.com/news/importance-of-seminars-and-workshops-for-students-in-higher-education-nid-1261.html

Rogoff, B. (1990). *Apprenticeship in thinking: Cognitive development in social context*. Oxford University Press.

Voice, A., & Stirton, A. (2020). Spaced repetition: Towards more effective learning in STEM. *New Directions in the Teaching of Physical Sciences, 15*. https://doi.org/10.29311/ndtps.v0i15.3376

Wenger, E. (1999). *Communities of practice: Learning, meaning, and identity*. Cambridge University Press.

Willingham, D. T. (2004). *Ask the cognitive scientist: Practice makes perfect—But only if you practice beyond the point of perfection*. American Federation of Teachers. Retrieved March 25, 2023, from https://www.aft.org/periodical/american-educator/spring-2004/ask-cognitive-scientist-practice-makes-perfect-only-if-you

Industry Professionals in the Classroom

If you asked the American Association of University Professors (AAUP) what their number one concern is, it might very well be the slow but steady erosion of tenure-track positions in higher education. A 2018 study using data from 2016 suggests that 73% of the instructional positions in higher education were off the tenure track. This reflects the unbundling of the traditional faculty role and, for many, is viewed as an attack on those professional values and academic freedoms that serve as the foundation for higher education.

From this perspective, industry professionals might be viewed as a *substitute* for professionally trained and credentialed faculty. They represent a low-cost alternative to traditional faculty members and therefore a threat to the heart of higher education. These contingent faculty members are not trained to advance knowledge, nor do they have a vested interest in the future of their institution. The resulting fear is that the elimination of tenure-track positions is tantamount to handing institutions of higher education over to a class of administrators who, rather than preserving the traditional mission of an institution, make decisions that focus more on revenues than the public good that flows from an educational institution.

When the mission of an institution is broadened to include the development of a work-ready graduate, the role of industry professionals in the educational process and how they are viewed changes dramatically. They become a *complement* rather than a substitute for traditional faculty

N. B. Niman, J. R. Chagnon, *The Work-Ready Graduate*,
https://doi.org/10.1007/978-3-031-33910-3_9

members. The goal is not to replace a highly credentialed full-time faculty with a part-time substitute. Rather, it is to carve out a place where the industry professional is welcomed into the Academy to enhance the educational experience of the typical undergraduate student. They become a net addition by bringing their unique perspective and experience to enhance learning.

Perhaps the best way to view this role is to think in terms of a different division of labor. The division would be between those who create and disseminate core knowledge with a new class of faculty able to place that knowledge into practice. In other words, traditional faculty would still engage in their primary role of creating the next generation of *thinkers.* In coordination, industry professionals would be invited into the academy with the primary responsibility of creating the next generation of *doers.*

By inviting industry professionals into the academy and providing them with an important role that emphasizes context and the application of skills in a meaningful way, colleges and universities can accelerate the professional development of their students and help them achieve professional success.[1] To prepare students for the working world, we need to go beyond fulfilling a traditional set of requirements, performing to a rubric, or thinking that actions result in nothing more than a grade at the end of the semester. Students need to transition to a professional mindset where the associated standards represent an approach to thinking and doing that represents a solid break from the past. The goal is to build a bridge between what tenure-track faculty believe their students need to know and what employers wish graduates would understand.

Opportunities for Professionals in the Classroom

Working professionals can add a dimension to the educational experience. Many tenure-track faculty have never worked for any appreciable length of time outside of academia. While their mastery of and contribution to the development of core knowledge is unsurpassed, many have little first-hand experience of putting that knowledge into practice. The same holds true for many contingent faculty who are in graduate school, where they are working on an assistantship with little prospect of a future tenure-track position, or are employed as the equivalent of journeymen instructors who must teach at multiple institutions to cobble together enough income to enjoy a modest life. Even those full-time lecturers who may have held an important position in industry will see that their skills and experience diminish in value over time as they become less familiar with the current state of how things are done in their previous occupation and often become entrenched in the existing academic system.

Fortunately, there exists a myriad of opportunities to have a working professional involved in the classroom in a way that lends their knowledge and expertise as an enhancement to the professional development of undergraduate students. Opportunities might include something as simple as attending a class as a guest speaker to something more complex such as assuming the role of an instructor with either a shared or full responsibility for a course. Starting from the least to most in terms of commitment, the following can serve as a list of potential opportunities:

- Panelist
- Guest speaker
- Judge/Evaluator
- Project client
- Mentor
- Instructor

Being part of a panel that is speaking to a specific topic in an existing course is perhaps the easiest way for an industry professional to get involved in the classroom. Rather than being asked to carry the entire conversation, they are part of a discussion where they can share their views and expertise on a particular topic. It is a single appearance that often requires the working professional to take some time out of their day to attend a single class.

Another possibility is their involvement as a guest speaker. Here, the working professional has sole responsibility to cover a particular topic. Because they are contributing to someone else's course, they have limited responsibility. Often as a guest speaker, they can repurpose an existing slide deck or just speak off the cuff.

Working professionals make for great judges in competitions or evaluators to provide commentary on course projects, presentations, or final papers. This calls for some engagement from the working professionals as they will need to take the time to observe, react, and respond to an assignment. The assignment, however, is designated by the faculty member and already exists within the parameters of an established course. Industry professionals can serve in a similar fashion as a project client for a corporate consulting project. They engage with students at specific intervals in the course structure, with the principal interactions occurring at the onset of that project and during the final delivery of the consulting work.

Many of the above roles are clearly defined and offer a limited, formal interaction between the students and industry professional. It seems like a much easier or less risky ask for an external individual to serve on a panel or as a guest speaker while keeping the interactions at arm's length. In contrast, mentorship is resurging as a way to establish relationships between students and industry professionals to provide professional development and career advice. Again, the dynamic does not necessarily lend itself to transferring knowledge or feedback on the skills and capabilities of the student in its current form—usually a conversation or dialogue to support what the student is doing to reach their career aspirations. In addition, many mentorship programs have difficulties of scale and are therefore limited as a support mechanism for particular student cohorts.

Whatever the role, industry professionals can become valuable partners who should be welcomed into the learning process. At first, collaborating with external practitioners may seem like a more difficult or riskier proposition to collaborate with external practitioners. However, from our experience it is just like other types of engagements: you just need to find the right people to ask and provide them with the right support.

Recruiting Professionals

For administrators who are accustomed to recruiting contingent faculty to fill existing gaps, it can be daunting to be asked to recruit a different type of professional to fill a new role within a system steeped in tradition. It need not be, though, because a surprising number of working professionals will jump at the opportunity to give back or are seeking to engage with students. There are many industry professionals who appreciate and value an opportunity to have a positive impact or help a student to develop their skillset. According to our program data, gathered from BiP instructor surveys taking place from Fall 2020 through Fall 2022, 54% of instructors cited "impacts on students' lives/skill development" as their initial motivation to participate in the program. In addition, another 22% of instructors indicated "giving back" as their motivation.[2]

Here, the strength of an existing alumni network will have a large impact on the level of difficulty in recruiting working professionals to assist in the classroom. Many alumni have fond memories of their time at university and are willing to help as long as the ask is tailored to meet their existing set of personal and professional constraints.[3] With the increased utilization of remote technologies, it has become possible for someone on an opposite coast to guide a class and interact with students.

The local business community is another great resource. They are often more accessible and interested in building relationships with universities/ colleges. Creating meaningful experiential learning opportunities forges new connections to their organization and local career opportunities. Business community members have a vested interest in developing valued skills and capabilities in graduates who will become the new talent pool from which they recruit.

For roles that require less commitment, the motivation underlying why someone is interested in getting involved is not as significant. Some may be looking to leverage the reputation of a college or university to further their professional ambitions. For a mentorship or instructor role, it is important to explain upfront the time commitment and responsibility to the students, and to gauge how this may align or conflict with pursuing their personal or professional goals. The most successful recruits are those who have past coaching or volunteer work, have a passion behind what they wish to teach or their industry, and have a realistic understanding of the commitments involved.

There is also a significant population of professionals who are interested in getting even more involved by becoming an instructor as part of their own professional development. While a few may have taught in a limited way in the past or flirted with the idea of changing careers to become a university instructor, others find it appealing to develop coaching, mentorship, or training experience that they can demonstrate on their résumés or use in their professional lives. Whether it is from a desire to give back, the satisfaction that comes from making a meaningful difference in someone's life, or because they tried it in the past and enjoyed it, the size of this population of professionals is large enough that is not too difficult to find individuals who will fit this type of engagement to enhance the educational experience.

For the Business in Practice program, the initial discovery process is integral to determining the appropriate role for a working professional. An industry professional's first foray in becoming involved most likely happened through contact with another unit, such as career services or the development office. Often they are provided with a long list of potential options and, little information about what each opportunity entails. We gauge all those possibilities and try to place them in a role that meets their needs. In addition, we use that initial contact to pinpoint their professional passion and assess whether or not it makes sense for them to enter into the course development process. It is their passion in a current or previous position that can sustain a learning experience that will last for an entire semester and ultimately determines the fit with our program. We want them to feel motivated and comfortable engaging with students, while concurrently providing current, relevant context and skills that can accelerate our students' professional development.

While there is a level of enthusiasm that sets these working professionals apart—after all, they are participating because they want to rather than have to—life often gets in the way. In terms of priorities, their personal and professional lives take precedence (for obvious reasons). A change in jobs, a baby that arrives for new parents, a sudden career opportunity, and an illness in the family are just some of the life changes that can prevent someone from being able to put in the necessary time and effort to fulfill planned obligations. In some instances, these are foreseen, and adjustments or postponements can be made. Occasionally, these events arise after the semester has started and affect the experience for both instructor and students. As with any organization, it is important to acknowledge and plan that this will eventually occur.

Working with Industry Professionals

When nurturing work-ready capabilities, a different type of course is needed, or existing courses must be retrofitted with a learning experience designed to elevate the development of human capabilities. The industry professional is brought on board to focus and accelerate the development of capabilities that, when combined with subject area knowledge, create a graduate prepared to enter the workforce. Hence, their professional experience and tacit knowledge, rather than their educational background, is of primary importance. Yes, they should be familiar with the subject matter, but their key contribution is guiding students to put both concepts and skills into practice.[4]

While many professionals have spent years mastering their craft and developing strategies for achieving professional success, few have had to distill their professional journey and experience into a series of organized steps. Often, what they have to offer does not scratch the surface of what is possible, and far exceeds what is needed to construct a worthwhile learning experience for a group of university students. Understandably, it can be a taxing exercise to extract tacit knowledge, as well as to streamline and organize their experiences and knowledge into course content that flows naturally from one stage to the next. Even when they can lay out the necessary steps to a process, it is one thing to understand how it all works and something else entirely to transform it into a learning experience that fosters active engagement by both students and the instructor.

Here, we apply a simple principle that we call the Rule of 3. The Rule of 3 is a gentle reminder that the goal is not to cram as much knowledge into a limited amount of time (seven or 14 weeks, in our case). Instead, it is to think in terms of the minimum amount required to spark the discovery process that takes place as part of an active learner-centric process.[5] After all, the more time spent introducing concepts, the less time available to provide opportunities for the development of soft skills. When the focus is on how to do something, trial and error become a natural part of the learning process.

The Rule of 3 reflects the basic divisions that are part of the learning experiences developed using the STAR^2 approach. The learning experiences can be divided into thirds. One third encompassing the concepts required to understand the basic subject matter being presented. The second third consisting of the applications/activities/guest speakers that bring the basic course material to life. The last third capturing how students will actively engage with the material and each other to complete a learning experience that often culminates in a final project.

Supporting the Learning Process

Most of the working professionals who become instructors in the Business in Practice program have no teaching background. From our experience, we have found that those who have taught before often have approaches more suited to highly structured, lecture-based courses rather than the informal, experiential learning experiences we offer. There is a tendency to revert to the familiar in new and uncertain situations, which, in this case, is often exemplified by speaking at the students for the majority of the time, giving quizzes, and assigning homework.

The STAR^2 design process, as illustrated in the previous chapter "Working With Industry Professionals", is essential for ensuring that instructors understand the structure of the learning experience, set expectations and purpose, and plan how students will engage with the course. As part of this process, we map out what is going to happen in the overall course and each individual class session. The syllabus template used for our learning experiences blocks out each week with pre-work, in-class activities, post-work (the preparation that needs to be completed to engage in the upcoming class), and those deliverables that represent significant milestones. Also included are the activities that occurs in the allotted class time, and the wrap-up work/progress point related to that class session. We pay particular attention to how the instructor will guide the in-class learning process and which active learning techniques are most appropriate for each stage of the experience. While we are involved in planning the essentials of each class session, we do not moderate each class or specific content. We are respectful of the fact we are part of a collaborative process and thus, leave much of the context and content to the expertise of the industry professional.

When we feel comfortable with the design, our efforts shift to preparing the instructor to step into the classroom environment. We host a boot camp and an orientation customized to our program. We have a resource library that focuses on techniques and tools that further the goals of the program. This includes videos, briefs that showcase supportive software tools, active learning techniques, engagement strategies, and a variety of carefully sourced links. By providing a curated set of offerings, busy professionals are more likely to dip in and explore what fits their course.

No design is perfect and sometimes problems arise. There are always unexpected issues that may well take a learning experience off course. It becomes beneficial to set the expectation, especially with new instructors, that they will need to be flexible, and they may even need to seek early feedback from their students in order to make real-time changes. Setting this expectation and having support structures in place (which we will discuss shortly) will better position the program and instructor to make necessary changes to deliver a beneficial course experience.

The best resource is often the other working professionals who participate in the program. They have learned from their own experience and are more than willing to share their insights.[6] We therefore hold community-wide check-ins three times during the semester where instructors can share struggles, insights, and best practices. Some sessions include a professional development segment that focuses on a particular topic. We also hold debriefs at the end of the semester and take what we have learned to add to a document which captures our 'collective wisdom' that is also included in the resource library. This "collective wisdom" is our recounting of what we have learned and contains a number of tips that we have gleaned from conversations with BiP instructors.

All of this is done as part of a collaborative process similar to what our instructors will be asking of their students. We provide structure with some guidelines, give support and insight, but ultimately, must enable them to become doers. Key areas as part of this work include the following initiatives.

Creating Community

From our experience, one of the most important qualities that ultimately sets the tone and success of the learning experience is whether or not time and attention is taken to build a sense of community. It has become a common pitfall of new instructors to want to hit the ground running with students, which often involves loading up the beginning of a course with too much background information. This comes at the expense of developing a sense of community and risks losing student interest and engagement before the course has really begun. This need to cover a lot of ground in a short period results in one-way communication rather than a dialogue, which is essential for active learning to take place.[7]

It is not possible to talk about building community without discussing icebreakers. We acknowledge that this can be an eye-rolling worthy word, especially for students. On the other hand, it provides an opportunity for increased bonding which pays off in terms of greater engagement and productivity.[8] We encourage the utilization of all activities with purpose or design- this applies to icebreakers and warm-up exercises. They should relate directly to the task, whether by context or to warm up the use of a skill that may be needed in the session. In fact, many of our instructors use the time when students are filtering into the classroom to initiate the community building process. This may take the form of playing music as they arrive, word clouds, polls, news related questions, or informal conversation.[9]

Similar low-stakes activities over the next couple of sessions help establish that student participation is essential and respected and that, with everyone contributing, the classroom experience becomes more valuable.[10] This may involve pairing students on the first day and then having them introduce each other. It might involve placing students in teams and then having one student speak for the group (students are less reluctant to speak if they are sharing ideas that are not exclusively of their own making).[11] Another successful technique is to have students submit their response to a question, reading, or speaker in advance of class and then invite the students with interesting submissions or that encapsulate many similar sentiments to share. We have found that since students have already prepared a response, they are more likely to contribute to the conversation.[12] The one-minute paper is another effective tool to have the students pause, reflect, and then share their thoughts as part of a class discussion.[13] All of these techniques are designed to break down barriers and establish a degree of comfort.[14]

Having students work in small teams additionally aids in developing work-ready capabilities. It often allows for camaraderie among students and a shared sense of purpose as they work to complete the deliverable. The instructor guides the student teams over multiple weeks, and much of the ongoing effort is workshopped during class. We try to set up these teams to perform and support each other. If students do not feel comfortable with each other and the instructor, they are reluctant to share work in progress, or give or accept feedback on their efforts. This community and open dialogue is essential to achieve the developmental goals and realize the full potential of the learning experience.

Active Learning and Encouraging Engagement

Each of our learning experiences is designed to place the instructor in a position where they have the opportunity to share insights into how something is actually done. Specialized knowledge gained through experience is best disseminated by having students actively working on a task. As everyone participates in some form of active learning, the industry professional has a natural opportunity to give feedback and to share industry or professional standards, as well as what might have happened if things were done differently. The goal is to guide the students in a direction where they can reach their own conclusions with a more nuanced understanding of how to progress towards a specific goal.[15]

While this interactivity is baked into the design, it is perhaps the most difficult concept for our working professionals to execute. Many of them are of a generation where the reigning pedagogy was "chalk and talk."[16] They were socialized to think that a student's role in the classroom is to sit, listen, and ask questions at the appropriate time.[17] Others think in terms of their professional experience and, rather than approaching the classroom as a learning environment, think more in terms of corporate training where certain concepts are delivered as efficiently as possible. Even for those who understand the value of active learning, if things are not going well, they often retreat to something that feels more comfortable, which is usually lecturing.

Overall, lack of engagement may have little to do with the students themselves and may have more to do with the structure and delivery of an individual class that is devoid of active learning or relevancy. Instructors are competing to hold students' attention for any extended period of time.[18] This is why we like to think of the time in class in terms of blocks where different activities take place. These blocks are usually 10 or 20 minutes long but can extend to an hour depending on the format of the class that day. We encourage a mix of guest speakers, teamwork time, workshopping, class discussion, and a minimum amount of lecturing. By breaking up the class into segments and having students participate and move in and out of them, it is easier to maintain their attention and engage with the instructors and activities.

We want our instructors to let the students drive the experience, by having them do as much as possible. Many of the active and experiential techniques we recommend incorporate communication and collaboration. Again, these are both capabilities that need to be practiced in a variety of ways for them to be developed. Pairing students up or using small teams encourages the use of these skills, especially if it is part of the task at hand. One technique that we have used successfully is to have each team member write down two ideas related to a task and then put them forward for discussion in a small group. Each group discusses the various ideas and collectively selects which to present with a brief explanation.

This can all be for naught if there is a failure to engage because students are unfamiliar with a topic, bored with the topic, or do not have an entry point to engage. The consequence is that time will seem to drag on and on or students will seek out other distractions. It is important to meet students where they are when possible. This often involves using relatable examples that capture their interests or that relate to their own lives. One of our instructors tackles this by giving each team of students responsibility over one of the course's weekly topics. The students assume the role of a panelist/subject matter expert (SME) and must select a subject related to the topic to present to the class. This includes sourcing at least two or three articles and connecting these to what they think their classmates need to know. The panelist/SME must also field questions from the other students in the class and the instructor. As a result, the students drive an aspect of the class and focus on what areas interest them (within broad parameters).

As with driving, it is often better to start someone on a closed course or local road, rather than heading to a highway or complicated downtown. It is intimidating for a student to be asked to contribute an opinion in a classroom with other students they don't know. It is more productive and inclusive to ask smaller groups to work together to propose an idea or solution to the larger group- mirroring the professional world that students will soon enter.

Minimum Viable Information

One challenge that appears frequently in the design and delivery of course material as mentioned is the tension between needing to provide a baseline amount of knowledge and the desire to hit the ground running by actively engaging with the students in a course. Avoiding a great deal of lecturing requires a creative approach to getting the students up to speed when they do not have a complete understanding of key concepts or are not yet comfortable with the tools to be used.

With more technical experiences that presume familiarity with a software tool, theoretical concept, or mathematical expressions that students have either forgotten or never learned, there can be apprehension from the onset. We work collaboratively with the instructor to identify ways to bring students up to a level where the learning goals underlying the course design can be met rather than lowering the bar. Sometimes this involves abandoning superfluous content, and other times involves the curation of videos or articles that can quickly get students relevant background information. Creating this bridge enables students to engage, build a community, and increases the chance of the course's success. Providing supplemental support allows students to move past confusion or the minutia of an element they don't fully understand.

Some new instructors will invest a great deal of time preparing each class with many resources and content while not fully building out activities. It is important to ensure there is sufficient time for activities to unfold or opportunities for students to interact with the content and each other. As part of the design process, we encourage instructors to think in terms of what is essential, what they can live without, and, if they find themselves with an abundance of time, what they would like to add.

Curation that highlights what is most important and provides a wide range of optional information is key for supporting a spectrum of learners.[19] To encourage students who are extremely interested in the topic or industry, instructors will often post additional resources, such as blogs, publications, articles, and videos that may continue to develop a more "career-ready" knowledge base.

Guide Program

We created a student guide program as a support mechanism for our industry professionals and the students enrolled in their courses. Many of the newer professionals have long forgotten what it is like to be a college student, or their memories do not match up with the changes that have turned the collegiate experience into something that only bears a passing resemblance to their own life story. By assigning them a student guide to help them understand the current student mindset and what they are likely to encounter in the classroom, we can proactively head off potential issues that may arise once the course begins. This also provides a mechanism that informs the instructor about potential approaches that will resonate with their students.

Each student guide goes through an application process, must have previously taken a Business in Practice course, and participates in a training program. The training program covers the various technologies used, addresses active learning, troubleshooting issues, best practices, and how to give feedback. This provides instructors with important help when navigating the classroom environment, utilizing the university's learning management system, obtaining the temperature of the room, and receiving advice on issues when they come up. Often, small adjustments can lead to improvements in the experience for all involved.

In addition to pairing a student guide with instructors new to the program, we also pair instructors who are teaching remotely to a classroom of students.[20] Remote instruction to a classroom of students has its own challenges, particularly with active learning. It can be difficult for an instructor to identify which student has a question, move the students into groups, sense the progress or mood of the room, interact with an individual or small group of students, or transition to an activity without support.

We meet with the guides on a weekly basis to listen to their experiences or coordinate action plans, or to decide if we will intervene if they are potentially dealing with a more sensitive issue or if an issue remains unaddressed by the instructor. This is an opportunity for all of the guides to hear from one another and work collaboratively to fashion solutions if problems are detected in a course. We discuss strategies on how to best communicate when they perceive things are not going well and lend additional support if needed. We are constantly reminded that the guides themselves are students and that being part of the program is a beneficial opportunity to support their professional development.

In addition to all that the guides do during the course, they play an important role in helping us determine the viability of the course—whether the instructor and/or the course should continue to be a part of the program. This also helps with the redesign process. Nothing goes perfectly the first time and, after reviewing course evaluations as well as debriefs with the instructor and student guide, it becomes possible to identify changes that will lead to an improved experience.

Complements Rather than Substitutes

The key to success when working with professionals turned part-time instructors is to intervene early and as much as necessary if things are not going well. With a good course design and adequate preparation, problems are minimal. However, they do happen. We therefore like to make adjustments in real time while the course is unfolding, rather than waiting until the end of the term.

Just as experience is perhaps the best teacher for our students, the same holds true for the way in which we support our course instructors. Regardless of whether they have taught before, everyone is new to the goals of our program and the unique approach that exemplifies all of our learning experiences. After designing 70+ experiences, we have developed a better understanding of what works. It has also become easier to judge who will likely have a great deal of success and who might struggle once the semester begins.

Ultimately, success or failure depends to a large extent on whether the execution of a course design leverages the working professional's own unique understanding, developed through years of actual experience. What they have to offer must complement the knowledge that is part of the core curriculum in order to serve as an effective counterpoint and provide a significant value add based on their work history and experiences.

When faculty and industry professionals work hand-in-hand to offer a more comprehensive learning experience that both disseminates core knowledge and puts that knowledge into practice, each professional can do what they do best. This new form of partnership can supercharge the development of work-ready capabilities while ensuring that the core concepts essential to the understanding of a particular academic discipline are met. In this way, industry professionals are not an alternate source of labor but rather are brought on board so that traditional faculty can do what they do best while at the same time providing for the dissemination of that special knowledge that only comes from working at a particular job or in a specific industry.

Notes

1. Gilbert et al. (2021).
2. Data taken from internal BiP surveys.
3. BiP Instructor Profile Survey, December 2021: UNH alumni represented approximately 54% of the instructors in the program.
4. Guest speakers help break down the barriers of the classroom walls to deepen learning and allow students the opportunity to connect with professionals to create meaningful learning connections (Percy et al. 2019; Shane 2022).
5. If we were thinking in terms of the Agile way of doing things, it might be called the minimum viable product: What is the minimum that needs to be done to get something up and running so that we can observe the response and quickly intervene to iterate and eventually achieve a fully developed product that best meets the needs of the client?
6. Wenger et al. (2002).
7. To revisit the ineffectiveness of lecturing, or one-way communication, see Freire (1968). To explore further the idea that learning is largely a social and interactive phenomenon, see Bourdieu (1977), Rogoff (1998), and Vygotsky (1978).
8. For more on how a sense of belonging and comradery affects motivation, see Walton and Cohen (2011).
9. One of the more recent polls given to students was in Mural to select the image of what type of cooked potato they enjoyed the most.
10. For more on how a sense of belonging and comradery affect motivation, see Walton and Cohen (2011).

    For a theoretical exploration of how and why community is an important aspect of learning and education, see Bourdieu (1977, 1987), Rogoff et al. (2016), and Vygotsky (1978).
11. Nasir and Cooks (2009).
12. Metzger and Via (2022).
13. See Stead (2005) for a discussion on one-minute papers. See also Chizmar and Ostrosky (1998).

14. For more on community and identity see Nasir and Cooks (2009) and Wenger (1999).
15. Dewey (1963) and Rogoff, et. al. (2001).
16. Within the field of economics, since 1995, a national survey of introductory economics instructors has been undertaken. The most recent results (2020) show little change from the first survey. Roughly the same percentage (83%) rely on lecture to teach principles of economics. The one large change over that 25-year time period has been the increased use (50%) of PowerPoint slides (Asarta et al. 2021).

    For information on the theory behind reproduction in education and educational processes, see Bourdieu and Passeron (1977).
17. Again, for reproduction in education see Bourdieu and Passeron (1977) and Freire (1968).
18. Bradbury (2016).
19. Young (1993).
20. All of our courses are taught synchronously in real time regardless of instructor location. Most have the students in a classroom. A limited number are taught completely remote.

References

Asarta, C. J., Chambers, R. G., & Harter, C. (2021). Teaching methods in undergraduate introductory economics courses: Results from a sixth national quinquennial survey. *The American Economist, 66*(1), 18–28. https://doi.org/10.1177/0569434520974658

Bourdieu, P. (1977). *Outline of a theory of practice*. Cambridge University Press.

Bourdieu, P. (1987). *Distinction: A social critique of the judgment of taste*. Harvard University Press.

Bourdieu, P., & Passeron, J. C. (1977). *Reproduction in education, society, and culture* (R. Nice, Trans.). Sage.

Bradbury, N. A. (2016). Attention span during lectures: 8 seconds, 10 minutes, or more? *Advances in Physiology Education, 40*(4), 509–513. https://doi.org/10.1152/advan.00109.2016

Chizmar, J. F., & Ostrosky, A. L. (1998). The one-minute paper: Some empirical findings. *The Journal of Economic Education, 29*(1), 3–10. https://doi.org/10.1080/00220489809596436

Dewey, J. (1963). *Experience and education*. New York: Touchstone.

Freire, P. (1968). *Pedagogy of the oppressed*. Bloomsbury Press.

Gilbert, F. W., Harkins, J., Agrrawal, P., & Taylor, A. (2021). Internships as clinical rotations in business: Enhancing access and options. *International Journal for Business Education, 162*(1), 125–140.

Metzger, K. J., & Via, Z. (2022). Warming up the cold call. *The American Biology Teacher, 84*(6), 342–346. https://doi.org/10.1525/abt.2022.84.6.342

Nasir, N. S., & Cooks, J. (2009). Becoming a hurdler: How learning settings afford identities. *Anthropology & Education Quarterly, 40*(1), 41–61. https://doi.org/10.1111/j.1548-1492.2009.01027.x

Percy, C., Rehill, J., Kashefpakdel, E., & Chambers, N. (2019). Insights and Inspiration: Exploring the impact of guest speakers in schools. *Education and Employers.* Retrieved March 26, 2023, from https://www.educationandemployers.org/wp-content/uploads/2019/10/Speakers-for-Schools-Report.pdf

Rogoff, B. (1998). Cognition as a collaborative process. In W. Damon (Ed.), *Handbook of child psychology: Vol. 2. cognition, perception, and language* (pp. 679–744). John Wiley & Sons, Inc..

Rogoff, B., Turkanis, C. G., & Bartlett, L. (Eds.). (2001). *Learning together: Children and adults in a school community.* Oxford University Press.

Rogoff, B. M., Callanan, K., Gutierrez, & Erickson, F. (2016). The organization of informal learning. *Review of Research in Education, 40*(1), 356–401. https://doi.org/10.3102/0091732X16680994

Shane, S. (2022, March 2). Leveraging guest speakers to increase student learning. *Edutopia.* Retrieved March 26, 2023, from https://www.edutopia.org/article/leveraging-guest-speakers-increase-student-learning/#:~:text=Guest%20speakers%20are%20fundamental%20in,and%20create%20meaningful%20learning%20connections

Stead, D. R. (2005). A review of the one-minute paper. *Active Learning in Higher Education, 6*(2), 118–132. https://doi.org/10.1177/1469787405054237

Vygotsky, L. S. (1978). *Mind in society: The development of higher psychological processes.* Harvard University Press.

Walton, G. M., & Cohen, G. L. (2011). Sharing motivation. In D. Dunning (Ed.), *Social motivation* (pp. 79–101). Psychology Press.

Wenger, E. (1999). *Communities of practice: Learning, meaning, and identity.* Cambridge University Press.

Wenger, E., McDermott, R. A., & Snyder, W. (2002). *Cultivating communities of practice: A guide to managing knowledge.* Harvard Business School Press.

Young, M. F. (1993). Instructional design for situated learning. *Educational Technology Research and Development, 41*(1), 43–58. https://doi.org/10.1007/BF02297091

A Practice-Based Journey

The choices that a student makes throughout their undergraduate experience will have a significant impact on where they end up in the future. Academics obviously dominates the choices made because students must earn a set number of credits to graduate and much of their focus is centered on their major. As part of that journey, they take courses that contain assignments and examinations that are determined by the instructor, and must devote a certain number of hours to studying (if they are going to meet all of these deadlines). With the time remaining, students are provided with multiple opportunities to make friends, have fun, possibly volunteer in an effort to create a better society, and for many, hold down a job just to pay the bills.

What sets the social experience apart from the others is that the rewards are more immediate. Going to a party, joining a campus organization, making friends, and just hanging out all come with immediate gratification (or disappointment). This stands in stark contrast to the professional experience. Here, students are asked to make an investment in their future by joining professional networks, creating a résumé, and taking certain courses that translate into the acquisition of knowledge that *may* be valuable upon graduation. The operative concept with respect to the professional experience is the time frame where many of these benefits are not realized until sometime in the future.

It should come as no surprise that for many students, preparation for an uncertain professional future is given less emphasis than academics, which

N. B. Niman, J. R. Chagnon, *The Work-Ready Graduate*,
https://doi.org/10.1007/978-3-031-33910-3_10

demand more attention and social experiences that provide an immediate set of rewards.[1] Self-regulation is a developed skill that comes with maturity and experience.[2] Without the capability to defer immediate gratification in light of more significant but future rewards, it is unsurprising that social endeavors dominates the decision process for many students.[3]

If academics can be made more relevant by focusing on practical applications, students may find themselves more interested in their future career than what they are going to do this weekend. It needs to help them develop a sense of purpose that when combined with tangible accomplishments, produces a feeling that is something more than a series of checked boxes. In other words, institutions need to actively dispel the notion that merely graduating somehow automatically prepares students for the career of their dreams and a life well lived.[4]

A Work-Ready Journey

One of the principal challenges in designing a journey that elevates the professional sphere is that many students focus on averting losses rather than taking risks during the learning process.[5] Examples of losses include earning a poor grade on an assignment, looking foolish in class, or the embarrassment that is associated with an unacceptably low grade point average. To avoid such losses, some students are attracted to those courses that offer an opportunity to spread risk over multiple assignments to minimize the chance that one assignment could result in a low grade for a course. Alternatively, they may select a course or instructor that has the reputation of being 'easy.' Loss aversion is one possible explanation for why many students prefer a highly structured learning environment with many assignments that individually contribute to a small percentage of the final grade.[6]

By reducing the chance that any single assignment will adversely impact their grade, students can effectively minimize their potential losses.[7] Learning, however, is very much about taking a risk. It entails thinking about something new, trying something different, and in some cases, pushing boundaries in uncomfortable ways. Moreover, when a student enters the professional realm, what constitutes taking a risk changes dramatically. There is not a syllabus to spell out their assignments and corresponding weight associated with their performance. This increases the probably of experiencing anxiety and therefore may demotivate exactly the behavior that needs to be encouraged. As a result, the fear of failure might become so strong that they choose not to engage in their own professional development.

Creating educational opportunities that promote personal, intellectual, and professional growth may define the undergraduate experience, but whether or not a student realizes all that such an experience has to offer depends on the connections and touchpoints built into an experience where students can pause, reflect, and enjoy the benefits associated with active participation. Any class, club, or social opportunity can contribute toward the development of a skillset that will have value throughout one's professional journey. The goal is to help students understand that by embracing new opportunities, they can turn skills into capabilities and, as a result, enjoy a more robust undergraduate experience with fewer losses and a clearer pathway to life after graduation.

For a graduate to become truly work-ready, those skills must be cultivated into a set of capabilities that goes beyond simple exposure to constructing a professional email, delivering a presentation, writing a report, or having an opportunity to work in a team environment. Being work-ready means developing a deeper understanding of how those skills are to be applied in a professional context in current and future endeavors. It uses those skills to enhance the capacity to think and apply knowledge within a nuanced understanding that is required in an authentic professional situation.

While repetition is important for the development of capabilities, it is not the same as solving one homework problem after another similar to what a student might experience in a typical digital learning platform. Instead, it comes from a carefully crafted sequence of experiences that are designed to apply those skills in a structured environment that provides insight into why a skill might be used in a particular context and how it might be applied to yield the best result. In other words, the learning environment becomes a substitute for the experiences that traditionally have served to instruct how best to approach a given situation. Whereas employers traditionally look at skills tempered by experience as an indicator of how well a candidate will be able to contribute to the organization, a set of comparable experiences along a practice-based journey can produce a similar result.

Gaming the System: A Student-Centered Design Approach

When creating learning experiences designed for students to promote the development of work-ready capabilities, context is crucial. The STAR² approach immerses the student in a situation that requires them to assume a role or the responsibility of a working professional. If students are to learn by doing, and for that activity to contribute toward the development of work-ready capabilities, then much needs to be done to reframe the experience so that students are open to new approaches to learning where the focus is more on how to do something than on the mastery of a set of ideas.[8] By including real company norms, evaluative processes, projects, and general ways of doing things that reflect the work history of the practitioner turned instructor, it becomes possible to interject authenticity into the course design process.

We found that the most successful experiences are those that are carefully planned and leave as little as possible to chance. By acknowledging the various components working collectively to create a quality learning experience, it is possible to stack the odds in terms of a successful outcome. Here, some fundamental game design principles can provide an effective framework for understanding the underlying issues.[9] There are five basic elements that work together to deliver an effective experience.

In the context of developing a successful game, we might talk about **The Players**—who they are, why they are interested in playing, and what they hope to achieve as an outcome. In the context of learning experience, our players are the students who participate to bring a particular design to life. [10] To get the maximum buy-in, it is important to remind them of why they are being asked to interact with a working professional and the goal of becoming better prepared to enter the workforce after graduation. At the same time, it is important to remind the working professional of the importance of meeting the students where they are. What is it they are most interested in? How will the topic impact their own personal lives?

For example, in a BiP course we developed called *Disruptions in the Supply Chain*, students were, for the most part, unfamiliar with the basic concepts and enrolled in the class more to fulfill a requirement than because they possessed an interest in the topic. What made the experience a success was helping students understand the significant role the supply chain plays in stocking store shelves, how and where products are produced, and how much they cost. By personalizing the material, students were quickly able to understand why the supply chain is important and how disruptions were affecting their lives on a daily basis.[11]

To encourage risk-taking and participation, all of our courses are credit/fail, but this is a double-edged sword. Because they are not awarded a letter grade, many students respond by minimizing the amount of effort they put into the experience. This is why we encourage instructors to think of possible non-grade rewards they might offer that recognize achievements and exceptional performance in order to provide encouragement for students to perform to a higher standard.

One of our instructors, for example, writes a professional recommendation on LinkedIn for the students who finish on the top team at the end of the experience. Another instructor highlights the top contributions to the entire class, in an effort to set expectations for quality work. A few instructors have offered a recommendation to their organizations' internship programs. Some courses are designed so that higher-performing teams get first selection in the choice of preferred client, industry, or component that contributes to the end of the term deliverable.

The Rules are another element that will affect the students' potential engagement in the experience. Most students have been trained over many years to think of the learning process as listening, absorbing, and repeating what they are told.[12] Exercises fulfill the role of reinforcing knowledge that has been delivered primarily by lecture, and the goal is to complete an assessment with as few mistakes as possible.

As you can imagine, all of this can be a source of anxiety for the student who is now being asked to work outside of the framework they have grown accustomed to over many years in the educational system.[13] In contrast, the STAR^2 approach is looking for them to take an active role in their education where what they learn and how much is dependent on the degree of their participation. Habits are hard to break, and students grow confused when they are asked to enter the equivalent of uncharted territory.

This poses a difficult challenge for our working professionals. The whole point of their involvement is to challenge students to work outside their comfort zone as they navigate an experience that replicates what they might encounter in a particular work environment. It is not that what they are asked to do is extremely complicated or cumbersome. Instead, the challenge comes from having to meet a different set of expectations assessed not by a set of rubrics but by those same professional standards found in an actual work environment.

Setting the stage acclimates the student to this new learning environment. Industry professionals explicitly lay out the basics—explaining who they are, why they are involved in the program, the purpose of the experience, and what will be expected from the students.[14] We encourage our industry partners to intersperse the course with professional work standards and aspects of their organizations' cultures and norms. Our aim is to introduce more structure at the onset and then gradually relax it as a student progresses through the experience.

While we are essentially designing bespoke learning experiences around the industry professional and our students, we embed common structures and elements that span all of our courses. We strive to deliver particular forms of consistency and repetition, or threads, that weave together and connect our courses. This contributes to a consistent experience that reinforces program goals and enables students to quickly get up to speed when they enroll in a new course.

The next element is **The Magic Circle**. This is the place where the "magic" happens, or, in learning parlance, the space we are creating for students where they are able to put ideas into action, strategies are executed, and outcomes are realized. It is possible to turn the classroom into a magical place with "aha" moments within a structure that embraces ISA^2—learning that is informal, situated, authentic, and active.

To maximize the amount of time available for active learning to take place, we frequently utilize the concept of the flipped classroom.[15] Students need to know enough to put ideas into practice, but we want to ensure that they have the maximum amount of time to interact with their classmates, workshop ideas, and gain insights from guest speakers or the instructor. This mimics a work environment where there is more onus to prepare before collaborating or taking action, instead of showing up with no familiarity or without the ability to contribute.

The prework also serves as warm calling for the discussion that is planned to ensue during the class or as part of a team task. To overcome the reluctance to talk, however, it is important to create a sense of community and a feeling of camaraderie among all involved.[16] The goal is to create a feeling that we are all in it together. How much I learn depends on how much you learn, and hence to get the most out of the experience, everyone needs to participate.

Once it is time for class, role playing is a common tool we use to replicate what our students are likely to encounter in a real work environment. Most of our activities have students interacting as part of a team. Taking matters one step further, the construct of a multi-disciplinary team lends itself to defining roles and responsibilities in ways that can enhance the experience. We have also found that skill-specific roles that can rotate and allow each student to develop a specific work-ready skill—such as team lead, presenter/spokesperson, researcher, or analyst—are also useful for creating an authentic learning environment. Assuming multiple roles provides opportunities to realize strengths and weaknesses, see alternate approaches, and share or understand different perspectives.[17]

Fundamentally, the role should require that each student has a responsibility to the team and to work collectively.[18]

The Magic Circle appears when students are given an opportunity to interact, and the working professional is able to guide the students by providing valuable insights and feedback so that learning progresses. This involves creating moments where students have an opportunity to respond and react to a guest or a work in progress, or determine the best pathway forward. It provides students with a feeling of agency—that they have some control over outcomes—and reinforces that the experience is a joint effort between the industry professional and the students.[19] As a result, each class must be carefully choreographed to ensure that there is ample time for ideas to coalesce and create a community of practice, where peer-to-peer learning emerges organically.[20]

With everything in place, it is time to **Play**—a set of activities that essentially bring the underlying $STAR^2$ narrative to life. Here, students encounter the situation and purpose, take up their tasks, and act. The students are the players, and as such the approach should be learner-centric. As we discussed in the chapter titled "Industry Professionals in the Classroom", this is where the keys are handed over to the students to drive the experience. Even though the experience is designed around the industry professional, if the student is to gain all the experience has to offer, they must take some ownership of the process under the guidance of the instructor. The Play should include tasks the students need to work through but are not so challenging that the students are discouraged or overwhelmed to the point where they disengage from the learning experience.[21] Through careful monitoring and the flexibility built into the course design, a closer match between ability and action can be achieved that grows confidence and leaves the student with a sense of accomplishment.

We require first-time instructors, and highly recommend to our returning instructors, that they implement a pre-class survey of their students. The surveys are short, usually no more than 10–15 questions. They include basic student questions such as preferred name and major, as well as questions customized to ask about perceived skill levels, affinity for various team roles, and knowledge of certain topics/terminology/tools. We also recommend including a few questions that will help with community building in the first class session, such as personal interests, organizations they are active in, songs they listen to a lot, or last book they read (not for a class). This provides a snapshot helping to capture a clearer understanding of the students in the course and suggests possible opportunities to structure student engagement and build a greater sense of community.

It is important to create a flexible structure and help the new instructor identify those signals that suggest editing needs to occur or that a robust discussion should be allowed to continue. Ultimately, it is all about motivation. Games have the advantage of being fun, and while learning can also be fun, what makes the process rewarding and a strong motivating factor is when students come to the realization that what they are doing and how they are doing it has value.

This transitions to the final element, also known as the **Epic Win**. An epic win is the end result that validates the experience and makes it all worthwhile. It is the "aha" moment when students come to the realization that what they have accomplished will make a difference in how they approach life and learning.[22] In other words, it is the culmination of what we have tried to accomplish in the STAR^2 design. To further emphasize the importance of this experience, qualitative data from a BiP instructor profile survey revealed that 40% of instructors allude to this "aha" moment or the ability to make connections beyond the classroom as what they find most rewarding or what motivates them to keep teaching in the program.[23]

From the perspective of creating a work-ready graduate, it is about developing some mastery with respect to how to do something rather than a comprehensive understanding of a particular body of knowledge. It is not just about learning what to do, but the best way of going about doing something.

Because our learning experiences for the most part do not impart knowledge that is critical to the mastery of the material in a functional area of business, we view success a little differently. The central focus of all our courses is the ability to apply a tool, technique, or skill in an authentic context. We have no expectation that at the end of the term, our students will gain mastery. Instead, we expect them to have a better understanding of why, when, and how something should be used and what the benefits and limitations are within a specific context.

The Best of All Possible Worlds

If there is one work-ready capability to "rule them all," it might be the ability to learn. In a fast-paced world where the only constant is change, an employee who is ready and able to learn new technologies and ways of doing things, or to adapt to changing circumstances, is highly valued.

Those who are intellectually curious and willing to update their capabilities in the face of new challenges are the most highly sought after. What we are talking about is a special group of thinkers *and* doers who are intrinsically motivated.

To be intrinsically motivated is to do something for the sheer pleasure it brings rather than some external reward.[24] One lens for understanding the role that intrinsic motivation plays in the development of self-sustaining learning is through the application of Self-Determination Theory (SDT).[25] The SDT framework is less about control and more about the creation of structures that support the conditions required for the manifestation of intrinsic motivation. These three structures are 1] autonomy, 2] competence, and 3] relatedness.

Autonomy is associated with the ability to choose one's own path. Autonomy for a student occurs when they have the ability to determine what they are interested in and the freedom to pursue those interests. Autonomy in learning is about creation and interacting with the process rather than meeting the metrics of a rubric. Here, the fabric supporting learning weaves together a structure that sets clear goals, has consistency in how rules are applied, and fosters engagement and positive feedback while providing avenues for personal choice.[26]

Competence is associated with mastery of a body of knowledge, or a set of skills designed to make learning possible. Students have a sense of control within a learning environment that provides appropriate cues to help them gain a sense of accomplishment. The goal here is to establish an environment that challenges rather than frustrates and is married to the idea of improvement relative to established norms over time.

Finally, relatedness is associated with a sense of belonging and connection, or identity. It captures the student's position relative to others in terms of their underlying beliefs and understanding. It includes how a student is a cultural being and relates to the context in which material is presented. It is about sharing ideas in a way that is relatable to a student's interests and life experiences while drawing connections to others, to a range of ideas, and to the future.

SDT might be what Gallup had in mind when it found that one of the key factors leading to student success is whether they had an opportunity to engage with a project that lasted more than one semester.[27] Parallels can also be drawn to our BiP program where students take four courses that provide a series of opportunities needed to develop work-ready capabilities, but select those courses based on their own interests. None of the courses are required to advance discipline-based understanding (though they might accomplish that). The hope is that, over the four courses, students can see themselves progressing, thereby contributing toward the development of the intrinsic motivation necessary to continue the process of transforming skills into capabilities.

Almost all courses are team-based within a learning community where individual contributions are valued. Students are given responsibility for how to make progress on a project where creativity is encouraged, and unique approaches are lauded. Skills are developed by interacting with an activity and each other. Over the four courses, students receive feedback from working professionals that will enable them to make the adjustments needed to obtain sufficient mastery to (at least) begin the process of turning those skills into capabilities. The courses are designed to have low-stakes risks and contain elements of activity and engagement. Community is paramount so students feel comfortable relating to each other and the instructor. By using authentic contexts with real applications, it becomes possible for students to develop a better understanding of professional practices.

This actualization provides students with the opportunity to create the best of all possible worlds where they become empowered to put their newly developed capabilities into practice. Through the creation of a unified set of experiences that spans the professional, academic, and social spheres, students are provided with the means to advance both their personal and professional development for years to come.

Elevated Experiences

In addition to the guided experiences that we offer through our Business in Practice program, as a business school, we also provide what we refer to as elevated experiences. We reserve the term for those experiences that function on a high level of student motivation and engagement. They provide students with an opportunity to turn skills into capabilities over an extended period of time, are associated with a series of projects that encapsulate an authentic, structured work environment, and are primarily sustained and managed by students. For students with high intrinsic motivation, they offer a gateway to further fuel their professional development.

Elevated experiences enable a soon-to-be graduate to construct a compelling narrative that showcases skills and capabilities developed as part of the experience and provides examples of how they were put into practice and led to an improvement for a real, functioning business. They essentially level the playing field by enabling a student to gain experience comparable to what they otherwise might have accomplished a couple of years after graduation. The story for potential employers is that they can hire a student who has demonstrated capabilities and a record of accomplishment. Elevated experiences arguably send the strongest and clearest signal that a student is work-ready.

Examples can include student-run experiences such as research and consulting teams for corporate projects, angel investment firms, communication/PR agencies, and data analytics labs. Regardless of the form, the experience connects students with working professionals over an extended period of time and offers an alternative to the internship. The end result is a dynamic portfolio of professional experiences where students can illustrate their specific contributions and value to a potential employer.

Voice Z Digital

Voice Z Digital, a student-run digital marketing agency, is what we envisioned as the next step after Business in Practice. The initiative to build Voice Z Digital was launched from our conversations with HubSpot, an early partner in our search for an elevated experiential learning opportunity. Digital marketing is a field where there is an influx of new technologies, emerging markets, and changing social trends, which all make it difficult for an established faculty member to keep up with the latest innovations in the field. Early conversations with digital marketing agencies confirmed that for our students to be prepared to step into a digital marketing role, they would need to have a meaningful experience with real clients under the guidance of an industry professional who could help them navigate the intricacies of client work within a turbulent industry where there is no single pathway to the successful completion of a project.

The goal was to create a student-run agency where the structure, operations, and services mirror those of a professional agency. A group of students were recruited to form the agency, decisions needed to be made about what services the agency would provide, and clients acquired. Our student agency, just like any other business, needed to identify an area of need in the market that could be credibly filled by student members with limited (but growing) experience. Since the agency would be populated with students predominantly under the age of 23, it was thought they could best assist clients looking to reach that age demographic.

What makes Voice Z digital such a powerful learning experience is that the student members of the agency are situated within the context of a functioning agency that has real clients, projects, deadlines, resource constraints, and personalities that dominate the work just like in actual agencies. The agency is run by a student leadership team headed by a student who serves as managing director. A faculty member is assigned to the agency to ensure the integrity of the academic experience (credits are awarded), and a working professional from a local digital agency assists with matters related to client management and quality of work.

By working as an associate in the agency, students have an opportunity to work with multiple clients and projects that differ in terms of their complexity, some of which persist beyond a single semester. Students can see the consequences of their actions, respond accordingly based on feedback, and make further recommendations that are informed by experience rather than an abstract set of principles. With sufficient experience, skills turn into capabilities as students become more aware of what to expect and adept at responding to the needs of a client or market. This enables our students to understand the complexity of managing human relationships with clients that have different needs or needs that may change before the end of the project. With multiple clients/projects at any moment in time, students can be assigned to projects based on their current skill level, and as those skills develop over time, they are provided with opportunities to work on more challenging projects in their professional development. All of this sets the agency apart from a conventional classroom experience. Success or failure does not depend on the judgement of a faculty member but rather the collective and sustained performance of the agency, externally on client work and internally to develop new talent that will become the next set of leadership.

When students and agency alumni were asked why they joined the agency, what they hoped to gain most from the experience were the soft skills that come with doing real client work. The primary motivation for joining the agency was the ability to work in a team-based environment on meaningful projects that resulted in actionable consequences. In our conversations with a finance student who joined Voice Z Digital, we asked him about his particular decision to join since he is focusing on another major. Coming out of COVID-19, he wanted to join a student organization that would give him an opportunity for greater personal interaction. More importantly, he wanted experience doing client work—an experience that subsequently paid off when he interviewed with a New York financial firm. What surprised him the most in the interview process was how little time was spent discussing his course work, or interest in finance for that matter; what elicited the most questions were his experiences working with clients and the capabilities that he developed as part of that process.

Second to the development of soft skills, our survey revealed that many students joined to better position themselves for an internship or a first job. This is a great experience for students thinking about entering the field of digital marketing because it gives them a realistic taste of what it would be like and helps them to decide whether or not they want to pursue a career in the field. Learning what you don't like can be almost as important as determining what you do like. Regardless of whether the agency graduate decides to pursue a career in the field, they all acknowledge that they can enter the workforce with a great deal more confidence, and an enhanced understanding of what it is like to work for an external client and what it takes to be an effective member of a team.

Creating a Complementary Curriculum

All of these efforts are designed to create a practice-based student journey that is complementary to the core curriculum. As Figure 1 shows, the course experiences span a spectrum that runs from professor-driven to one that is guided by a working professional, and ends at one that is self-directed. Alternatively, the spectrum can be viewed as progressing from the conceptual to the applied and finally ends at an actual experience (Fig. 1).

Our core courses are able to take advantage of the tenure-track faculty who are knowledge creators and who are able to bring the latest research into the foundational courses that serve as the basis for the applied work we do in the BiP program. The BiP program adds an intermediary layer that imparts context-driven skill development that prepares students to utilize tools, approaches, and soft skills.

In the BiP program, smaller courses are designed and developed around the experiences of a working professional who is brought in to share their expertise—often within the context of how to do something. Learning experiences are interactive, as the students are guided through a series of steps that are often developed around a central course project involving a real company that takes place over the entire semester. All the courses rely on active learning, keeping lectures to a minimum, and use material that is

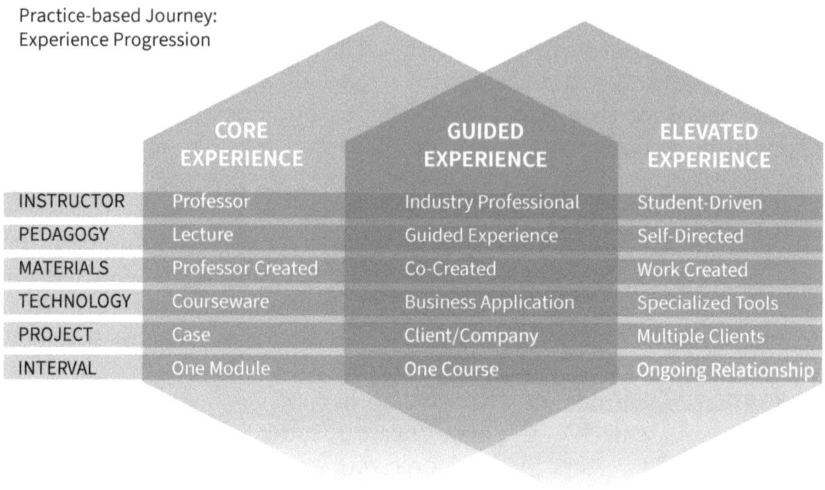

Fig. 1 The practice-based journey progression is shown as it extends from a traditional, core curriculum experience to a guided experience to an elevated experience. The figure displays the corresponding type of instructor, pedagogy, materials, technology usage, typical project, and interval

co-created with the students in the course. The technology used focuses more on business applications that students are likely to encounter in the workplace.

Finally, the elevated experiences, while having faculty and industry professionals on the periphery, allow the responsibility and progression to be dictated by the learners themselves—they set the expectations, skills, and capabilities in a domain that is essentially self-governed by the student organization. This gives them an opportunity to work on real projects, with real clients, using the standard tools found at real agencies. Because the experience most closely approximates a real working environment, students are able to take advantage of an experience that most closely replicates what they will find post graduation.

Realized Opportunities

Offering a wide range of experiences can provide an important contribution to the self-discovery process, which is one of the primary reasons students attend university. A program or set of meaningful experiences that goes beyond the occasional career night can help students develop a better understanding of what they like (and do not like), while introducing them to a new set of possibilities in time for them to determine how they might apply their knowledge and capabilities to do good or make a living.

Those same experiences designed to develop human capabilities can also introduce new possibilities and, in doing so, career opportunities to put those capabilities into practice.

Even business students who study the main functional areas such as finance, marketing, or management have a hunger to discover how business is actually done in the real world. Important business concepts, such as the supply chain, take on new meaning when a student has an opportunity to see how disruptions in the supply chain affect their daily lives and is exposed to professionals who share their work experience at different points along the chain.

Integrating working professionals into the campus experience can serve to either initiate or enhance the development of professional networks that both increase understanding and open doors to potential internship or employment opportunities. We encourage our students to connect with speakers or instructors on LinkedIn, which enables them to tap into professional networks built around a particular company or job function. Overcoming some of the simple barriers that prevent students from feeling comfortable reaching out or interacting with working professionals can pay large dividends in terms of refining the discovery process associated with finding an interesting career opportunity. Once they are ensconced in the world of working professionals, this affords students the ability to subsequently leverage those connections to identify additional opportunities.

Working with professionals allows for experiences that provide students with a structured narrative and demonstrated capabilities they can utilize as evidence (signals) when they reach out and form connections as part of their professional network. For students who take part in elevated experiences, such as Voice Z Digital, it provides an opportunity to connect in new ways and illustrate a more fully developed skillset and an ongoing level of motivation to develop capabilities in oneself and the people who will follow.

Employers are looking for students who have a familiarity with the professional world and are doers—who have a set of experiences that make them work-ready. They are seeking graduates who can step in and hit the ground running and integrate themselves into their organization.

Notes

1. Present bias reflects the observed behavior that most people prefer an immediate reward and will put off costs (opportunity or real) until sometime in the future. This may explain why students would rather spend time with their friends than visit their career services office. Spending time with friends has an immediate reward (fun) but while the payoffs to a visit to career services might have a larger reward (a job), that reward is only received sometime in the distant future. O'Donoghue and Rabin (1999) demonstrate that sophistication (understanding they might have self-control problems in the future) can mitigate procrastination and from the perspective a work-ready graduate, it suggests that if a student's understanding of what is required to secure a quality job placement early in their undergraduate career, they might procrastinate less and invest in those activities that will increase their work readiness.
2. Self-regulated learning (SRL) and its impact on time management is discussed in Wolters and Brady (2021).
3. Hoch and Loewenstein (1991) explain time inconsistency as the result of sudden changes in desire that lead to choices that represent a transient alteration in tastes. From the perspective of the student who must choose between studying for an exam and attending a party with friends, they might understand the importance of studying to receive a grade that is needed to satisfy degree requirements, maintain good academic standing, preserve or earn a scholarship or award, or garner the attention of a favored professor. However, a sudden increase in desire triggered by the smell of alcohol, social media posts, texts from friends, or loud noises down the hall creates a set of conditions that may prompt them to act inconsistently. In other words, while the student understands they would be better off studying, the struggle between desire and willpower is a losing one for them and they end up attending the party with friends.
4. This notion may stem from a transactional mental model identified by Fischman and Gardner (2022).
5. For more information on college student risk aversion, see Tversky and Kahneman (1991) and Nalley and McKenzie (2011).
6. Where class enrollments, promotion, or salary increases depend on the outcome of student evaluations, there is a positive incentive for faculty to accommodate this desire by offering a portfolio of assessment options.
7. One way of looking at this is that students choose between different prospects (outcomes) and choose those that minimize the chance they will come up short (incur losses). See Kahneman and Tversky (1979).
8. Erickson et al. (2020) explored situational interest, motivation, and engagement across different learning modalities. They found that the

learning environment can have a large impact on these factors. Students involved in hands-on laboratory stations experienced the most interest, motivation, and engagement. Second were students involved in problem-based case studies. The lowest levels were seen with video lectures. See also Cajiao and Burke (2016).

9. A review of the evidence-based literature on serious games can be found in Lameras et al. (2017).
10. An example of how active learning can develop leadership/followership is the use of The Arena as an in-class exercise. See McCauley (2021).
11. Interest that is motivated by the learning environment (situational interest) in contrast to personal interest (inherent in the learner) can have a large impact on learning outcomes. Hunsu et al. (2017) look at the impact of innovative teaching methods, the relevance and applicability of what is being taught, and personal interest as descriptive variables that increase situational interest and hence improve learning outcomes.
12. Within sociology, Huggins and Stamatel (2015) discovered that there was no difference in learning outcomes between lecturing and team-based learning. However, students engaged in team-based learning thought they improved their oral communication and creative thinking skills more than the lecture students.
13. A report released by Gallup and the Lumina Foundation found that 36% of bachelor's degree students considered stopping their course work. In 2022, 69% reported emotional stress as the number one reason why they might stop (Gallup and the Lumina Foundation, 2023).
14. To assist, we developed a first day slide deck to help ensure consistency and approachable tone, and a customizable section for expectations from the start.
15. Using data from 317 studies, Bredow et al., (2021) demonstrate the efficacy of the flipped classroom.
16. A great resource for why community building is important and how one might go about building community within the classroom can be found in Columbia University Center for Teaching and Learning (2023).

    The importance of learning communities is discussed in Wenger (1999).
17. Bonwell and Eison (1991).

    Role playing is more effective than lecture in Acharya et al. (2019).

    Also see McCarthy and Anderson (1999).
18. Johnson and Johnson (2011).
19. Co-creation: the effectiveness of a partnership model where students are co-creators of their learning experience is demonstrated in Billett and Martin (2018).
20. More about cultivating communities of practice can be found in Wenger et al. (2002).

21. Martin et al. (2008) found that engineering students prefer courses that are more challenging as long as the challenge can be met.
22. Ryan and Deci (2000).
23. In a December 2021 BiP Instructor Survey (sample of 25 current instructors), respondents submitted qualitative information to open text questions such as "What do you find most rewarding about the teaching experience?" or "What motivates you to continue teaching in the program?" Ten of the respondents specifically cite or directly allude to "aha"/ lightbulb moments or students engaging in content and making impactful connections.
24. Technically, intrinsic motivation pertains to activities done "for their own sake," or for their inherent interest and enjoyment (Ryan & Deci, 2000). Extrinsic motivation is often needed when someone is required to do something rather than from the joy or satisfaction that comes from doing it well. A sports analogy might illustrate the point best. Some athletes participate because of the sheer joy they receive from playing the game. They would play in extreme cases without compensation because of their love of the game. This is in contrast to other athletes who play for another reason such as fame, status, a scholarship, or financial stability.
25. SDT has been used to understand the intrinsic motivation associated with computer game play (Ryan et al., 2006).
26. Ryan and Deci (2000).
27. Gallup and Purdue University (2014).

References

Acharya, H., Reddy, R., Hussein, A., Bagga, J., & Pettit, T. (2019). The effectiveness of applied learning: An empirical evaluation using role playing in the classroom. *Journal of Research in Innovative Teaching & Learning, 12*(3), 295–310. https://doi.org/10.1108/JRIT-06-2018-0013

Billett, P., & Martin, D. (2018). Engaging students in co-creation of sociological knowledge and curriculum design as a form of deep engagement. *Journal of University Teaching & Learning Practice, 15*(5), 1–15.

Bonwell, C. C., & Eison, J. A. (1991). *Active learning: Creating excitement in the classroom*. School of Education and Human Development, George Washington University.

Bredow, C. A., Roehling, P. V., Knorp, A. J., & Sweet, A. M. (2021). To flip or not to flip? A meta-analysis of the efficacy of flipped learning in higher education. *Review of Educational Research, 91*(6), 878–918. https://doi.org/10.3102/00346543211019122

Cajiao, J., & Burke, M. J. (2016). How instructional methods influence skill development in management education. *Academy of Management Learning & Education, 15*(3), 508–524. https://doi.org/10.5465/amle.2013.0354
Columbia University Center for Teaching and Learning. (2023). *Community building in the classroom*. Columbia University. Retrieved March 26, 2023, from https://ctl.columbia.edu/resources-and-technology/teaching-with-technology/teaching-online/community-building/
Erickson, M., Marks, D., & Karcher, E. (2020). Characterizing student engagement with hands-on, problem-based, and lecture activities in an introductory college course. *Teaching & Learning Inquiry, 8*(1), 138–153. https://doi.org/10.20343/teachlearninqu.8.1.10
Fischman, W., & Gardner, H. (2022). *The real world of college: What higher education is and what it can be*. The MIT Press.
Gallup and Purdue University. (2014). *Great Jobs great lives: The 2014 Gallup-Purdue Index Report*. Gallup, Inc. Retrieved March 23, 2023, from https://www.gallup.com/services/176768/2014-gallup-purdue-index-report.aspx
Gallup and the Lumina Foundation. (2023). *Stressed out and stopping out: The mental health crisis in higher education*. Gallup, Inc. Retrieved March 26, 2023, from https://www.gallup.com/analytics/468986/state-of-higher-education.aspx?utm_source=public_sector&utm_medium=email&utm_campaign=lumina_state_of_higher_education_email_1_march_03222023&utm_term=report&utm_content=download_report_cta_1
Hoch, S. J., & Loewenstein, G. F. (1991). Time-inconsistent preferences and consumer self-control. *Journal of Consumer Research, 17*(4), 492. https://doi.org/10.1086/208573
Huggins, C. M., & Stamatel, J. P. (2015). An exploratory study comparing the effectiveness of lecturing versus team-based learning. *Teaching Sociology, 43*(3), 227–235. https://doi.org/10.1177/0092055X15581929
Hunsu, N. J., Adesope, O., & Van Wie, B. J. (2017). Engendering situational interest through innovative instruction in an engineering classroom: What really mattered? *Instructional Science, 45*(6), 789–804. https://doi.org/10.1007/s11251-017-9427-z
Johnson, D. W., & Johnson, R. T. (2011). *Learning together and alone: Cooperative, competitive, and individualistic learning* (5th ed. [Repr.]). Allyn and Bacon.
Kahneman, D., & Tversky, A. (1979). Prospect theory: An analysis of decision under risk. *Econometrica, 47*(2), 263. https://doi.org/10.2307/1914185
Lameras, P., Arnab, S., Dunwell, I., Stewart, C., Clarke, S., & Petridis, P. (2017). Essential features of serious games design in higher education: Linking learning attributes to game mechanics: Essential features of serious games design. *British Journal of Educational Technology, 48*(4), 972–994. https://doi.org/10.1111/bjet.12467

Martin, J. H., Hands, K. B., Lancaster, S. M., Trytten, D. A., & Murphy, T. J. (2008). Hard but not too hard: Challenging courses and engineering students. *College Teaching, 56*(2), 107–113. https://doi.org/10.3200/CTCH.56.2.107-113

McCarthy, J. P., & Anderson, L. (1999). Active learning techniques versus traditional teaching styles: Two experiments from history and political science. *Innovative Higher Education, 24*(4), 279–294. https://doi.org/10.1023/B:IHIE.0000047415.48495.05

McCauley, K. D. (2021). The arena: An activity to foster teamwork, communication, and cooperation in and across teams. *Management Teaching Review, 6*(3), 199–209. https://doi.org/10.1177/2379298119883356

Nalley, L., & McKenzie, A. (2011). How much is that exam grade really worth? An estimation of student risk aversion to their unknown final college course grades. *The Journal of Economic Education, 42*(4), 338–353. https://doi.org/10.1080/00220485.2011.606085

O'Donoghue, T., & Rabin, M. (1999). Doing it now or later. *American Economic Review, 89*(1), 103–124. https://doi.org/10.1257/aer.89.1.103

Ryan, R. M., & Deci, E. L. (2000). Self-determination theory and the facilitation of intrinsic motivation, social development, and well-being. *American Psychologist, 55*(1), 68–78. https://doi.org/10.1037/0003-066X.55.1.68

Ryan, R. M., Rigby, C. S., & Przybylski, A. (2006). The motivational pull of video games: A self-determination theory approach. *Motivation and Emotion, 30*(4), 344–360. https://doi.org/10.1007/s11031-006-9051-8

Tversky, A., & Kahneman, D. (1991). Loss aversion in riskless choice: A reference-dependent model. *The Quarterly Journal of Economics, 106*(4), 1039–1061. https://doi.org/10.2307/2937956

Wenger, E. (1999). *Communities of practice: Learning, meaning, and identity.* Cambridge University Press.

Wenger, E., McDermott, R. A., & Snyder, W. (2002). *Cultivating communities of practice: A guide to managing knowledge.* Harvard Business School Press.

Wolters, C. A., & Brady, A. C. (2021). College students' time management: A self-regulated learning perspective. *Educational Psychology Review, 33*(4), 1319–1351. https://doi.org/10.1007/s10648-020-09519-z

Outcomes

For higher education to maintain its premier position as *the source* for professional, entry-level job candidates, it must turn its attention to developing work-ready capabilities for its graduates. Similarly, it must do a more effective job of demonstrating this improved value proposition to potential employers. Employers will recruit students from campuses that are doing a better job of preparing their graduates to step into the workforce, and in turn, those institutions will find it easier to attract students within a declining population of potential applicants.[1] This will only happen if employers perceive that greater value exists and if university efforts are rewarded in the form of more, better, and/or higher-paying placements and rates of satisfaction from recent graduates.

The question is how to evaluate whether a program is accomplishing its goals. Measuring discipline-based knowledge can be as straightforward as asking applicants to take an exam. The results would provide some measure of how much a student has learned. In contrast, when the evaluation turns to whether the applicant has developed a desired set of work-ready capabilities, the evaluative process is more subjective in nature, making it challenging to identify, let alone quantify.[2] That has not stopped many institutions from publishing their placement rates as a proxy for how well they are preparing their graduates, but these rates are only part of the story.

Measures of program outcomes need to encompass more than mere statistics on graduate job placement rates and starting salaries. Placements are only one proxy for whether graduates have developed a set of

N. B. Niman, J. R. Chagnon, *The Work-Ready Graduate*,
https://doi.org/10.1007/978-3-031-33910-3_11

work-ready capabilities that will serve them well along their entire career. Moreover, success in securing employment today may not translate into similar success tomorrow if a curriculum remains static and does not reflect a changing landscape driven in part by AI and other technologies. That is why assessment needs to be coupled with a plan for continuous improvement based on a broad collection of datapoints that provide both direct and indirect measures of program effectiveness.

Assessment Planning

Effective assessment requires a plan.[3] An assessment plan provides an opportunity to revisit program goals and reflect on what you are trying to accomplish and how you are going about it. More importantly, a good plan will lay the groundwork for continuous improvement that can help raise a program to the next level.[4] Program assessment will vary from program to program and institution to institution based on the stakeholders, goals, and values of the respective programs and institutions. Throughout our discussion, we will use the Business in Practice program to illustrate how an assessment plan is constructed. Based on our experience, we created an assessment plan containing the following:[5]

- Program Outcomes

Program goals should be translated to outcomes specifically related to what the program aims to achieve. Each program's outcomes will provide the cornerstones for continuous improvement. What is the program's purpose at its core? What are the desired outcomes and what are the action plans that will lead to continued development of that purpose?

- Program Elements

With program goals/outcomes in hand, the next step is to identify the components that are instrumental to the program—whether affecting or affected by the program. Who are the stakeholders and how are they being served? What are the design elements of your program that lead to the desired outcomes?

- Data and Methodology

Once you have identified the elements that serve to define each outcome, it is time to pinpoint the data, tools, and timing that will provide information related to those outcomes. Attention and recalibration may be needed to determine how the method, instrument, and timing will contribute to the evaluation process. Based on the desired results, some data will be readily available, some will require the development of a specialized instrument, and still other data might require the cooperation of other groups on campus.[6] Identifying what is possible, what is likely, and what may never happen is required for the data collection process to move forward.

- Assessment Map

An assessment map is a planning tool integral to understanding and coordinating a program's assessment. It is a visual representation that facilitates the assessment process by plotting the where, when, and how of assessment (particularly when it is a program-level plan and includes a number of stakeholders, elements, and outcomes). It also provides a level of transparency and integrity to the process that is essential for establishing credible results.

- Continuous Improvement

The purpose of assessment is essential for providing a sense of how well the program's goals are being fulfilled. It is invaluable for identifying areas of strength and weakness, and then creating an action-oriented plan for improvements designed to enhance program operations and outcomes.

Program Outcomes

Every program should be based on a set of goals. These goals define what the program is designed to accomplish, inform the outcomes, and set the direction for the assessment plan. The plan will contain the essential elements of the program and the types of data to be collected that are needed to assemble a picture of how well the program is performing relative to the desired outcomes.

The four core outcomes of the BiP program are:

- The effectiveness of practice-based learning
- The currency and value of the courses offered
- How well the program has contributed to the development of work-ready capabilities
- The overall level of professional preparedness upon completion of the program

With respect to experiential learning in general and Business in Practice specifically, how outcomes are generated has more to do with the process than with whether a sufficient level of mastery of a core set of principles was reached. While an individual course will have developmental goals that might encompass specific skills (which are difficult to measure under the best of circumstances), the goal for the entire program is to turn those skills into capabilities. This is a process that takes place over time and is the result of multiple attempts to put various skills into practice. As a result, a simple exam at the end of the program or some other similar measure will not suffice to measure the effectiveness of the program. What is required is a collection of indirect measures designed to assess how well a student might collaborate, construct a narrative, adapt to a changing set of circumstances, or read a room to determine an effective strategy designed to persuade key decision-makers.[7] A more holistic approach must be taken with the relevant question (from an assessment perspective) of how to measure work-ready capabilities.

Program Elements

With program outcomes in mind, it is time to think about those elements that will guide the assessment process. Ultimately, the goal is to demonstrate that the program has created a positive impact for key stakeholders. The stakeholders for BiP are those groups that are either affected by or have a positive impact on the program. They provide essentially the lenses that will be used to evaluate the program. Key stakeholders include the students served by the learning experiences, the working professionals guiding those experiences (serving as a proxy for those experiences), and the business community that finds itself as the beneficiary of a program designed to develop work-ready graduates.[8]

Our first element looks at the program from the student perspective. This includes both students who are currently part of the program and those who have graduated from the program. They are primarily impacted by the courses they take, and the capabilities developed through their participation in the program. The success of the program ultimately rests on whether, at the time of completion, they are in a better position to meet the challenges of their first job and beyond. Our students and alumni are perhaps in the best position to evaluate program effectiveness. Relevant questions to be asked pertain to student experiences while in the program (context-driven experiential learning), program impacts resulting in the development of work-ready capabilities), and the extent to which they have expanded their professional networks and formed tighter connections to potential career pathways.

The second element adopts the lens of our industry professionals partnering in the program. They essentially represent the course experiences and therefore have the largest impact on program outcomes. Relevant questions here closely evaluate the program design and seek to understand the extent to which various components effectively contribute to the attainment of program outcomes. This includes the courses that form the foundation for our learning experiences and the effectiveness of the working professionals who execute on a course design. It also evaluates the projects and activities that contribute toward those learning and developmental goals that foster the growth of work-ready capabilities.

The third element encompasses the broader business community. The business community is a large beneficiary of the program and can provide an external measure of program effectiveness. They are in a prime position to speak to the work-readiness of our graduates in terms of the capabilities developed and their relevance. They are also in the best position to compare the readiness of our students relative to graduates they recruit from other programs. Questions here might include whether the courses are current and relevant, processes and projects align with what actually exists, recent graduates transitioned more easily or with less training time, and if the level of capabilities of graduates is noticeable or leads to a higher level of contribution to their organization. All of this is reflected in the reputation a program earns after it has a chance to turn out a number of graduates.

Data and Methodology

After establishing program elements and outcomes, the assessment plan needs to address what data points are required for evaluation. A work-ready program defies many traditional assessment approaches because outcomes include soft or fuzzy skill areas rather than hard skills, and several outcomes related to developing a more work-ready graduate will not be realized until some point in the future (rather than within a single semester). This presents added challenges. Because it is challenging to collect some of the needed data, we have separated data collection into three categories: the first (accessible) captures data that is currently available or may already have been collected as part of another protocol; the second (attainable) category consists of data that is within reach with modest effort; and the last category (aspirational) is data that we aspire to collect.[9] The categories address the challenges of collecting/extracting the data as it relates to timing, methodology, resources, and complexity. Figure 1 illustrates where specific data sources and methods fall according to our assessment environment (Fig. 1).

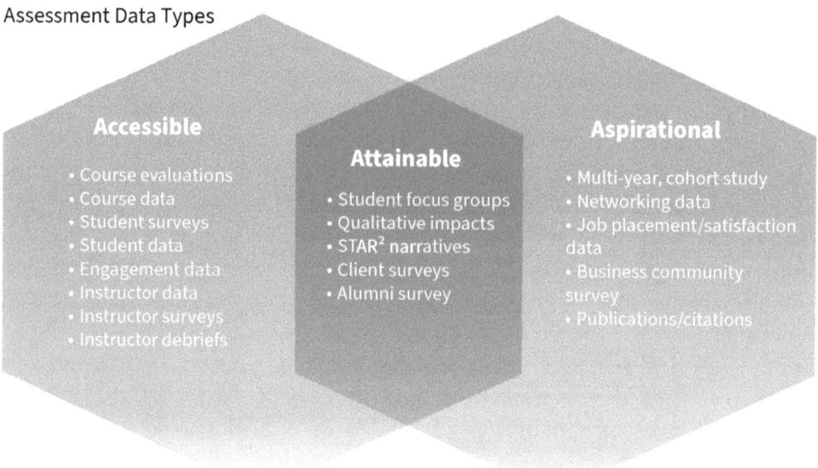

Fig. 1 Assessment Data Types classifies outcome-related data points into three categories that represent the challenges—timing, methodology, resources, and complexity—of collecting quality data. The three categories are accessible, attainable, and aspirational

Many of the mechanisms required for data collection need to be designed, tested, and then modified as new data is acquired or program changes are implemented. To a large extent, it is about careful planning and testing before rolling out an extensive plan to prevent issues like survey fatigue from interfering with the collection process. Having a map to assist in the development of a comprehensive plan can minimize the number of times a stakeholder group is asked to take the time and respond.

Assessment Map

Any data collection plan is enhanced with the construction of an overarching visual map that displays the assessment outcome/purpose and corresponding data collection point(s). The general guiding principle is to keep it simple. The more complicated the framework, then extra time will need to be spent on data collection and assessment and less time will be available for action plans and program improvement. It is easy to forget that assessment is only meaningful if it results in impactful program improvements.[10]

A variety of assessment instruments for both direct and indirect measures need to be employed to capture a more informed and complete picture. Some of these measures will be easy to collect and others will represent a serious challenge. As a first step, the assessment map should include a complete list of data points. The second step is to evaluate what data can be easily collected and what may take the development of a specialized instrument or require the cooperation of other groups on campus.

A simplified version of a map we have created for our Business in Practice program is illustrated in Figure 2. What is important to recognize is that while some assessments serve a single purpose, others can provide data that may be useful to evaluate multiple outcomes or program elements. As we continue to discuss the assessment map, we will be directing the conversation around the elements (or lenses) that provide the assessment data (Fig. 2).

The Student Lens

Asking students whether they perceive the program to be of value is an important first step in gaining a measure of whether it is generating desired outcomes. However, students, like anyone else, may not perceive how well or to what extent a program has impacted them until they have actually embarked on a career. Present student satisfaction or awareness may reveal

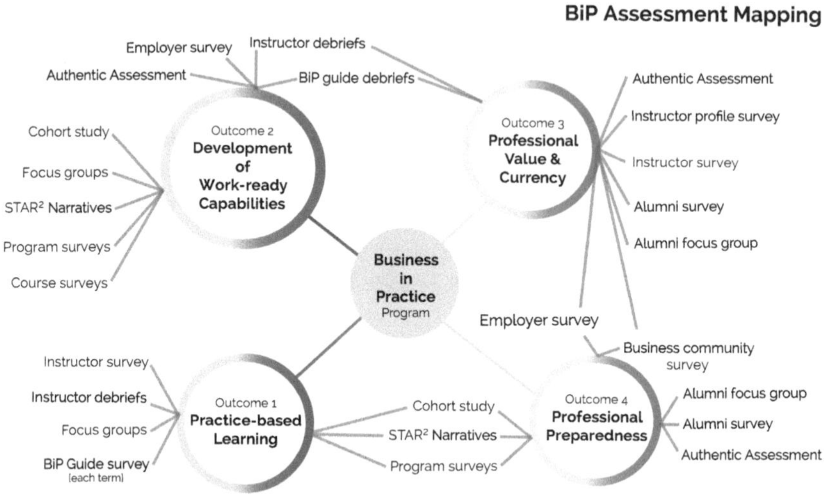

Fig. 2 When designing a program-level assessment plan, it becomes essential to map data collection to program-level outcomes. Some data sources (stakeholders) will be able to provide information on more than one outcome. This is a more simplified version to serve as an example of a starting point

only a portion of what is needed to assess the program. It will be important to also collect data when students become alumni to capture a potential change in perspective that only comes from additional experience and reflection. This particularly applies to outcomes addressing what we might think of as professional buoyancy—how well work-ready capabilities rise to the top and play a role in accelerating their professional development.

We use some traditional assessment tools to identify student perceptions of the program. These include a student survey that is designed to capture program-level data that cannot be included in the university's standard course evaluations.[11] We supplement this data with student focus groups, where a sampling of eight to 10 students share their impressions as part of a structured dialogue.[12] To capture student development over time and gain a greater understanding of program impact, a cohort study can be a valuable tool. By following a group of students from the time they arrive on campus until they graduate (and possibly a year post graduation), it becomes possible to gain a better understanding of how the program has influenced their professional development.

Moving on to assessing the effectiveness of the courses, we return to course evaluations to gain a better understanding of what students thought about their experience. Data speaking to the effectiveness of the instructor and course design, which skills students utilized, what connections they made to the professional world, and whether they found the course/projects to be relevant are all areas that contribute to our understanding of each individual course component. We also interview students one-on-one to gain a better understanding of their individual learning experience and ask follow-up questions if we see trends in other assessment data. To gain an even better understanding of the effectiveness of each element, we cross-check student impressions with the assessments we created for our working professionals turned instructors.

To supplement views compiled from students and instructors, we ask our student guides, informally through our regular meetings and formally as part of an evaluation process, to describe positive elements and areas for improvement. In their role as a guide and student peer, they often provide a voice for the students in the class. In this way, their account of how the course experience unfolded week to week has a significant weight on whether we should welcome back an instructor or make substantial changes in the course design.

Given the challenges associated with evaluating work-readiness, we have developed additional measures. One approach is to ask students to reflect on their course experience and try to explain what they did and learned as if they were describing it to a potential employer. We are looking to see how well they can articulate the $STAR^2$ narrative to demonstrate their skills, knowledge, and behaviors through the situation they encountered, the tasks they planned, and the specific actions they took to contribute to the results, and lastly to reflect on those accomplishments or failures as part of the experience.[13]

Beyond the $STAR^2$ narratives, a carefully designed authentic assessment provides an alternate means for obtaining similar information.[14] Authentic assessments are particularly well suited for evaluating soft skill development. They provide a means for evaluating how a student might respond to a given situation. They also provide an opportunity for gaining a better understanding of how a student problem solves and provide insight into the level of confidence they exhibit in managing a challenging situation.

After students have completed the program, gathering data and viewpoints from alumni is particularly enlightening and allows for a clearer picture of impacts. An alumni survey enables graduates to reflect on their experience, more accurately recognize what capabilities they developed through the program, and share their perspectives after they have entered the workforce and can speak about how well they were prepared to embark for entry into the workforce.

The Working Professional Lens

For working professionals, course evaluations, debriefs, and instructor surveys play an outsized role in determining whether instructors or courses will or should return. The debrief provides a deeper understanding, from the instructor's perspective, of what went right and wrong in the course.[15] We also ask them to complete an instructor's survey which provides an additional opportunity for them to reflect and share additional insights or concerns about the experience.

We ask our instructors, either directly in a debrief or through our instructor survey, to evaluate the capabilities of their students both prior to the start and after the course has been completed. Given the experience level of our instructors, they are perhaps in the best position to evaluate student performance across the program and to provide insight into how well prepared students are to enter the workforce. They can also identify shifts in overall baseline knowledge and ability, general progression and development, and comparative quality of applying knowledge and skills between cohorts of students. Here, once again, we use the university's standard course evaluation tool to gather additional data from the student perspective—both quantitative and qualitative. The quantitative data also provides us with a standardized framework that we can use to compare the quality of instruction relative to other academic programs on campus.

Regardless of whether it is through an evaluative process, a focus group, debrief, or individual interview, we are trying to understand whether the learning experiences have accomplished their design goals. Students or instructors are generally willing to talk about their experiences, and while this may be less formal, these measures in total allow us to gain a more comprehensive assessment of what is working and where further attention needs to be directed as part of a continuous improvement program.[16]

At the end of the evaluative process, an additional indicator of success is whether an instructor chooses to return and teach again in the program.[17] In rare cases, we have chosen not to ask someone back, which causes us, as program designers, to reflect on the quality of the job we are doing. That being said, if someone chooses not to return, it is often because of factors beyond the control of program staff or the instructor. A change in personal or professional commitments can make it challenging for a professional to stay engaged with the program.

The External Business Community Lens

The business community is an important stakeholder in determining the success of the program. Ultimately, they will provide an important measure of success through who they choose to hire and how well our graduates perform in the job. Without a direct stake in what or how our students are taught, employers can provide an arm's length assessment based on their perceptions of how well our students are prepared to meet current and future challenges. Again, a survey or focus group provides an opportunity to gain a greater understanding of what skills and practices are most in demand by employers and whether or not we are delivering on that collective vision of what is needed from a work-ready graduate. Of additional value is their ability to compare our graduates relative to those who are hired from other institutions.

Where the external business community does play an important role in the program is through their willingness to provide real projects that can be integrated into a specific course design. With respect to our Business in Practice program, the project often involves a client component.[18] After the learning experience ends, a client survey is an effective way to gain external information on student performance relative to professional standards and expectations.[19] The client survey can be supplemented by a student survey that provides a glimpse of project outcomes from an internal perspective. An additional element is the informal student stories that capture the process as it unfolds and provide an understanding of the effectiveness of both a project and the student learning experience.

Ultimately, student/alumni satisfaction and the reputation that a program develops within local business community are perhaps its most valuable assets. Here, job placements and alumni satisfaction provide an important measure of program success.[20] An alternate or supplemental measure is networking data that can demonstrate an expansion of professional networks beyond that first job.[21] One of the valuable aspects of attending college can be the connections made that may provide opportunities in the present or future.

Continuous Improvement

Data collection and assessment are important in obtaining the evidence that justifies the resources needed to sustain a work-readiness program. The real value, however, is found in the development of a continuous improvement program. Ideally, we utilize an iterative approach where changes are made in real time to ensure that both our working professionals and students have a beneficial experience. Effective assessment creates strategically located checkpoints to stop and reflect on what we have done and need to do to make positive improvements in the program. Real-time adjustments are matched with those that occur at the end of the year, as we have an opportunity to systematically go through all the data collected and have time to reflect and think creatively. Annually, we evaluate whether we have the right mix of courses and whether those offered are responsive to relevant business needs. The goal is to ensure that the curriculum is positioned to prepare our students for conditions that *currently* exist (or will in the near future).[22]

This process also provides an opportunity to take the responses from various surveys and instructor debriefs and produce what we refer to as the "collective wisdom." The collective wisdom is a distillation of everything we have learned from the previous year shared in an accessible manner with everyone participating in the program. Its purpose is to provide helpful suggestions that can be incorporated as courses are redesigned or lead to changes in how developmental goals are achieved. These modifications improve the quality of instruction by our current collection of working professionals, assist us to refine the design process, and help us to improve the initial design process for new learning experiences to the benefit of all.

Assurance of Learning

Employers want to hire graduates who possess a set of soft skills that are well suited for their organization. However, as we have seen, traditional signals such as courses taken, grades earned, and extracurricular activities do not necessarily provide a clear indication of whether these skills have been fully developed. The hiring process is designed to ascertain the potential of new hires, and the success of such a process is especially important when the organization will make a substantial investment in developing that talent after they are hired.

We believe that it is not skills but capabilities that are truly what companies should be looking for in a candidate. These are hard to evaluate because they are not developed in a single experience but require a progression that occurs over time. The rise of alternate credentials in the form of badges, certifications, or micro-credentials provides additional evidence, but they are also limited in terms of what is communicated with respect to those essential skills or capabilities possessed by the graduate.

Assessment is traditionally the cornerstone for assurance of learning. Did the courses, experiences, or overall program meet the stated objectives? More importantly, can one reasonably expect that, upon completion, students have acquired the skills and capabilities that are the intended result? In other words, the purpose of assessment is to ensure that the subsequent signals sent to employers mean something other than a series of boxes that have been checked with the hope (rather than the reality) that the program has accomplished its goals.

In this way, assessment is critical to the success of any program designed to make students more work-ready. It can reassure employers that they are actually hiring who they think they are hiring (a work-ready graduate). Where capabilities cannot be measured through a simple test, the reputation of an institution established through the collection of evidence (here, evidence of capability development) can be very motivating as employers try to differentiate graduates from those at competing colleges and universities, or individuals with alternate experience and credentials.

Notes

1. Grawe (2021).
2. Direct observation is an unrealistic goal, particularly if a program includes a large number of students. It is therefore important to look for indirect measures that require looking more closely at a select combination of variables. One such measure might be reflected in the degree of confidence that a student exhibits.

   The degree of confidence is a reflection of their experience level and associated capabilities that are too difficult or costly to measure directly. However, a recruiter might look at a graduate's résumé for leadership opportunities and might listen carefully to the degree of confidence expressed in an interview to infer whether the candidate possesses the specific capability. What this means for program assessment is that carefully crafted instruments must be created to tease out the same information that a recruiter is trying to infer from a list of accomplishments articulated on a résumé and in an interview (Creswell, 2014).

3. DePaul University (2023).
4. Eisner (2001).
5. A useful starting point that helped us think about how to create our own plan is the EvaluLEAD framework (Grove et al., 2005).
6. We chose our methods based on principles of methodological integrity as outlined by Levitt et al. (2017) and Creswell (2014). Methodological integrity concerns all aspects of research, from the delineation of the topic to selection of methods, data analysis, and articulation. Integrity is established when

   > Research designs and procedures…support the research goals (i.e., the research problems/questions); respect the researcher's approaches to inquiry (i.e., research traditions sometimes described as world views, paradigms, or philosophical/epistemological assumptions); and are tailored for the fundamental characteristics of the subject matter and the investigators. (Levitt et al., 2017, pp. 9–10)

   Both our research questions and our conception of methodological integrity inform our assessment map, which includes program goals, program elements, and our instruments of data collection.
7. Rogoff et al. (2016).
8. What might be surprising is the intentional omission of university administrators. The university administration is the beneficiary of a successful program, but other than providing financial support, it does not truly play a role in the design and delivery of the program. If the students, working professionals, and business community have a positive view of the program and the program itself is delivering on its promise, administrators can gain comfort that a program is well managed and effective.
9. Collection that is aspirational includes data that is either too challenging to obtain or requires the passage of time before they can be collected. For example, a business community survey is not difficult to construct but has limited value until a program has been in existence for several years. Evaluating whether the program is having an impact on higher education also requires the passage of time; papers need to be written, and the regular publication cycle takes time.
10. Simplicity is why much of what we discuss above comprises groups of three. This is an intentional effort to capture only what is most important and convey that there are other significant elements that, while valuable, are not important enough to deserve much time and effort. If you lose focus, what at first appears to be a simple exercise can turn into something quite complicated.
11. Every university has a standard set of questions that are asked as part of the institution's course evaluation process. We value that data as both a measure of how well the course went and as a basis for comparison across campuses. Unfortunately, these course-specific questions do not truly address how well things are going at the program level.

12. Focus groups are particularly effective in triangulating data (Boateng, 2012).
13. STAR[2] narratives provide an opportunity for students to reflect on their experience and require agreement on the part of instructors to make time available within the course, and are included as one of the course requirements. There is no reason for these narratives to expand beyond a single page, and they can follow the structure that was used as part of the design process.
14. Authentic assessment can best be defined as assessment activities that comprise replicas of that real professional world. For more about authentic assessments, see Baron and Boschee (1995), Larkin (2014), and Torrance (1995).
15. The debrief provides an opportunity to dig deeper into whether the original design was effective, what changes (if any) are needed, and how much engagement took place, and to conduct an overall assessment of the course project. Course delivery, the ability to be flexible, and overall attitude are the key indicators of whether it is worth investing time in creating a version 2.0.
16. See Boateng (2012) again for the power (and drawbacks) of focus groups.
17. From the pilot of the program through Spring 2022, the BiP program experienced an 87% return rate (instructors who taught a second time).
18. Applied and experiential learning references: Dewey (1906, 1963), Gilbert et al. (2021), Prince (2004), and Rogoff (1990).

    Consulting project references: Grossman (2002) and Heriot et al. (2008).
19. A client survey is not something that is too challenging; however, past clients are inevitably very busy, and it can be difficult to get them to take the time to fill out a written survey. Often, a phone call and verbal responses serve the process instead. In addition, alumni surveys with suitable tweaking over time can provide valuable information when a program has grown to the point where the sample is too large to generate meaningful results.
20. Often a university is already collecting this data in the form of a First Destination Survey. The challenge is not necessarily in constructing an instrument to collect the data but in obtaining sufficient institutional buy-in where it becomes possible to add some of the questions to tease out some of the relevant data.
21. At the most basic level, we try to obtain this information through questions on our student survey; we directly ask whether they connected with their instructor or guest speakers on LinkedIn. To expand upon this, you might gather attendance data from networking and other professional events.
22. Returning to the 2023 Wiley report on Closing the Skills Gap, their survey indicates that hard skills have a useful life of four years or less, and the same holds true for soft skills (p. 14). This suggests that imparting skills or developing capabilities is a process that is subject to constant renewal as needs change and organizations evolve (Wiley University Services, 2023).

References

Baron, M. A., & Boschee, F. (1995). *Authentic assessment: The key to unlocking student success.* Technomic Publishing Company, Inc.

Boateng, W. (2012). Evaluating the efficacy of focus group discussion (FGD) in qualitative social research. *International Journal of Business and Social Change, 3*(7), 54–57.

Creswell, J. W. (2014). *Research design: Qualitative, quantitative, and mixed methods approaches* (4th ed., international student ed.). SAGE.

DePaul University. (2023). *Assessment planning.* DePaul University. Retrieved March 27, 2023, from https://offices.depaul.edu/center-teaching-learning/assessment/assessing-learning/Pages/assessment-planning.aspx#:~:text=An%20assessment%20plan%20provides%20a,responsibilities%20and%20the%20overall%20timeline

Dewey, J. (1906). The experimental theory of knowledge. *Mind Association, 15*(59), 293–307.

Dewey, J. (1963). *Experience and education.* Collier Books.

Eisner, E. W. (2001). What does it mean to say a school is doing well? *Phi Delta Kappan, 82*(5), 367–372. https://doi.org/10.1177/003172170108200506

Gilbert, F. W., Harkins, J., Agrrawal, P., & Taylor, A. (2021). Internships as clinical rotations in business: Enhancing access and options. *International Journal for Business Education, 162*(1), 125–140.

Grawe, N. D. (2021). *The agile college: How institutions successfully navigate demographic changes.* Johns Hopkins University Press.

Grossman, T. A. (2002). Student consulting projects benefit faculty and industry. *Interfaces, 32*(2), 42–48. https://doi.org/10.1287/inte.32.2.42.66

Grove, J. T., Haas, T., & Kibel, B. M. (2005, January 1). *EvaluLEAD: A guide for shaping and evaluating leadership development programs.* W.K. Kellogg Foundation. Retrieved March 27, 2023, from https://wkkf.issuelab.org/resource/evalulead-a-guide-for-shaping-and-evaluating-leadership-development-programs.html

Heriot, K. C., Cook, R., Jones, R. C., & Simpson, L. (2008). The use of student consulting projects as an active learning pedagogy: A case study in a production/operations management course. *Decision Sciences Journal of Innovative Education, 6*(2), 463–481. https://doi.org/10.1111/j.1540-4609.2008.00186.x

Larkin, T. L. (2014). The student conference: A model of authentic assessment. *International Journal of Engineering Pedagogy (IJEP), 4*(2), 36. https://doi.org/10.3991/ijep.v4i2.3445

Levitt, H. M., Motulsky, S. L., Wertz, F. J., Morrow, S. L., & Ponterotto, J. G. (2017). Recommendations for designing and reviewing qualitative research in psychology: Promoting methodological integrity. *Qualitative Psychology, 4*(1), 2–22. https://doi.org/10.1037/qup0000082

Prince, M. (2004). Does active learning work? A review of the research. *Journal of Engineering Education, 93*(9), 223–231. https://doi.org/10.1002/j.2168-9830.2004.tb00809.x

Rogoff, B. (1990). *Apprenticeship in thinking: Cognitive development in social context.* Oxford University Press.

Rogoff, B., Callanan, M., Gutiérrez, K. D., & Erickson, F. (2016). The organization of informal learning. *Review of Research in Education, 40*(1), 356–401. https://doi.org/10.3102/0091732X16680994

Torrance, H. (Ed.). (1995). *Evaluating authentic assessment: Problems and possibilities in new approaches to assessment.* Open University Press.

Wiley University Services. (2023). *Closing the skills gap 2023: Employer perspectives on educating the post-pandemic workforce.* John Wiley & Sons, Inc. Retrieved March 23, 2023, from https://beyond.wiley.com/resources/skills-gap-report/

Forces of Change

Higher education has thrived because of both the implicit and explicit promises of higher wages and more fulfilling careers for its graduates.[1] The question now is whether the value higher education has to offer still merits a high price in the face of new, less expensive alternatives. In response, some institutions are abandoning traditional majors, while others are looking to catch the next big wave with the hope of growing enrollments.

Stories abound that reflect the current trend to shut down academic programs in response to falling revenues.[2] One headline appearing in the *Washington Post* reads "Marymount University cuts English, several other majors" with the subtitle "The Catholic university in Northern Virginia says it is restructuring to expand fields that draw more students."[3] The article follows an earlier one with the headline "Rural universities, already few and far between, are cutting majors." The subtitle for the latter is more explanatory, stating, "with budgets and enrollment crashing, some schools cut humanities in favor of 'workforce needs.'"[4]

What is missing from this conversation is recognition that budget-cutting exercises that limit the number of majors or make draconian cuts in other areas very rarely solve a revenue problem. They often merely weaken an institution by making it even more difficult to put in place those reforms needed to place an institution on sound footing. If higher education is to be responsive to applicants and employers alike, it must graduate students who employers are both interested in, and excited about, hiring.

N. B. Niman, J. R. Chagnon, *The Work-Ready Graduate*,
https://doi.org/10.1007/978-3-031-33910-3_12

In their influential book *The Race Between Education and Technology*, Claudia Goldin and Lawrence Katz explain how skill-biased technological change (SBTC) has created a seemingly insatiable demand for graduates who could meet the challenges created by the Industrial Revolution.[5] This has created a set of conditions where the demand for more educated workers has outstripped the supply of college graduates, leading to a large wage premium for those who graduate with a bachelor's degree.[6]

In an updated framework, they demonstrate (along with David Autor) that the premium associated with higher levels of education grew rapidly from 1980 to 2000, suggesting that the development of digital technologies that have changed almost every facet of our daily lives has increased the need for college graduates even more. In the later period, from 2000 to 2017, they show that the premium has continued to grow, however, much of the increase in the premium occurred *within* the category of college graduates rather than between those with a degree and those without.[7]

These findings suggest that employers value some degrees more than others.[8] One possible explanation is that as the economy is shifting away from general-purpose technologies to those that are more specialized, graduates who can meet these more specific needs will find themselves choosing between a larger set of higher-paying opportunities. In doing so, it provides a rationale for why some administrators believe the key to success for their institution is in picking winners and losers among their offerings in response to a "new reality" that represents what they perceive to be a sizable shift that values some majors more highly relative to others.

Universities should be responsive to external changes in order to stay both current and relevant. In fact, our own program, Business in Practice, emerged as the result of just such an effort. It represents a path forward that does not entail closing down programs, eliminating majors, or losing touch with the traditional mission of a university. Rather, it is the creation of a complementary experience that can accelerate the professional development of any institution's graduates. By doing so, it offers a response to those who question the value of an undergraduate degree and provides a stronger rationale for why someone should be willing to pay the price and take on the debt to earn a bachelor's degree.

Pathways of Change

To create the next generation of thinkers *and* doers, higher education must elevate the development of work-ready capabilities as part of its mission and ultimately value proposition. It has little to do with promoting STEM majors or eliminating the liberal arts. What is required is a rethinking and recalibration of how colleges and universities should approach the undergraduate experience. More resources need to be invested in preparing students for what will happen after graduation.

Our solution entails opening up the academy to working professionals as part of the creation of an expanded curriculum that supports the development of work-ready capabilities. Institutions need to expand their mission and embrace the concept of a work-ready graduate in response to changing perceptions and the creation of new alternatives that are more attuned to the needs of perspective students. It may represent the best path for closing the wage gap between majors while preserving those traditional values that are the hallmark of an undergraduate education.

From a work-ready perspective, there is no such thing as a 'right' or 'wrong' major.[9] Learning best occurs when students are interested in the subject matter and work-ready capabilities can be developed from any major or at any institution. It is not that the world needs more business, STEM, or other highly specialized majors. Instead, what is needed are curricula that support a wide spectrum of students by offering them meaningful opportunities to put their knowledge into practice. It is not what is optimal or best in the abstract, but rather what will make the strongest contribution to an organization's workforce needs. Employers repeatedly state that they want to see students with applicable skills and not necessarily specific knowledge.[10]

Majors across all disciplines are better served when students are provided with an opportunity to develop work-ready capabilities that can be used to launch a career and establish the foundation for a life well lived. Whether a student is studying computer science, pre-med, marketing, or history, they should be encouraged to participate in structured experiences that help to develop relevant skills that over time morph into capabilities. Students need many opportunities to practice (and receive feedback) as part of this journey if they are to learn how to collaborate, become situationally aware, and construct a compelling narrative that can be shared with a recruiter. Any and every major can contribute to the development of work-ready capabilities to prepare the next generation of doers.

That being said, progress will not be made unless we can dispel, the notion that regardless of how a student approaches their studies, they will necessarily graduate work-ready. Thinking critically about ideas from 100 years ago does not necessarily mean that a student can understand how a similar set of ideas can be applied directly toward solving a current business issue. Just as higher education acknowledges and invests in the student's social and academic transition to post-secondary education, it needs to make a comparable investment in a deliberate and concerted plan to cultivate the student's professional development and transition to the world of work.

Students in any major can make a positive contribution to any organization if, in addition to bringing an elevated understanding of the world as it is or was, they have developed in-demand capabilities that can support an organization's mission. Because well-defined career paths may be more elusive for some majors than others, an opportunity to put ideas into practice can create opportunities that previously might have been unattainable. From our perspective, context provides the spoonful of sugar that helps turn work into something that can be personally fulfilling and contribute to a life well lived. By creating an overlay to the major that promotes the development of work-ready capabilities, learning can become more engaging, and by helping the average student to see what they are learning in the context of why they are learning, affords an opportunity to translate knowledge into actions that can support their own personal and professional goals.

Seeds of Change

The extent to which a graduate is work-ready depends in large part on the experiences they participate in while they earn their degree. This requires that students are presented with a coherent set of experiences where they can apply their skills and knowledge by actively engaging with peers and working professionals.

To embrace the concept of a work-ready graduate and empower others, we offer three guiding principles:

Principle 1: Embed working professionals in the curriculum.

Many entry-level jobs require two to three years of work experience. The right internship can contribute to meeting the qualifications for an entry-level position, but many are out of reach for some students and other students choose not to participate despite the opportunity.[11] To create a more integrated and accessible alternative, institutions should welcome working professionals as partners in the curriculum. While there may be no substitute for direct experience, a working professional can share their own experiences to help students understand a real work environment. By having students collaborate on projects guided by a working professional, it becomes possible to add a level of authenticity that approximates what they are likely to find on the job.

Principle 2: The interactions between students and professionals must be significant.

While working professionals are not the only ones adept at explaining the world outside of the academy, these interactions create opportunities that enable the transfer of their tacit knowledge to students who can then benefit from their experience in a way that accelerates their own professional development. This exchange requires more than brief appearances in the form of a guest speaker, judge, or panelist. Transforming skills into capabilities calls for repeat interactions and feedback over an extended period of time rather than during a single class session or an organized event.

Principle 3: Experiences need to be active rather than passive.

From the perspective of creating a work-ready graduate, experiences need to be structured in a manner where students are asked to accomplish something they are likely to encounter once they graduate and enter the workforce. To develop work-ready capabilities, a student must assess the problem and understand how to take the necessary steps to implement solutions of the sort that potential employers would find to be of value.

Dynamics of Change

Taking the steps required to produce a work-ready graduate requires leadership from the top and buy-in from each part of the organization. It requires broad participation to execute on such a shared vision. We recommend the following.

All Aboard

Before any change can happen, it is important to get everyone on board. When we say everyone, that means faculty, staff, and administrators. Creating work-ready graduates requires an approach that integrates all facets of the undergraduate experience. On many college campuses, the faculty control the academic experience, the staff oversees what happens outside the classroom, and the administration allocates resources between different campus groups. This typically occurs in various siloes or collections of disconnected islands with limited interaction between the different groupings.

A siloed approach will not work. Faculty, staff, and administrators need to work in concert if graduates are to become truly work-ready. Who to bring to campus, where to include them in the curriculum, and how to make it a great experience for everyone involved needs to be part of a collective and well-orchestrated effort.

Open Up the Curriculum

The challenge in creating a work-ready graduate is developing opportunities for working professionals to have a meaningful role at the intersection of the academic, social, and professional spheres. A good starting point is with the curriculum. The curriculum needs to be viewed as a scaffold that has a number of opportunities for working professionals to interact with students, whether within a traditional course structure or as an organized set of experiences.[12]

There are at least three opportunities to introduce practice-based learning into a well-established curriculum. One possibility would be to introduce an in-practice set of courses that can "sit on top" of the core curriculum. It does not compete with the dissemination of core knowledge but rather complements the core by placing key concepts into practice. A second possibility would be to expand existing courses by adding a fourth hour (an additional credit) to existing three-hour/-credit courses. In this model, the in-practice component would act as an enhancement, similar to a lab component found in many science or introductory courses. The third alternative is to retrofit existing courses by adding an in-practice component directly into the course itself.

The third option is both the easiest and the most difficult to implement. It is easiest because all that is required is for faculty to reconfigure their own course design. This in turn also makes it extremely difficult because faculty may already struggle to fit their own required materials into the allotted time. Covering required topics often leaves few, if any, opportunities to invite working professionals into the classroom, let alone make time for active learning approaches.

One strategy for creating space within an already full class is to adopt a flipped approach. Important course concepts could be covered outside of the classroom while allowing guided learning under the auspices of a working professional during class time. Students are introduced to important concepts outside of class, thereby focusing on active learning during class. Here, class time can be split between teaching approaches designed to enhance core knowledge and integrated active learning that promotes putting those concepts into practice.

Craft Meaningful Experiences

Meaningful experiences can take place in the classroom, but there is no reason to limit the opportunity for turning skills into capabilities to the core curriculum that defines an academic major. We have been fortunate at the University of New Hampshire to create an entire program that sits on top of the core curriculum and is staffed by working professionals. We also understand that other institutions may not be able to create a similar experience.

An additional approach we have implemented is to include an experiential component to the academic minors the college offers to the rest of the campus. For example, Paul College's leadership minor requires students to participate in a leadership experience. This might involve taking on a leadership role in a campus organization or participating in structured experiences such as leadership camp where students participate in an intensive program designed to teach and put into practice leadership skills.

Capabilities develop over *time* and hence what is needed is a structured series of touchpoints where, skills have an opportunity to mature, and students are able to apply those skills in a variety of ways. Hence, advisors need to not only track courses taken to ensure that students are making progress toward their degree, but also monitor experiences across the entire campus that reinforce what is taught in the classroom and provide students repeated and sustained skill development.[13]

Welcome Working Professionals on Campus

Making space for working professionals on campus, in substantial roles other than guest speakers or participants at a career fair, necessitates acceptance of the idea that their contributions are pivotal in the development of a work-ready graduate. This is predicated on the idea that those who engage in business on a daily basis offer something of value that cannot be replicated in a textbook, case, or laboratory experiment.

Working professionals must be welcomed to campus as collaborators and partners, rather than invited guests. Their professional experiences are different, and as a result, have something to contribute that is often beyond the reach of the current faculty, staff, and administrators. An approach that welcomes working professionals into the curriculum is one that acknowledges those differences and embraces them as a positive force for developing a work-ready graduate.

It is important to think of this relationship as a two-way street. As working professionals have an opportunity to engage with students, they, in turn, are more likely to welcome graduates to join their professional endeavors. It is important to invest time and energy in nurturing these relationships. From our experience, moving from an expression of interest to a willingness to make sacrifices and participate on a deeper level is cultivated by a shared investment in the experience.

Create a Connected Community

Fashioning opportunities where students can form a meaningful relationship with a working professional that extends beyond a single event might lead to an internship or job. The benefit associated with repeated interaction is that, over time, students become less intimidated by, and more familiar with, individuals who are professionally well established. In turn, a working professional can help breathe new life into a curriculum by demonstrating how core principles are used in a work environment. In doing so, what a student might do with a particular major becomes more tangible, with students beginning to see themselves in a professional role in which they use what they have learned in a meaningful way. To realize their professional goals, students need to become connected with local businesses, alumni with related interests, and recruiters from local and national firms. Work-readiness is not something that can be developed without establishing a strong network. To facilitate these connections, a collective effort among faculty, career services, student and residential life, the alumni office, and the development office is required to nurture relationships with working professionals who can make a substantial contribution to the success of the institution.

Embrace Innovation

To develop a work-ready graduate, innovation needs to become a guiding principle. Innovation means experimenting with and testing new approaches. Each experience, learning opportunity, or identified skill does not have to be overtly baked into the design or fixed in place and time. The power of innovation is unleashed when stakeholders collaborate with each other and have the support and flexibility to try something new, to invent something that does not currently exist, and to integrate it into an existing structure. This keeps the system fresh, vibrant, and, most importantly, applicable to a dynamic and changing world. There must be a willingness to take risks and understand that some new initiatives will not be successful. After all, it is precisely these new initiatives that lead to improvement or spark further ideas to keep the curriculum current and help students develop new capabilities that will position them for the future.

Agents of Change

Colleges and universities are at an inflection point—do nothing and run the risk of becoming irrelevant as changes beyond their control enable others to provide what employers are demanding. The choice could not be any clearer. Either open up the academy to working professionals and expand its mission, or sit on the sidelines as demographics, changing labor markets, and the rise of alternatives lead to only a select list of institutions able to survive. Higher education was at one time thought to be the path to a life well lived, but now it risks remaining rooted in a past that no longer meets the needs of prospective students and those employers who hire them when they graduate.

Looking ahead to the future, especially as AI continues to permeate the workplace, there will be an even greater need for graduates who are both *thinkers* who can recognize new opportunities and *doers* who can leverage them to make an even greater impact. This is perhaps the strongest reason why change must happen now. To create the next generation of thinkers *and* doers, higher education must elevate the development of work-ready capabilities as part of its mission and ultimately value proposition.

It is time to plant the seeds of change in order to re-envision the traditional undergraduate experience and to cultivate new pathways capable of fashioning integrated experiential learning opportunities. These seeds represent our dedication to those principles that support the development of a graduate who can find meaning in what they do and place them in a strong position to make an impact on both business *and* society.

To reach that future requires an educational experience that constructs a bridge to the professional world, fosters real-world connections regardless of major, and invites students and working professionals to work collaboratively as part of the learning process. While the path is full of twists and turns, there is nothing insurmountable that cannot be overcome. Anyone working in higher education can be an agent for *this* kind of change.

Moreover, we hope to convey the message that if we can do it, so can you. Change is not easy.[14] But it is possible. Like experiential learning, it is all about taking that first step. It does not have to be a huge, disruptive one. Rather, it requires a clear vision and a strong enough push to generate some momentum. Enough of a step to build upon, and enough to demonstrate a level of success that will motivate others to join in the process. To create the next generation of thinkers *and* doers, higher education needs to embark on a *transformative* experience that requires its very own thinkers *and* doers.

Notes

1. Of course it is also important to note that many high-paying jobs do not require a college degree and many graduates with a bachelor's degree are employed in jobs where the degree is not required. See, for example, Carnevale et al. (2020).
2. A sobering look at the future is provided by Nathan Heller, who chronicles the fate of English and other liberal arts majors (Heller, 2023).
3. Anderson (2023).

4. Marcus (2022).
5. Goldin and Katz (2008).
6. See Ma and Pender (2023, pp. 18–28).
7. Autor et al. (2020, p. 7).
8. See Figure 2.9, page 26, of the report produced by the College Board that shows earnings by major. Computer science topped the list with early career earnings of $70,000 and mid-career earnings of $100,000. At the bottom were those in the performing arts with early earnings of $34,000 and mid-career earnings of $60,000 (Ma & Pender, 2023).
9. Advice that Robert Frank likes to give to job seekers based on his reading of the happiness literature goes as follows: "Find something you enjoy doing because then you will want to put the hours in to become an expert. As time goes by, your services will become very valuable to those who have an interest in what you can provide. As technology extends the reach of those who might purchase your services, the number of buyers may become so large that you become worth a fortune. If in turn, what you do contributes to something that you and others find to be important, it will not matter as much how you are compensated because the fulfillment that comes with doing something that is morally satisfying will offset any wage differentials you might experience" (Frank, 2016).
10. In a study undertaken by researchers at the University of Wisconsin who actually went out and interviewed employers in the state of Wisconsin, their results "highlight the need for a systemic approach to skills-related problems that places the use of active learning techniques by educators and employers as a central focus." "Instead of solely focusing on technical mastery of a field, employers and educators value a variety of technical expertise, interpersonal competencies, and personal attributes that they believe will enable students and employees to succeed in the workplace over the long term" (p. 3). The educational programs that best cultivate these capabilities utilize experiential, hands-on teaching methods while exposing students to multiple disciplines (Hora et al., 2016).
11. That, however, is not necessarily the case for everyone (Carnevale et al., 2020).
12. The concept of an ecosystem forms the foundation for the first-year experience called FIRE (First Year Innovation and Research Experience) that we created at the Peter T. Paul College of Business and Economics. The program is designed to help smooth the transition from high school to college while bringing a sense of excitement to learning and providing a firm foundation for educational achievement. In addition, it emphasizes the importance of becoming work-ready by helping students understand what they will need to accomplish over the next four years if they are to

have a successful entry into the workforce. We accomplish this goal in part by having our students work in teams to grapple with some of the larger problems of the day and providing them with the tools they need to achieve academic success.

13. Repurposing existing activities can provide a framework for putting skills into practice, but it requires either the rethinking of existing activities or the design of specialized activities to promote the development of work-ready capabilities. Without some intentionality in the design, students will find themselves busy doing things while still not taking the necessary step to develop skills into capabilities. For example, in our first-year experience (FIRE) we have students working in teams to solve a grand challenge by identifying a commercial solution to one aspect of the problem. See Niman et al. (2017).
14. The greatest challenge perhaps has been a cultural one. Students have been trained to ask what is expected of them and to perform within a rigid set of guidelines. Faculty have been trained within a model that rarely extols the virtue of experiential learning. All of this is characterized by a great divide between the faculty who dominate academics and the staff who are charged with everything else. The challenge is one of changing mindsets.

References

Anderson, N. (2023, February 24). Marymount University cuts English, several other majors. *The Washington Post*. Retrieved March 26, 2023, from https://www.washingtonpost.com/education/2023/02/24/marymount-university-humanities-majors-eliminated/

Autor, D., Goldin, C., & Katz, L. (2020). *Extending the race between education and technology* (No. w26705; p. w26705). National Bureau of Economic Research. https://doi.org/10.3386/w26705

Carnevale, A. P., Cheah, B., Van Der Werf, M., & Gulish, A. (2020). *Buyer beware: First year earnings and debt for 37,000 college majors at 4,400 institutions*. Center on Education and the Workforce, Georgetown University.

Frank, R. H. (2016). Distilling career advice from the happiness literature. In D. W. Harward (Ed.), *Well-being and higher education: A strategy for change and the realization of education's greater purposes*. Bringing Theory to Practice.

Goldin, C. D., & Katz, L. F. (2008). *The race between education and technology*. Belknap Press of Harvard University Press.

Heller, N. (2023, February 27). Enrollment in the humanities is in free fall at colleges around the country. What happened? *The New Yorker*. Retrieved March 26, 2023, from https://www.newyorker.com/magazine/2023/03/06/the-end-of-the-english-major

Hora, M., Benbow, R., & Oleson A. (2016). Beyond the skills gap: How the lack of systemic supports for teaching and learning undermine employer, student, and societal interests (WCER Working Paper No. 2016-9). University of Wisconsin–Madison, Wisconsin Center for Education Research. Retrieved March 26, 2023, from https://wcer.wisc.edu/docs/working-papers/Working_Paper_No_2016_9.pdf

Ma, J., & Pender, M. (2023). *Education pays 2023: The benefit of higher education for individuals and society*. College Board. Retrieved March 26, 2023, from https://research.collegeboard.org/media/pdf/education-pays-2023.pdf

Marcus, J. (2022, December 16). Rural universities, already few and far between, are cutting majors. *The Washington Post*. Retrieved March 26, 2023, from https://www.washingtonpost.com/education/2022/12/16/rural-university-college-major/

Niman, N. B., Rury, T., & Stewart, S. (2017). *What makes the first-year seminar high impact? An exploration of effective educational practices* (T. L. Skipper, Ed.). University of South Carolina, National Resource Center for The First-Year Experience & Students in Transition.

Index[1]

[1] Note: Page numbers followed by 'n' refer to notes.

N. B. Niman, J. R. Chagnon, *The Work-Ready Graduate*,
https://doi.org/10.1007/978-3-031-33910-3

FSC
www.fsc.org
MIX
Papier | Fördert
gute Waldnutzung
FSC® C083411

Kolibri 360 GmbH
Ferdinand-Jühlke-Straße 7
99095 Erfurt, Deutschland
produktsicherheit@kolibri360.de